Student Workbook

for use with

Prepared by M. LOUISE WINTERSTEIN
CENTENNIAL COLLEGE

NELSON / EDUCATION

Workbook for use with Procedures for the Canadian Legal Office, Seventh Edition
by M. Louise Winterstein

Associate Vice President, Editorial Director:
Evelyn Veitch

Editor-in-Chief, Higher Education:
Anne Williams

Marketing Manager:
Shannon White

Developmental Editor:
Tracy Yan

Content Production Manager:
Imoinda Romain

Proofreader:
Liba Berry

Senior Manufacturing Coordinator:
Charmaine Lee-Wah

Printer:
Webcom

COPYRIGHT © 2009 by Nelson Education Ltd.

12   16

For more information contact Nelson Education Ltd., 1120-Birchmount Road, Toronto, Ontario, M1K 5G4. Or you can visit our Internet site at http://www.nelson.com

ALL RIGHTS RESERVED. No part of this work covered by the copyright herein may be reproduced, transcribed, or used in any form or by any means—graphic, electronic, or mechanical, including photocopying, recording, taping, Web distribution, or information storage and retrieval systems—without the written permission of the publisher.

For permission to use material from this text or product, submit all requests online at www.cengage.com/permissions. Further questions about permissions can be emailed to permissionrequest@cengage.com

Every effort has been made to trace ownership of all copyrighted material and to secure permission from copyright holders. In the event of any question arising as to the use of any material, we will be pleased to make the necessary corrections in future printings.

ISBN-13: 978-0-17-644087-9
ISBN-10: 0-17-644087-9

This workbook is intended as a procedural guide only; it does not offer legal advice. A lawyer should be consulted whenever expert legal advice is required.

Please note that all names of law firms, clients, and other individuals in this text are fictional and are not based on any real-life individuals; any similarities are entirely coincidental.

To my family:
My husband Ed, for his staunch support as always,
My children Lee, Shannon and Amanda for the joy they bring,
And in memory of my parents, Adam and Mabel Grant
Standynge Fæste

TABLE OF CONTENTS

Preface — v

Part One – Legal Office Procedures, Documentation and Terminology
Chapter 1 The Legal Environment — 1
Chapter 2 Procedures and Practices in the Law Office — 5
Chapter 3 Client Records — 9
Chapter 4 Legal Correspondence: Memoranda and Letters — 13
Chapter 5 Client Dockets and Accounts — 19
Chapter 6 Legal Citations — 27
Chapter 7 Introduction to Legal Documents — 35
Chapter 8 Introduction to Civil Litigation — 45
Chapter 9 Preparing Court Documents — 53
Chapter 10 The Originating Process — 59
Chapter 11 Serving and Filing Court Documents — 67
Chapter 12 Responses to the Originating Process — 71
Chapter 13 Consents, Requisitions, Notices, and Notices of Motion — 81
Chapter 14 Proceeding to Trial: General Actions — 91
Chapter 15 Application Proceedings — 99
Chapter 16 Orders, Judgments, and Costs — 111
Chapter 17 Disposition of Actions without Trial — 119
Chapter 18 Introduction to Family Law — 123
Chapter 19 Family Law Proceedings — 131
Chapter 20 Introduction to Real Estate — 139
Chapter 21 Transfer/Deed — 143
Chapter 22 Charge/Mortgage — 147
Chapter 23 Discharge of Charge/Mortgage — 151
Chapter 24 Commencing the Real Estate Transaction — 155
Chapter 25 Acting for the Vendor — 165
Chapter 26 Acting for the Purchaser — 175
Chapter 27 Closing the Real Estate Transaction — 185
Chapter 28 Introduction to Corporate Practice — 191
Chapter 29 Incorporating an Ontario Corporation — 195
Chapter 30 Corporate By-Laws, Meetings, Minutes, and Resolutions — 199
Chapter 31 Corporate Securities, Records, and Changes — 207
Chapter 32 Wills and Powers of Attorney — 211
Chapter 33 Administration of Estates — 217
Chapter 34 Settling the Estate — 227

Part Two – Legal Transcription
Introduction — 231
Commonly Misspelled / Misused Words — 234
Index to Legal Transcription Files — 235

Part Three – Reference Material
Areas of Legal Practice Codes — 248
Staff List — 249
Index of Forms — 250
Matter/Client Numbers — 251
Address List — 255
Proofreader's Marks — 262

PREFACE

WELCOME to the offices of Hill, Johnston & Grant, a law firm that practices in many areas of law, including corporate, estates, family law, litigation, and real estate.

The assignments in this workbook are intended to provide experience in applying the legal procedures and documentation discussed in the *Procedures for the Canadian Legal Office, 7th Edition*. Your instructor will advise you which assignments you are to complete and how such assignments are to be carried out.

There are practice files to accompany this assignment book which may be accessed at **http://www.legaloffice.nelson.com** by clicking on **Student Resources.** Some of the required office forms and rough drafts for some of the exercises are located in these practice files. All materials have been prepared in Microsoft Word 2003. The disk contains two folders: Drafts and Forms. As these files are required a reference will be made in the assignment book to the appropriate folder and file name. In addition, you will require prescribed legal forms to prepare some of the documents. Your instructor will advise you how this material may be secured.

The first section of this book is the assignments for you to complete as instructed. You will frequently be required to refer to or use information from material provided by the instructing lawyer. You are expected to select the appropriate material from that provided to complete a particular item in the assignment. You will also find assignments that relate to the same files and matters. You should maintain a file of completed assignments, since on many occasions you will be instructed to refer to previous work in order to secure the necessary information to complete a new assignment. There are also legal terminology exercises at the end of each chapter to enable to you build your legal vocabulary.

The second section of this book contains instructions and support material for the transcription of a variety of legal documentation. Your instructor will advise you how to access the necessary audio files to accompany this material

At the end of the assignments there is a reference section of material in connection with the law firm of Hill, Johnston & Grant which you will need to refer to frequently when completing assignments.

As you will note, there is revised and handwritten material. The ability to read handwriting of all kinds is a requirement for a legal assistant. Perfect handwriting is rarely encountered in the real world!

The names used for parties and law firms in the assignments in this workbook are fictional and no reference to existing persons or firms is intended. The exercises and material included are intended for educational purposes only.

In these assignments, I have endeavoured to provide an opportunity for you not only to exercise judgment and initiative but also to demonstrate good basic skills. I hope that the experience you gain in completing assignments will lay the foundation for a successful career in the legal environment.

Louise Winterstein

CHAPTER 1 – ASSIGNMENTS
The Legal Environment

A. LEGAL OFFICE PROCEDURES

1. REFERENCE MATERIAL

At the end of this assignment book, there is a section containing reference material for the Hill, Johnston & Grant law firm. You will need to refer to this material when completing many of the assignments. You should become familiar with what information is available and where it is located.

All references to precedents or figures in this assignment book indicate the precedents and figures contained in the textbook to accompany this assignment book, Procedures for the Canadian Legal Office, 7th Edition.

B. LEGAL DOCUMENT PRODUCTION

1. ARTICLE FOR OFFICE PROCEDURES MANUAL

It is your first day at the Hill, Johnston & Grant law office and the office manager, Margaret Aspin, has requested that you complete the following material that has been written by Peter T. Grant for the Hill, Johnston & Grant Office Procedures Manual. Peter Grant has drafted the document on his computer and then made handwritten changes.

You should note that when people handwrite material, they often use shortcuts, such as abbreviations and acronyms, and that the material may contain errors in grammar, spelling, or punctuation. When preparing any handwritten material (including material in a "handwritten font") in this assignment book, you should key all words in full and proofread carefully for all omissions and errors to ensure that a document reads sensibly and correctly. A guide to proofreaders' marks is located in the reference material at the end of this assignment book.

As you work through the assignments in this book, you will be provided with a notation such as the one shown below advising where any applicable drafts or forms are located for the practice files that accompany this assignment book. These practice files are located on the internet at: **http://www.legaloffice.nelson.com** *by clicking on* **Student Resources.**

Note that not all drafts are available in the practice files.. Most documents will need to be fully keyed to encourage the development of keyboarding and formatting skills.

(Practice Files: Drafts Folder – File: Draft 1)

SECURITY OF CLIENT INFORMATION — BOLDED

Client's affairs are to be treated as completely confidential so that a client may safely disclose information to the lawyers of this firm in order to carry out the legal services required by any such client. A client's confidence must be respected at all times, and, accordingly, except in the course of professional duty, the affairs of a client should not be discussed outside the office with anyone not directly involved with the file.

No material is to be taken from any file even temporarily without a memorandum as to its location being placed in the file. Anyone printing or photocopying material for a precedent for his or her use should ensure that sufficient deletions are made so that the client's affairs remain completely confidential. No precedent material is to be given to anyone not an employee of this law firm without the prior consent of the lawyer responsible for the file.

It is recognized that a matter which is in general knowledge such as a major litigation, is often the subject of discussion by members of the public. The best practice when such matters are discussed is not to participate in the discussion. This is the rule for all members of the staff other than lawyers. If a lawyer feels obliged to participate, it should be on a very general basis so that there is no possibility whatsoever that any matter that a client might consider to be confidential is disclosed.

No discussion of clients' affairs should be carried on in the reception area, the elevators, or public hallways where information might be overheard by anyone not a member of the staff. No discussion of clients' affairs should be carried with any member of the staff not connected with work on the file. Any necessary discussion should be limited to information required for that person to perform his or her responsibilities.

Great care should also be taken when files are left on a desk – or being carried from one office to another – to ensure that material is not inadvertently exposed to view of anyone not working on the file.

All employees of Hill, Johnston & Grant, whether a lawyer, law clerk, legal administrative assistant or support personnel, are required to sign a confidentiality agreement as part of the terms of their employment with the firm. By executing this contract, the employees promise not to reveal any information that they acquire while working for the firm to anyone outside the firm during and following there term of employment with the firm. Two copies of the agreement will be executed in the presence of a witness. One copy will be kept by Hill, Johnston & Grant and the 2nd copy is for the employee to keep for his or her records.

A person who breaks any of the above rules involves this firm in a breach of the trust accorded to it by the clients and in a breach of professional ethics of the most serious nature. Whether such breach occurs wilfully or carelessly, it will be regarded as sufficient grounds for immediate dismissal from the employ of this law firm.

C. LEGAL TERMINOLOGY

At the end of each chapter of this assignment book, there is a legal terminology exercise such as the one below. Each of these exercises will focus on the legal terms contained in the related chapter; however, there may be additional terms not specifically related to the chapter in order to increase your general legal vocabulary. The glossary at the back of your text contains most, but not all of the legal terms in these exercises; some will need to be looked up in a legal dictionary (either hard copy or on-line)

After completing this exercise you should be able to spell and define the following legal terms. Read the definitions shown below. Then select the correct term and match it with the words or phrase that best matches it in meaning, and write the correct term in the space provided. There are more terms than definitions.

Legal Terms

associate	attorney	fiduciary
legal aid	barrister	tariff
commissioner	council	sole practitioner
CBA	counsel	LLP
CLA	notary public	LTD.

Definitions

1. one who is entrusted _____

2. one who administers oaths _____

3. a person who authenticates a copy of a document _____

4. a lawyer who is a member of a firm but not a partner _____

5. a fee schedule that may be used to calculate legal services _____

6. a lawyer who practice largely involves court work _____

7. acronym for law firm partnership that has limited liability _____

8. a lawyer who practices on his or her own _____

9. acronym for national association for lawyers in Canada _____

10. financial assistance program to provide legal services to qualified individuals _____

CHAPTER 2 – ASSIGNMENTS
Procedures and Practices in the Law Office

A. LEGAL OFFICE PROCEDURES

1. USE OF INITIAL CAPITALS

Consider each of the following sentences to determine whether the guide to capitalization set out in your text has been followed. Use proofreader's marks to make any corrections. Write a "C" at the end of the any sentence that you believe does not require any corrections.

1. In view of your pending Marriage, you will need to make a new Will.
2. The proper name of the act is the courts of justice act.
3. He lives in the city of Kingston, in the County of Frontenac.
4. It is expected that judge Harris will give Judgment shortly.
5. Many latin terms are still used in legal work.
6. After you prepare the Cheque, please do the five Letters.
7. The Defendant has asked for damages in his statement of claim.
8. The word "testator" is used to describe a man who makes a will.
9. The public guardian and trustee is assuming responsibility for Joe's affairs.
10. There are many lawyers employed in the office of the children's lawyer.

2. USE OF NUMBERS AND SYMBOLS

Consider each of the following sentences that appeared in <u>legal correspondence</u>. Underline each incorrectly expressed number of symbol, and show on the line provided the proper form for such number or symbol. If no revision is required, write the letter "C" on the line provided.

1. We are claiming damages of fifty-four thousand dollars. _____
2. We will have to pay 15 percent interest on the loan. _____
3. The agreement was dated 14 February, 20__. _____
4. There are 2 very large boxes of material. _____
5. Our office hours are 9:30 to 1:00, and 2 to 5. _____
6. Her cheque was for one hundred dollars ($100.00). _____
7. The statement that he is unmarried is in paragraph four. _____
8. The letter was dated June 24, 20__. _____
9. 100 km is the maximum speed limit on Highway 427 _____
10. He has an appointment with you at ten a.m. tomorrow. _____

B. LEGAL DOCUMENT PRODUCTION

1. CONFIDENTIALITY AGREEMENT

As a new member of the firm, you are asked to prepare the following confidentiality agreement for your signature in front of a witness. This document should be prepared double spaced.

CONFIDENTIALITY AGREEMENT

I, YOUR NAME, understand that during the term of my employment with the law firm of Hill, Johnston & Grant, I will come into contact with & acquire information that is of a confidential nature regarding the clients of the law firm. Such confidential information may be in written, verbal, or electronic format & I acknowledge that I am responsible for maintaining the confidentiality of such information.

I understand and agree that such information is subject to the rules of lawyer-client confidentiality. I therefor undertake to treat confidentially all such information & agree not to disclose any such information to any persons either during the term of my employment with Hill, Johnston & Grant (except as may be necessary in the proper discharge of my employment duties) or at any time after the date of the termination of my employment.

I agree not to make personal use of any such confidential information or to remove any client information or documentation from the offices of H-, J- & G- except in the performance of my duties. I further agree to report any violations of the confidentiality of client information to my supervisor.

I agree that upon termination of my employment with H-, J- & G- that I will return to the firm any and all records that may have been in my possession during my employment.

I understand and agree that in addition to any other rights and remedies of H-, J- & G- to enforce its rights arising from this agreement, in the event of a breech by me of any undertaking and agreement herein, Hill, Johnston & Grant may immediately terminate my employment with the firm.

This agmt shall be governed by the laws of the province of --name of your province.

IN WITNESS WHEREOF I have executed this confidentiality agreement to be effective as the date set out below.

DATED this _____ day of (current month, year).

_____   _____
Witness   *Your Name*

2. DRAFT ARTICLE

Peter Grant asks you to make the necessary changes to the draft of the following item on annual paid vacations for inclusion in the office manual. (Practice Files: Drafts Folder – File: Draft 2)

Annual Paid Vacation

Employees are entitled to annual vacations depending on his or her length of service as of January 1, 20___, as follows:

1. Less than ~~one~~ one (1) year's service: one (1) week after completing six (6) months' employment
2. ~~One~~ (1) year: two (2) weeks
3. 2 – 8 years: three (3) weeks
4. 9 – 15 years: four (4) weeks
5. 16 – ~~20~~ 19 years: five (5) weeks
6. 20 or more years: six (6) weeks

Vacation periods of more than four weeks shall be taken in two sections with exceptions only if approved by the Management Committee. *as one vacation period*
On completion of 25 years continuous employment with this law firm, an employee will be granted a one-time vacation of eight weeks which may be taken together at mutually-agreed upon time.
All requests for vacations ~~may~~ should be presented to the Office Manager on the Vacation request form at least two weeks before the requested vacation period. Every effort will be made to grant such requests depending on the personnel needs of this office.

3. FAX COVER PAGES

Peter Grant has requested material be delivered by fax and you are asked to prepare the fax cover sheets. The necessary fax and file numbers may be found in the reference section of this assignment book. (Practice Files: Forms Folder – File: FaxCover)

(a) The first fax is a two-page letter to Smith, Fraser, Hamid & Lee LLP to the attention of John A. Hamid, in connection with the Crenwood re Staufferdale file.

(b) The second fax is to Armstrong, Ward & Siegel to the attention of Burt M. Ward and consists of a one-page letter which is attached to a five-page document in connection with Greglon Estates re sale to Veneracion file.

C. LEGAL TERMINOLOGY

After completing this exercise you should be able to spell and define the following legal terms. Read the definitions shown below. Then select the correct term and match it with the words or phrase that best matches it in meaning, and write the correct term in the space provided. There are more terms than definitions.

Legal Terms

client	privilege	Children's Lawyer
Public Guardian and Trustee	*sic*	addendum
principle	agreement	prescribed form
principal	guarantee	guarantor

Definitions

1. office that administers justice on behalf of minors

2. protects the interests of mentally incapable people

3. binding exchange of promises between parties

4. individual who employs a law firm

5. an established fundamental rule of law

6. one who promises to answer for the debt of another

7. a legal document for which the format and basic content has been set by an act or statutory regulation

8. indicates an error in quoted material that appears in the original material

9. an attachment to a written document

10. protects confidential communications between a client and his or her legal advisor

CHAPTER 3 – ASSIGNMENTS
Client Records

A. LEGAL OFFICE PROCEDURES

1. INDEX OF CLIENT RECORDS

Most law offices have computerized client records and provide an up-to-date printout to each lawyer at regular intervals which shows his or her active matters at that time. However, some still maintain this information on a paper index as well. Your records for matters will be in the form of an alphabetical paper index as shown in the reference section at the end of this assignment book. There is also an index of the code numbers that the Hill, Johnston & Grant law firm assigns to the various areas of legal practice.

2. FILING

Although Hill, Johnston & Grant assign a number to each new file, most lawyers and their legal assistants maintain their current files in cabinets near their desks and keep the files in alphabetical order.

(a) Naming Files

You are given a list of matters for which new files to be opened. Suggest a suitable name to conform to good alphabetical filing rules. Set out your suggested name in the space provided.

Our client Gino Mancuso is suing Monarch Construction Inc.

Our client City of Eagleton is entering into a lease at Woodbine Centre

Our client East Hardware Limited is selling property located at
25 Trafford Road, Stratford to Applegate Holdings

(b) Arranging Files

You are asked to prepare a list in proper alphabetical order of a number of recently opened files (including those listed above). Set out your list in the space provided.

CBC and Martin Construction Ltd.

WCB re de Nardo v. Preston

WCB re Dennis v. MacIntosh and others

Juliette's Boutiques and Mercer

098567846 Ontario Limited re Corporate Matters

Juliette's Boutiques and McDonald

CBA re Mid-Winter Conference

East Hardware re Humber Manufacturing and Stone

Province of Ontario, Ministry of Social Services re Matthewson

B. LEGAL DOCUMENT PRODUCTION

1. ACTING FOR HENRY DELOS-RAYES

Sylvia has prepared the new matter form and tickler slips for Henry Delos-Rayes (see Figures 3.2B and 3.4B). Peter Grant asks that you prepare a retainer for this client, following the template shown in Precedent 3.1, and provides you with his notes.

> To: Hill, Johnston & Grant
> Attention: PTG
>
> I, Henry Armand Delos-Rayes, of the Township of Georgian Bay in the District Municipality of Muskoka --- to represent --- in a claim for personal injuries against me by John J. Williamson of the Township of Severn, in the County of Simcoe.
>
> Retainer being paid -- $500.00
> Fees on an hourly basis of $350.00 an hour for Peter T. Grant and $250.00 an hour for Michael D. Colucci
> Interest @ 6% per annum

2. ACTING FOR JULIETTE'S BOUTIQUES LIMITED

You are asked to open a file for a new matter for an existing client. You are to prepare a new matter form/label and a tickler slip. Refer to Figures 3.2 and 3.4 and the notes on the following page. **(Practice Files: Forms Folder – Files: Matter Form, Tickler)**

> Client: -- Juliette's Boutiques Limited
> Other Party -- Nancy White
> Other Solicitors - John A. Hamid at Smith, Fraser, Hamid & Lee LLP
> Number has already been assigned - see client index
> Fee will be on an hourly basis
> Tickler for 1 month from today - reminder to commence action if not settled - no limitation date

3. ACTING FOR MARYLYNN PALMER

Peter Grant has been retained by Marylynn Palmer, who recently suffered serious personal injuries in a fall from a horse after it was bitten by a dog. You are asked to open the file. Refer to Figures 3.2A and 3.2B to prepare the new matter form/label. You also need to prepare a retainer (Precedent 3.1) and an authorization (Precedent 3.2) and are provided with the notes on the following page to use in preparing this material. **(Practice Files: Forms Folder – File: Matter Form)**

Marylynn Palmer   3346 Walton Avenue, Apt 807,
Mississauga L6D 7PZ
Res: 905-239-6001
File Number has been assigned - see client index
Other Party: Gerald Rose (of Mississauga)
Other Solicitors: Brianna T. Wolfe at Fox, Wolfe & Lyons

Retainer - describe client as of the City of Mississauga in the Regional Municipality of Peel -- represent her in a claim against Gerald Rose for personal injuries as a result of a fall from a horse -- on an hourly basis. Retainer of $1,000 received and interest to be at 6%

Prepare an authorization to:
Dr. Jane Bragna, 46 Kenwood Road, Toronto M4V 7C2
-- for information on Marylynn Palmer's medical condition as a result of a fall from a horse

4. DRAFT ARTICLE

Michael Colucci asks you to make the necessary changes to the draft of the following item on document references for the office manual. Prepare this article double spaced.

Document Identification or ~~Document~~ Reference

As all computers in the law firm are networked and files often shared, the following standard method of document identification is to be used when preparing any lengthy draft material. This will allow ~~any~~ all members of the firm to be able to locate and retrieve any document. The document identification may be removed before the final version is printed out for signature at the option of the author.

The document reference is to appear at the bottom left corner of every page as a footer. Insert the authors initials and then use the Insert Field, File Name (and check off the box – Add path to file name) to insert the name and location of the document. Use Insert, Date (and check off the box – Update automatically) to insert the date of the draft. Any reference to draft numbering is optional. Document identification references may be keyed in a smaller font size as shown in the examples below ~~as follows~~:

JA\c:\London\declaration
September 1, 20___
Draft No. 2

PTG\h:East\corporate\agmt1-01/09/20___

C. LEGAL TERMINOLOGY

After completing this exercise you should be able to spell and define the following legal terms. Read the definitions shown below. Then select the correct term and match it with the words or phrase that best matches it in meaning, and write the correct term in the space provided. There are more terms than definitions.

Legal Terms

tickler date	authorization	et al.
due date	conflict of interest	v.
limitation date	retain	vs.
retainer	notary public	ats
index	table of contents	dockets

Definitions

1. client accounting records

2. the date by which certain steps should be taken

3. at the suit of

4. and others

5. any inconsistency between the interests of the lawyer and his or her client.

6. document signed by a client employing the law firm

7. the date on which something must be done or the right to do so is lost

8. document that allow release of information to other parties

9. versus (preferred acronym)

10. the date which is a reminder of something to be done

11. listing of material in alphabetic order

12. listing of material in the order in which it appears

13. to employ a lawyer or law firm to act on your behalf

CHAPTER 4 – ASSIGNMENTS
Legal Correspondence

A. LEGAL OFFICE PROCEDURES

You have been asked to prepare several memoranda and letters for Peter Grant, Lynda Ritchie and Michael Colucci. Review the following extract from the Hill, Johnston & Grant Office Procedures Manual regarding preparation of outgoing correspondence before preparing the letters:

OUTGOING CORRESPONDENCE

The correspondence that leaves this office represents this law firm and creates an image reflecting our standards of work. The Management Committee therefore requests that the following guidelines be followed in the preparation of all outgoing correspondence:

1. The letter style to be used is full block, left justified, with mixed punctuation.

2. Our file/matter number must appear on all correspondence.

3. Show the date in month, day, and year order (e.g. January 1, 20xx).

4. Prepare inside addresses in initial capitals and do not use any courtesy title with the name of a law firm.

5. Use the courtesy title Mr., Mrs., Ms. or Miss when addressing individuals; use Dear Sirs & Mesdames when the letter is addressed to a firm or company.

6. Key the firm name (unless it is a personal letter) in all capitals a double-space below "Yours very truly"; do not use "Per" (unless specifically requested by the writer). Three lines below, key the writer's name in initial capitals; if the writer is not a partner or associate, their position should be shown beneath their name in initial capitals.

B. LEGAL DOCUMENT PRODUCTION

1. MEMORANDA TO FILE

On the following page there are drafts of two memoranda to file for you to prepare. Remember to include the file number in the memorandum subject line and to proofread carefully. Refer to Precedent 4.1.

(a) **Memo to File – From PTG – Re Palmer and Rose**

I had a lengthy telephone conversation today with Dr. Irene Harrison who has been treating Marylynn Palmer.

Dr. Harrison said that the x-rays showed no break in the shoulder or arm. There is a great deal of deep bruising. The deep cut in her right hand required eighteen stitches to close. She is suffering a great deal of discomfort from these injuries as well as the whiplash to her neck & the pulled tendon in her shoulder rotator cuff area.

At present she is taking percodan to control the discomfort. Dr. H- proposes to prescribe a less potent narcotic-type drug now that the initial period of discomfort has been dealt with.

Mrs. Palmer is now having physiotherapy treatment for her neck, shoulder & back. When her hand heals, she will also require physiotherapy treatment to overcome any residual problem with finger dexterity – an important point since Ms. Palmer was a costume designer. Dr. H- pointed out the very real possibility of arthritic change as she grows older.

Dr. H- will put her report in writing & will forward it together with her account.

(b) **Memo to File – From PTG – re Juliette's Boutiques & White**

I had an interview with John Jason, Pres. of Juliette's Boutiques yesterday about some collection matters, particularly the Nancy White matter.

Apparently during her employment as manager of it's 2478 Prince Andrew Drive South store, their was a shortage of $8,426.65. John told me that Mrs. White had been an excellent manager but had had some very difficult personal family problems. They did not wish to make her situation even more difficult & therefore agreed to let her repay this shortage by monthly payments of $500. At that time her employment was terminated.

To date she has repaid $3,500 but has failed to make payments for the last 2 months. John advised me that there Human Resources people had tried to talk to her, but she refused to meet with them or provide any info. to explain her defaulted payments.

John feels they had been as generous in their treatment of Mrs. White as possible. In view of her consultation with John Hamid (see letter attached) Juliette's wish Mrs. White to repay the balance as soon as possible. ¶ I am to write to Smith, Fraser to clarify the situation. If no satisfactory assurance repayment will be resumed we are to commence legal proceedings.

2. LETTERS

Your instructor will advise you on the use of letterhead. Only the letter to Smith, Fraser is available to be retrieved from the practice files. The other letters must be fully keyed. Refer to Precedent 4.4. (Practice Files: Drafts Folder – File: Draft 3)

(a) Today's Date

Send by registered mail & SS

John A. Hamid
Smith, Fraser, Hamid & Lee LLP
75 Victoria Street, Suite 503
Toronto ON M5C 2B1

Dear Mr. Hamid:

Juliette's Boutiques Limited and White
Our Reference ????
Your Reference 5012/JAH

We act on behalf of Juliette's Boutiques Limited in respect of its claim against Sarah White in the sum of $8,426.65 for shortages that occurred while Mrs. White was employed as manager of its store at 2478 Prince Andrew Drive South. I understand from your recent letter to John Jason, President of Juliette's, that you act for Mrs. White.

We understand that Mrs. White agreed to make up those shortages by monthly payments of $500.00, but that as of the end of last month she was in arrears to the extent of $1,500.00. A total of $3,500 has been repaid to date.

We would appreciate your advising us whether it is your clients' intention to settle this claim in full in due course by not only bringing the payments up to date but also continuing to make the monthly payment as they fall due until the total amount has been repaid.

Unless we hear from you within 10 days with your client's undertaking to take immediate steps to meet her obligations, it will be necessary for us to advise our clients to institute legal proceedings herein to recover the amount owing.

Yours very truly,

PTG

Send a copy to John Jason, President, Juliette's Boutiques Limited

(b) ~~DRAFT~~

~~Yesterday's~~ today Date

Send By Fax
& Without Prejudice
& SS

Colin W. King
Armstrong, Ward & Siegel

Dear Sir

Henry P. Jones – 24 Mohawk Blvd. Toronto
Expropriation by City of Toronto

I have considered at length with my client the matters that I discussed with you last week. I am satisfied that the figure of $185,000 that I used is a realistic one if the legal question is resolved in favour of Mr. Jones. I am unable to say that your figure is unrealistic if it turns out that the city's position is right on the legal question.

If we are going to avoid prolonged proceedings to determine the legal question, and keeping in mind that a result adverse to the city might require ~~the City to~~ an appeal, because of its effect on other expropriations proceedings, it seems that a compromise settlement is ~~appropriate~~ should be considered. In other words, I suggest we agree to settle the matter at ~~$175,000.00.~~ that figure.

I am authorized to offer to settle the matter at $175,000, ~~subject to adjustment~~ with respect to the matter of the payment to be made on account, and subject to the usual adjustments on closing. Mr. Jones will let me know within a week whether he wishes to retain possession, but this will not (effect?) the question of the quantum of compensation, and Mr. Jones' decision on the matter of possession will be known before any agreement that might be ~~arrived at between us~~ reach has been approved by the authorities.

It is going to be difficult for me to ~~see~~ meet with you in the next two weeks, since I ~~accept~~ expect to be in Ottawa for two appeals in the Supreme Court. However, ~~you might be good enough to~~ please call my office and leave a message as to when you might be able to see me. I will do my best to meet at your convenience. I know you are as anxious as Mr. Jones and to bring this matter to a conclusion.

If we cannot arrange a mutually convenient time, my partner Mr. Johnston is available. He has worked closely with me and mr. Jones on this matter and is fully conversant with all the particulars of our discussions.

Send a copy to Henry P. Jones with the following letter:

Dear Henry

I am enclosing a copy of my letter to Colin King for your information. Either Mr. Johnston or I will keep you informed on this matter.

PTG

(c) Letter to
Dr. Jane Bragna, Suite 2608, Medical Arts Building, 46 Kenwood Road, Toronto Ontario M4V 7C2
Re: Marylyn Palmer
We have been retained to act on behalf of Mrs. Marylynn Palmer, who was seriously injured last month. ¶ We understand that you are treating her for her injuries as a result of the accident. It would be appreciated if you would provide us with a medical report indicating the nature and probable duration of Mrs. Palmer's injuries, together with your account to date. We enclose an authorization permitting us to receive such information. ¶ As you know, all medical reports must be provided to the solicitors for the other party if the dispute require legal proceedings and a trial. We would be pleased to speak to you about this at your convenience, either before or after receipt of your medical report.
Yours very truly
Michael D. Colucci

C. LEGAL TERMINOLOGY

After completing this exercise you should be able to spell and define the following legal terms. Read the definitions shown below. Then select the correct term and match it with the word or phrase that best matches it in meaning, and write the correct term in the space provided. Note that there may be more terms than definitions.

Legal Terms

release	jurisprudence	statute
Q.C.	per se	statue
Without Prejudice	per annum	ancillary
expropriation	per diem	bona fide
ante	age of majority	minor

Definitions

1. the philosophy of law

2. when an individual is deemed an adult

3. by itself; taken alone

4. individual not considered an adult

5. Queen's Counsel

6. to relinquish rights or interests

7. government seizure of title to property

8. government legislation

9. term used in correspondence to indicate document contents may not be used in court

10. by the day

11. auxiliary

12. in good faith, honestly, without fraud

13. by the year

CHAPTER 5 – ASSIGNMENTS
Client Dockets and Accounts

A. LEGAL OFFICE PROCEDURES

The Hill, Johnston & Grant law firm uses a computerized accounting system, and all lawyers, articling students and law clerks are required to record their time entries each day. In most law firms these entries may be keyed directly into the accounting system; however, for the purpose of these exercises, the entries will made into a daily time record sheet that requires essentially the same information as would a computerized time entry.

1. COMPLETING A DAILY TIME RECORD FROM DIARY NOTATIONS

WORK PERFORMED	
Juliette's re White - TF Jason re finalizing details;; LT Smith Fraser	25 m
Palmer and Rose - RD Dr.'s report; TF Bragna; memo to file	1 hr
Anderson, C. Power of Attorney RD file & RL on ancillary powers; DR PA	70 m
East Hardware - Corp. Affairs DR agmt & TT client CW Burnsley re terms	90 m
Chan re separation agmt. TT client; RD agmt.	35 m
Little & Clelland re agmt. engaged RS draft agreement	40 m
Vlasnezski re will AT your residence to execute will	90 m
Knight Mortgage EM Martin Brownlee re receipt of corrected cheque	6 m

Peter Grant is extremely busy today and asks you to prepare his daily time record sheet for yesterday. His diary page listing the work performed yesterday is shown at the left. You will need to locate the correct file/matter number and calculate the time as a decimal before keying the time entry.

The necessary form may be retrieved from your practice files.
(Practice Files: Forms Folder – File: Time Record)

2. ACCOUNTING REQUISITIONS

You have been asked to prepare the appropriate accounting requisition form for each of the items on the following page. The necessary forms are located in your practice files as follows:

Practice Files: Forms Folder   *– File: Petty Cash*   *(Petty Cash Voucher)*
                                           – File: Receipt   *(Cash Receipts)*
                                           – File: Cheque   *(Cheque Requisition)*

1. Re Little and Clelland - Petty Cash Voucher for postage of $3.68 including $0.18 of GST paid by Sylvia Sharpe yesterday.

2. Petty Cash Voucher - office expense (no disbursement code required) - plant for Mrs. Vlasnezski (file is V--- re Will) for $10.00 plus PST and GST paid by Peter T. Grant.

3. Prepare a cash receipt for cheque for $500 received from Marylynn Palmer as a retainer.

4. Cash receipt for the cheque shown at right which was received from Maria del Talfa paying an account.

```
                THE ROYAL BANK OF CANADA
                   Bailwood & King Branch
                      Toronto ON  M1F 9C3
    No. 97                         Yesterday's Date, 20xx

    PAY TO THE
    ORDER OF   Hill, Johnston & Grant         $ 519.65

    Five Hundred and Nineteen ———————— 65/xx DOLLARS

    Account No. 0000 0000 0000     M. del Talfa
    Re: RichardsonEstate    Estate of Jason Richardson
                            Maria del Talfa, Estate Trustee
```

5. Requisition a trust cheque to Grand & Toy (Invoice #97864) re East Hardware - Corporate Affairs for the purchase of a Corporate Box - $24.95 plus PST and GST. Their GST no. is R102171451. Have accounting forward cheque with the invoice.

6. Requisition a cheque, certified, payable to the Minister of Finance for $110.00 (filing fee) re Handel Estate. Have accounting return cheque to you.

7. Requisition a cheque to pay Dr. Bragna's account shown here. Have accounting forward cheque with the attached invoice.

```
DR. JANE BRAGNA                              Suite 2608
Orthopaedic Surgeon                     46 Kenwood Road
                                        Toronto ON  M4X 7C2

(416) 397-4680                          Date: Yesterday's Date

Peter T. Grant
Hill, Johnston & Grant
17 Princess Street South, Suite 2501
Toronto ON  M8Y 3N5

FOR PROFESSIONAL SERVICES RENDERED:

            RE  Marylynn Palmer
            Telephone consultation and report

                                             $150.00
                            GST                 7.50
                                             $157.50
            GST #R812457860
            Accounts are due when rendered
```

B. LEGAL DOCUMENT PRODUCTION

Peter Grant has drafted several accounts to be rendered to various clients. These accounts appear on the following pages of this chapter. Your instructor will advise you on the style and use of account paper. Refer to Precedents 5.2, 5.2 and 5.3.

1. ACCOUNT – APPLEGATE HOLDINGS

Peter Grant asks you to prepare the following short account in which there are no disbursements.

> Applegate Holdings Limited re Corporate Affairs
>
> TO PROFESSIONAL SERVICES ... Sept. 4 to Sept. 6, 20__
> To receipt of initial instructions; reviewing lease in question; revising authorities, to opinion provided Sept. 6 & reporting to you.
>
> FEE $300.00

2. ACCOUNT – VLASNEZSKI

This account, including the disbursements, has been drafted for you to prepare in final form.

> Mrs. Lillian Vlasnezski
> 794 Pemberton Cres. Toronto ON M4R 2C6
>
> Re: New Will
> File No. ??
>
> TO PROFESSIONAL SERVICES RENDERED for the period from October 2 to 14, 20__, connection with the above matter including the following:
>
> Interview with you on Oct. 2 to receive instructions for new will; drafting new will; attending on you to execute new will
>
> | | | |
> |---|---|---|
> | | OUR FEE: | $250.00 |
> | | GST: | ?? |
>
> DISBURSEMENTS SUBJECT TO GST
>
> | | | | |
> |---|---|---|---|
> | Photocopies | | $5.50 | |
> | Travel | | 16.08 | |
> | | | ?? | |
> | | GST | ?? | ?? |
>
> BALANCE DUE $??

3. ACCOUNT – MARTIN DROHAN LIMITED ACCOUNT

Peter Grant has given you the draft account for this client and the section of the billing report outlining the disbursement shown on the following page. He asks you to prepare the account in good form. He points out that the money being held in the trust account should be credited to the client on the account.

Martin Drohan Limited
??

in account with

Hill, Johnston & Grant

Suite 2501, 17 Princess Street South
Toronto, Ontario M8Y 3N5

GST Registration No. R9646802753

Re: Alistair Cormack
File ??

TO PROFESSIONAL SERVICES during the period May 1, 20xx to (last Friday):

To receiving your instructions to act for you in this regard; ¶ To obtaining necessary information from you to prepare statement of claim; preparation of statement of claim and attendances to file and serve the same;

Receiving & reviewing statement of defence and discussing the same with you,; ¶ Preparation of reply and and attendances to file and serve the same;

To preparation of record; attendance to pass record and set action down for trial

To telephone conversations and correspondence in connection with arranging examinations for discovery; ¶ Interview with you preparing for examination for discovery; attendance on discovery; including preparation and engaged one and one-half hours;

To numerous telephone conversations in connection with negotiations for settlement when action is settled for $46,832.00;

Preparing consent to the discontinuance of the action and arranging for execution by all parties; filing the consent;

To all other relevant telephone conversations and correspondence.

OUR FEE:	$3,500.00
GST:	?
DISBURSEMENTS (see billing report - next page)	
LESS: Transfer from Trust	500.00
BALANCE DUE:	?

Extract from Martin Drohan Limited re Cormack billing report -

DISBURSEMENTS

SUBJECT TO GST

JUN 15/20xx	PTG	PHOTOCOPYING	$ 11.50
JUN 11 20xx	PTG	SERVICE OF DOCUMENT	25.00
JUN 17 20xx	LCR	FAX CHARGES	7.50
JUN 17 20xx	LCR	PHOTOCOPYING	5.00
JUL 25 20xx	PTG	LONG DISTANCE	14.60
JUL 30 20xx	PTG	COURIER CHARGES	12.10
JUL 31 20xx	LCR	LONG DISTANCE	13.05
SEP 09 20xx	PTG	TRANSCRIPT OF DISCOVERY	115.75
		DISBURSED TOTAL SUBJECT TO GST	$204.50
		GST (5%)	10.23
		DISBURSEMENTS AND GST	$214.73

NOT SUBJECT TO GST

SEP 15 20xx	PFE	FILING FEES	450.00
		DISBURSED TOTAL NOT SUBJECT TO GST	$450.00

BILL AS IS ----ONLY BILL FEES/DISBURSED----DO NOT BILL-----ADJUST FEE/BILL TO-----CHANGE FEE ALLOCATION
BALANCE IN A/R $ 0.00   BALANCE IN TERM $ 0.00   BALANCE IN TRUST $500.00   TRANSFER FROM TRUST $

Extract from Humber Casualty re Etobicoke Automotive Corp billing report -

DISBURSEMENTS

SUBJECT TO GST

JUN 15/20xx	PTG	PHOTOCOPYING	$ 2.40
JUN 11 20xx	PTG	DELIVERY CHARGES	12.00
JUN 17 20xx	PTG	FAX CHARGES	8.00
JUN 17 20xx	PTG	PHOTOCOPYING	5.00
		DISBURSED TOTAL SUBJECT TO GST	$ 27.40
		GST (5%)	1.37
		DISBURSEMENTS AND GST	$28.77

NOT SUBJECT TO GST

JUN 10 20xx	PTG	COURT FEES	$19.00
		DISBURSED TOTAL NOT SUBJECT TO GST	$19.00

BILL AS IS ----ONLY BILL FEES/DISBURSED----DO NOT BILL-----ADJUST FEE/BILL TO-----CHANGE FEE ALLOCATION
BALANCE IN A/R $ 0.00   BALANCE IN TERM $ 0.00   BALANCE IN TRUST $750.00   TRANSFER FROM TRUST $

4. ACCOUNT – HUMBER CASUALTY COMPANY OF CANADA

Peter Grant has drafted the text portion of this chronological account on his computer and has provided you with the disbursement portion of the billing report shown on the previous page. He asks that you prepare the account in good form. (Practice Files: Drafts Folder: Draft 4)

Humber Casualty Company of Canada
Re: Etobicoke Automotive Corp. ats Consentino
Our File No. ??? Your Claim No. N-95-83533

[handwritten: Pick up disb'ts from previous page. Note money in trust account]

To our fee for professional services rendered as follows:

20__ (this year)

#	Jan. 8	Receipt & perusal of your file
	Jan. 10	Letter to you re payment into court;
	January 31	Undertaking to make payment into court and correspondence concerning same;
	Feb. 27	Letter to the court in order to ascertain whether or not our payment into court had been accepted *by the plaintiff;*
	March 7	Receipt of notification that the plaintiff had accepted the payment in to Court;
#	March 12	Letter to you reporting payment to date;
	March 21	Preparing final release and letter to the plaintiff requesting that he sign the same;
	March 31	Letter from you inquiring as to progress and letter in reply;
#	April 10	Letter to the plaintiff regarding signing of release;
	April 23	Letter to you advising that the release had not been returned;
	May 4	Letter from you with instructions to proceed as is deemed appropriate;
	May 23	Consultation with court regarding payment out of court *and obtaining copy of court ledger*
DS	June 2	Letter to you regarding payment out of court
	June 14	Telephone conversation with you discussing progress *of negotiations*
	June 21	Telephone conversation with you;
	July 10	Telephone conversation with you;
	July 27	Letter to the court requesting copy of court order;
	Aug 17	Receive copy of court order;
	Aug 25	Our final report to you and all matters incidental thereto.

Fee $3,000.00

5. ACCOUNT – CENTENNIAL CONSULTING RE CORPORATE AFFAIRS

Prepare the following draft account. Note that the disbursements have not been separated into which are subject or not subject to GST – you will need to do this before you prepare the account. There is no money being held in the trust account for this client.

Centennial Consulting re Corporate Affairs
File No. ???

TO PROFESSIONAL SERVICES RENDERED from Sept. 15 to Dec. 10, 20xx, in connection with a proposed development agreement with Durham Technology Inc. including:

To meeting with you to discuss proposed agreement; telephone discussion with solicitors for Durham T---; conducting searches against Durham Tech---; drafting agreement and forwarding same to you and Durham Tech—'s solicitors; telephone discussions with you and Durham T--'s solicitor; preparing revised agreement; registering partnership with Ministry of Consumer & Business Services; attending on execution of agmt; receipt and transmission of deposit monies; reporting to you; in all,

OUR FEE: $950.00
GST   ?

DISBURSEMENTS

Photocopying	$ 4.50
Courier Charges	72.50
Facsimile Charges	4.50
Photocopying	45.25
Search Fees	25.00
Registration Fees	125.00
Facsimile Charges	5.60

C. LEGAL TERMINOLOGY

After completing this exercise you should be able to spell and define the following legal terms. Read the definitions shown below. Then select the correct term and match it with the words or phrase that best matches it in meaning, and write the correct term in the space provided. There are more terms than definitions.

Legal Terms

trust account	billable time	general account
retainer	E. & O.E.	contingency fees
void	e.g.	escrow
accountable	receipt	time value
accounts receivable	petty cash	docket

Definitions

1. a client accounting records

2. legal fees that are paid if lawyers are successful in the claim being pursued

3. bank account containing monies held on behalf of clients

4. legal fees calculated on the number and amount of hours that the lawyer spends on the file

5. to hold in trust under until certain conditions are met

6. time spent by a lawyer for which a client will be charged

7. bank account containing monies belonging to the law firm

8. sum of money which is a deposit for legal services

9. acronym for errors and omissions excepted

10. acronym for *exempli gratia* (for example)

11. amounts owing by clients to the law firm

12. written acknowledgement for receiving money or property

13. small amounts of money kept by the law firm for expenses

CHAPTER 6 – ASSIGNMENTS
Legal Citations

A. LEGAL OFFICE PROCEDURES

1. CITING ACTS FROM REVISED STATUTES

In the space provided, cite each of the following acts in proper style:

1. the weed control act revised statutes of Ontario 1990 chapter w.5 section 27

2. Alberta income tax act revised statutes of Alberta 2000 chapter A-26 section 1 subsection a

3. Canada business corporations act revised statutes of Canada 1985 chapter c-4 section 1 subsections b iii

4. the divorce act revised statutes of Canada 1985 chapter d-8 section 9

5. rent review act revised statutes of Nova Scotia 1989 chapter 398 section 1 subsection a

6. courts of justice act revised statutes of Ontario 1990 chapter c.43 section 123 subsection 2 a

2. LAW REPORTS

Refer to the charts of law reports contained in Chapter 6 that provide information on the full name of various law reports, the appropriate abbreviation and the form of citation, i.e., by volume or year. Then indicate the required information for each law report in the following list:

LAW REPORT	ABBREVIATION	FORM OF CITATION FOR LATEST VOLUME
1. Carswell's Practice Cases		
2. Dominion Law Reports		
3. Ontario Reports		
4. Western Weekly Reports		
5. Supreme Court Reports		
6. Manitoba Reports		
7. All England Reports		

3. CITING CASES FROM LAW REPORTS – ONE LAW REPORT CITED

In the space provided, cite each of the following reported cases in good form.

1. Ayangma v. Wyatt 2001 198 Newfoundland. & Prince Edward Island Reports 126 PEISC

2. S. v. S. 2003 Reports of Family Law 5th 235

3. Macdonald v. Clark 2001 287 Alberta Reports 176

4. Regina v. Quesnel 1985 53 Ontario Reports 2d 338

5. Re National Trust Co. and Bouckuyt et al. 1987 59 Ontario Reports 2d 556

6. Eagle Creek Consultants v. Burke 2003 212 Nova Scotia Reports 2d 388

7. Kampus et al. v. Bridgeford et al. 1981 126 Dominion Law Reports 3d 175 at p 178

8. Allen v. Thorn Electrical Industries Ltd. 1967 2 All England Reports 1137

9. Heppel v. Stewart et al. 1968 1 Supreme Court Reports 707 at pages 710-11

10. Winner et al. v. S.M.T. (Eastern) Ltd. et al. 1954 13 Western Weekly Reports ns 657

4. NEUTRAL AND ELECTRONIC CITATIONS

1. Crystalline Investments Ltd. v. Domgroup Ltd. 2004 1 SCR 60

2. Rice v. Bleta 1986 OJ No. 136 QL H.C.J.

3. MacLeod v. MacLeod 1996 NSJ No. 578 QL N.S.S.C.

4. Hutchings v. Li 2001 CanLII 7576 ON S.C.

5. CITING CASES FROM LAW REPORTS – PARALLEL CITATIONS

1. Basarsky v. Quinlan 1971 24 DLR 3d 720 1972 SCR 380 1972 1 WWR 303

2. City of Kamloops v. Nielsen et al. 1984 2 SCR 2 10 DLR 4th 641 1984 5 WWR 1 60 BCLR 172

3. Edwards v. Law Society of Upper Canada 1998 156 DLR 4th 348 37 OR 3d Gen. Div.

4. Lafferty v. Brindley 2003 13 RPR 4th 181 2003 OJ No. 4256 QL CA

B. LEGAL DOCUMENT PRODUCTION

1. MEMORANDUM OF LAW – PALMER FILE

Prepare the following memorandum of law in good form. Remember to cite all statute and case law correctly and proofread carefully. Refer to Precedent 6.1.

MEMO to Michael Colucci from Patricia Emery
RE: Palmer and Rose - Liability of Dog Owners
File No. ???   } format properly

You asked me to review the applicable Ontario statutes to see if the following common law principal is in effect in Ontario:

At common law the owner of an animal such as a dog which is normally harmless, is not liable, in the absence of negligence, for a mischievous act which is not the animal's normal nature to commit usually.

Many jurisdictions have modified this common law principal set out above. In Ontario a strict liability has been imposed on owners whether or not there is any prior knowledge of the nature of the animal. The relevant provisions of the applicable act, the Dog Owners Liability Act Revised Statutes of Ontario 1990 chapter D.16, are as follows:

1. In this act, "owner" when used in relation to a dog, includes a person who possesses or harbours the dog and, where the owner is a minor, the person responsible for the custody of the minor.

2.(1) The owner of a dog is liable for damages resulting from a bite or attack by the dog on another person.

* * *

3. The liability of the owner does not depend upon *scienter* or fault or negligence on the part of the owner, but the court shall reduce the damages awarded in proportion to the degree, if any, to which the fault or negligence of the plaintiff caused or contributed to the damages.

I will be researching the following case which deals with liability of dog owners:

Moffat et al v. Downing et al 1981 22 or 2d 155

PFE

2. LETTER – PALMER FILE

Prepare the following letter in good form. Remember to cite all statute and case law correctly and to proofread carefully.

Letter to John A. Hamid, Smith, Fraser – Re: Palmer and Rose file

We act for Marylynn Palmer and understand that you act for Gerald Rose, the owner of a german sheppard dog.

Our client has advised us that she was seriously injured in an incident on the 16th of last month involving this dog. We are advised that she was riding her horse on the private riding trail adjacent to the side road when Mr. R-'s dog ran towards the horse and started to bite at it's front legs. As result of the dog's biting, the horse reared & Mrs. Palmer was thrown. The horse ran onto the adjacent road & was hit by a passing vehicle.

Mrs. Palmer suffered serious personal injuries to her neck, shoulders, arms & back, multiple lacerations & a deep cut to the back of her right hand that required eighteen stitches to close. The injuries to her horse required that it be destroyed.

Mrs. P- has been unable to return to her employment as a costume designer with Molson Theatrical Productions. It is not yet known weather surgery will be required to lessen the scarring on her hand. She is presently undergoing physiotherapy for her neck, shoulder & back & when her hand heals she will require physiotherapy to endeavour to regain the flexibility & strength.

Under the provision of the Dog Owner's Liability Act RSO 1990 Chapter D.16 your client is responsible for damages resulting from Mrs. Palmer's injuries as a result of this incident.

We would like to discuss settlement of this matter with you & we would appreciate hearing from you as to how your client proposes to settle this claim.

Yours very truly
Michael D. Colucci

3. MEMORANDUM OF LAW – PALMER FILE

Patricia Emery has now drafted the second memorandum of law in connection with the Palmer file. You are to prepare the final copy of the revised draft. Remember to correctly format all citations. (Practice Files: Drafts Folder – File: Draft 5)

Memo
To MRC
From PFE
Re Palmer and Rose

As requested by you, I have looked at the following cases dealing with property damages against the owners of a dog.

Moffett et al. v. Downing et al. 1981 32 Ontario Reports 2d 155

The case deals with a claim for damages as a result of a dog running towards a horse being ridden by Miss Moffett. The horse reared and Miss M. was thrown. The horse went on to the road and was struck by a car.

In his decision Brooke J. said at p. 157:

". . . the dog was allowed to run around playing with children and barking. They must have known that horses were regularly ridden along the highway, and that if a horse became frightened, an accident might occur. They ought to have foreseen that an accident might occur."

Wong v. Arnold et al. 1987 59 O.R. 2d 299 – cite properly

This was an appeal by the defendants from a judgement in favour of the plaintiff in an action for damages for personal injuries

The appeal was heard by Grange, Finlayson and Krever jj.a., and oral judgment was given by Finlayson j.a.

The plaintiff suffered personal injuries as the result of an attack by one of two dogs owned by the defendants. The plaintiff had gone to the defendants' home to speak to their son who delivered his daily newspaper. When he saw a large dog on a leash on the veranda, he stopped at the end of the veranda and called the boy's name. A dog inside the house started to bark and the large dog lunged at the plaintiff. It was restrained by the leash, but the claws of one of its front paws struck the plaintiff on his knee. The plaintiff took a step back, lost his balance and fell and broke his leg. The plaintiff sued the defendants as owners of the dogs, relying on s. 2(1) of the Dog Owners' Liability act, Revised Statutes of Ontario 1990 c. D.16:

> 2(1) The owner of a dog is liable for damages resulting from a bite or attack by the dog on another person.

The judgment at p. 300 set out:

> I am of the same opinion as Blair J. in Chittenden v. Hale et al. 1933 OR 836 ... that the statute has removed the necessity for the victim of an attack by a dog proving scienter on the part of the owner or that the injury was due to negligence on the part of the owner. This has been codified by s. 2(3) which reads:
>
> > "2(3) The liability of the owner does not depend upon scienter or fault or negligence on the part of the owner but the court shall reduce the damages awarded I proportion to the degree, if any, of which the fault or negligence of the plaintiff caused or contributed to the damages."
>
> Section 2 creates a *prima facie* liability on the part of the owner for injuries resulting from an attack by a dog, but it is still open to him to establish affirmatively, if he can, facts excusing him from liability.
>
> Looking at the case on appeal and accepting the findings of the trial judge, there are no such facts that exonerate the owners from liability. The plaintiff was not a trespasser, he did nothing to provoke the dog, and the suggestion that his calling out of the boy's name amounts to contributory negligence cannot be supported. The trial judge correctly disposed of this submission by stating:
>
> > " I find that a reasonable consequence of the actions of both dogs was a hasty retreat in a state of confusion by Mr. Wong to the extent that he fell."

The appeal was dismissed with costs.

If you want me to look at other decided cases on this point, the following would seem to be relevant:

Morsillo v. Miglano 1985 52 Ont. Rep. 2d 319

Kirk v. Trerise 1981 122 DLR 3d 60

Morris v. Baily 1970 3 Ont Rep 386

4. MEMORANDUM OF LAW – GEORGIAN TECHNOLOGIES INC.

You are asked to prepare the final copy of the revised draft. Remember to correctly format all citations. (Practice Files: Drafts Folder – File: Draft 6)

To: PTG
From: Howard Podoba
Re: Georgian Technologies Inc. ats ~~Lea~~side Electronics Ltd. [Bay] [File No.?]

As requested by you, I have reviewed the Flintoft v. The Royal Bank of Canada 1964 17 DLR 2d 630 case.

This appeal was he[a]rd by a court composed of Taschereau CJ and Hall, Abbott, Martland and Judson JJ. The judg[e]ment of the court was delivered by Judson J. and r[ea]d in part:

My opinion is that the majority judg[e]ment is correct. By agreement in writing between bank and customer, an express trust of ~~these~~ [this] account was created in favour of the bank . .

The judgment goes on to say:

In Union Bank of Halifax v. spinney and Churchill 1908 38 SCR 187, the proceeds of the sale of the bank[']s security came into the hands of Spinney, a third party, who was guarantor of the customer's account with the bank. The proceeds were in the form of ~~drafts~~ [cheques] drawn in favour of the guarantor instead of the bank, as they should have been. Spinney took [with knowledge] that the ~~drafts~~ [cheques] were in payment for meal, ground f[r]om corn, on which the bank held security, and he was held liable to account. I can find in the report no ~~motion~~ [mention] of any written agreement similar to the one in existence in the present case, but it is clear tha[t] the oral understanding between [the] bank and customer was to the same effect. See also Vail v. Murphy 1960 SCR 913 at page 920. —cite properly

The appeal therefore was dismissed.

C. LEGAL TERMINOLOGY

After completing this exercise you should be able to spell and define the following legal terms. Read the definitions shown below. Then select the correct term and match it with the words or phrase that best matches it in meaning, and write the correct term in the space provided. There are more terms than definitions.

Legal Terms

authorities	cite	J.A.
C.J.	case law	judge
JJ.	statute law	citations
Regina	Gazette	appeal
regulations	*stare decisis*	appellate

Definitions

1. a person who adjudicates matters within the court

2. previously decided cases that support a client's position in a legal matter

3. judge, court of appeal

4. judges

5. to refer to an act by name, statute and chapter

6. references to previously decided cases

7. Chief Justice

8. a government's official newspaper

9. review of decision of lower court by a higher court

10. decisions of judges; judge-made law

11. legislative law

12. legal principle of abiding by decisions of previous decided cases that are of a similar fact situation

13. rules outlining how the provisions of an act are to be carried out or administered

CHAPTER 7 – ASSIGNMENTS
Introduction to Legal Documents

A. LEGAL OFFICE PROCEDURES

1. GENERAL ADDRESS FOR USE IN LEGAL INSTRUMENTS

You should become familiar with how to locate general address information for your province or territory through the use of a reference book such as a municipal directory or the internet. Your instructor may provide you with a list of sample municipalities for you to use in practicing this procedure.

2. USE OF NUMBERS AND SYMBOLS

Consider each of the following extracts from a <u>commercial legal document</u>. You may wish to refer to the discussion on the use of numbers and symbols in Chapter 2 of your text. Use proofreader's marks to edit any incorrectly expressed number or symbol. Indicate by a 'C' any item that you believe is correct as presented.

1. In consideration of the sum of Twenty Five Thousand Dollars…

2. Interest will be payable at 7 percent per annum.

3. …in consideration of the settlement of the action commenced by court file no. 99-457892.

4. Upon receipt of one month's notice…

5. …being part of Lot 9 (nine).

6. …at an agreed price of One ($1.00) Dollar.

7. The invention is described as Canadian Patent number 49117611182 (the "invention")

8. FIVE HUNDRED------($500.00)-------DOLLARS

B. LEGAL DOCUMENT PRODUCTION

1. HEADINGS & ENDINGS TO AGREEMENTS

From the information provided on the following page, prepare the heading <u>and</u> ending for each agreement. Use the current date where necessary. Your instructor will advise which precedents from the text to use in formatting these headings and endings and if backs are to be prepared as well. Refer to Figures 7.2, 7.3, 7.4, 7.5 and 7.6.

1. For an agreement made the   day etc. between you (described by your last name) and East Hardware Limited (described as East).

2. For an agreement made as of the   etc. between Mary Jane Brocovich and Alexander Paul Brocovich, both of whom live in the capital city of your province/territory (described as the "purchasers") and you (the "vendor").

2. ARTICLE FROM A LONG AGREEMENT

Michael Colucci has drafted a new Article XIX for an agreement regarding a shopping centre. Peter Grant has now reviewed it and made several amendments as shown on the following page. You have been asked to review the draft to be sure that all errors have been noted and then retrieve the draft from disk and prepare in final form. Refer to Precedent 7.2.
(Practice Files: Drafts Folder – File: Draft 7)

Also prepare the following letter to forward the agreement to the Ingle, Henchman & Broder law firm for their consideration

Please send by Fax

Liam P. Broder
Ingle, Henchman & Broder

Preston re Centre Lease Agmt.
Further to our discussion yesterday, I have now drafted a new section relating to rent during reconstruction. A copy of the revised article XIX for this lease is enclosed for your review and comments. I would appreciate receiving your comments asap as time is becoming of the essence if our client is to move in by the lease commencement date. ¶ When I have heard from you, I will incorporate this section in the existing wording of the article and let you consider the entire agmt. with all revisions to date so that we may move forward on this matter.

PTG

Please copy John Preston on this letter

DRAFT NO. ~~1~~ 2
~~Yesterday~~'s Date
~~Today~~

ARTICLE XIX
DESTRUCTION OF LEASED PREMISES
SHOPPING DISTRICT

{ DS & BOLD }

2. In the event that centre reconstructs the leased premises or elects to reconstruct or repair the leased premises as hereinbefore in the article provided for, then and so often as such event shall occur:

(b) if the leased premises shall by reason of such occurrence be rendered untenantable only in part, the fixed minimum rental shall be abated proportionately as to the portion of the leased premises rendered untenantable, until Centre's work of reconstruction and/or repair is completed; or

(c) If the leased premises shall be reason of such occurrence be rendered wholly untenantable, the fixed minimum rent shall be abated in whole until Centre's work of reconstruction is completed but to the extent only of proceeds received by Centre from rent insurance for which the premiums have been paid by Lessee; and

(d) from and after the date upon which Lessee is notified in writing by centre that Centre's work of reconstruction and/or repair is completed, all rent under the lease shall commence and Lessee shall complete all Lessee's Work (as set out in Schedule "B") required to fully restore the leased premises and to enable Lessee to re-open the leased premises for business fully stet. Certificate of an architect appointed by Centre for such purpose shall bind the parties hereto as to the state of tenantability of the leased premises and as to the date upon which Centre's Work of reconstruction and/or repair is completed.

(a) If the leased premises are not by reason of such occurrence rendered untenantable in whole or in part, the rent shall not be abated.

Nothing in this section 2 shall be constructed to permit the abatement of the percentage rent or additional rent, but for the purposes of Article II 2(b) hereof the computation of percentage rent shall be based upon the revised fixed minimum rent as the same may be abated pursuant to this section 2.

3. SHORT AGREEMENT – EAST HARDWARE AND GRAHAM

Prepare a good copy of the following rough draft of an agreement between East Hardware and Martin Phillip Graham. Remember to show all amounts in words and figures and to be careful of initial capitalization of definitions such as "Retailer." Refer to Precedent 7.1 in your text.

This Agreement made as of the 1st day of January, 20__ (next year)

BETWEEN

EAST HARDWARE LIMITED

herein referred to as the "Retailer"

and

MARTIN PHILLIP GRAHAM

herein referred to as the "Associate"

Witnesseth that in consideration of the mutual covenants and agreements herein set out, the parties hereto agree:

1. The Retailer hereby engages the Associate as an associate buyer of hardware supplies for a period of 3 years commencing on the 1st day of January, 20__ and terminating on December 31, 20__. This term includes a paid annual vacation of four weeks to be taken at a time or times mutually agreed upon.

2. The Associate agrees to act as a buyer subject to the discretion of the Retailer of hardware supplies for the retailer and to act as an advisor and consultant in respect of the merchandising of hardware supplies.

3. The Retailer agrees to provide a recent model car for the use of the Associate in the performance of his duties as associate buyer & to maintain the necessary insurance thereon.

4. The Retailer agrees to pay the associate the sum of Forty-Five Thousand Dollars each year during the term of this agreement, payable $3,750.00 monthly, payable on the 25th day of each and every month until

the effective date of termination of this agmt. The first such payment to be made on the 25th day of January, 20__.

Key in Insert "A" here

~~5.~~ 6. The Associate agrees to lease from the Retailer the furnished office located at Suite 431, 17 Princess Street South, at a monthly rental of $500.00, which lease shall be terminated immediately upon the termination or cancellation of this agreement by either party for any cause whatsoever.

5. The Associate agrees to perform his duties subject to the direction of the Retailer, in an honest, ethical conscientious and businesslike manner.

6. This agmt. may be terminated by either party giving to the other three calendar month's notice in writing of a desire to terminate this agreement and upon giving of such notice this agreement and the lease between the parties referred to herein shall thereupon be terminated.

Insert "A"

5. The Retailer agrees that the associate will be provided with a credit card for the purpose of purchasing gasoline at the expense of the Retailer and that all other traveling expenses incurred by the Associate in the execution of his duties shall be paid by the retailer upon submission of expense vouchers.

IN WITNESS WHEREOF etc......

4. LONGER AGREEMENT – GAMS and PODOBA

Peter Grant has now reviewed and revised the draft agreement between Drs. Gams and Podoba shown on the following three pages. Retrieve this file from disk and prepare in good form. Once you have made the revisions shown, you should proofread the <u>entire</u> agreement to ensure that is reads sensibly and is correctly formatted. **(Practice Files: Drafts Folder – File: Draft 8)**

THIS AGREEMENT made in duplicate as of the 1st day of Jan, 20__

BETWEEN:

DR. HOWARD GREGORY GAMS
(herein "Gams")

- and -

DR. WALTER PODOBA
(herein "Podoba")

WHEREAS Gams carries on the practice of medicine in and around the City of Barrie, in the County of Simcoe, and has an office located at 468 Lady Emily Drive, in the City of Barrie;

AND WHEREAS Podoba is a duly qualified medical practitioner licensed to practise medicine in the Province of Ont.

AND WHEREAS Gams and Podoba are desirous of entering into a formal agreement regarding the terms of engagement of Podoba for a certain specified term.

NOW THEREFORE THIS AGREEMENT witnesseth that in consideration of the premises and mutual covenants herein contained, the parties hereby agree to & with each other as follows:

1.00 ENGAGEMENT — BOLD ALL HEADINGS

1.01 Gams hereby engages Podoba, and Podoba hereby accepts such engagement, to carry on the practice of medicine at Gams' office at 468 Lady Emily Drive, subject to the terms hereinafter set forth.

2.00 TERM AND RENEWAL

2.01 This agreement shall commence on the 1st day of January, 20__, and shall be in full force and effect for a period of three (3) months, up to and including the last day of ?, 20__.

3.00 DUTIES

3.01 Podoba shall be responsible for treating and caring for Gams' patients during the term of this agreement and shall provide the best available care to ensure that Gams' patients and others seeking & receiving treatment are adequately and competently cared for at all times.

4.00 TIME AND ATTENDANCE TO DUTIES

4.01 During the term of ~~the~~ *this* agreement Podoba shall perform ~~hs~~ *his* duties during Gams' posted office hours and shall diligently ensure that all appointments set up by Gams' staff and himself are kept and shall, *not* without the written consent of Gams, engage in any other business, *or occupation* that would in any way interfere with the performance of his duties. Podoba will at all *times* use Gams' office *facilities* and office staff, and Gams will at all times be responsible for payment of *the* charges *and salaries* associated with *use and* the operation of the office.

5.00 REMUNERATION *(In accordance with this agmt)*

5.01 Podoba agrees to promptly complete and submit to the Ontario Health Insurance Plan all of the patient billings in regard to treatment rendered by him, in his own name and under his own claim number, and immediately upon receipt *by him* of payment thereof from *the* (OHIP) agrees to transfer to Gams the *total* amount of such payment. The parties hereto, *specifically* acknowledge Gams' interest in and right to receive such payment *from Podoba* by reason of Gams' obligations hereunder to pay all office overhead expenses and the monies to Podoba hereinafter ~~set out~~ *described*.

5.02 Gams shall pay to Podoba for services rendered by him hereunder between *Jan. 1, 20-- and March 31, 20--,* monthly, in arrears the following minimum remuneration: the sum of Four Thousand Dollars ($4,000.00).

5.03 Gams further agrees to pay Podoba after receipt by him of the payment referred to in paragraph 5.01, (additional remuneration) as follows: for the services rendered during the three month period commencing the 1st day of January, 20__, and ending the last day of March, 20__, fifty percent of all payments in excess of $15,000.00 received by Podoba and paid to Gams *in accordance with para 5.01 herein.*

5.04 Podoba agrees that no other remuneration of any nature will be paid to him ~~or~~ by Gams on his behalf.

6.00 TERMINATION

6.01 (a) By Gams

This agreement may ~~be terminated~~ before the 31st day of March, 20__, upon ten (10) days written notice of termination ~~by~~ Gams to Podoba.

(b) By Podoba

This agreement may ~~be~~ terminated *stet* ~~by~~ Podoba at any time before the last day of March, 20__, for any reason, upon giving two (2) weeks' written notice of termination.

6.02 Podoba will not be entitled to any payment solely on account of this agmt.

7.00 NOTICE

Any notice of payment required to be given or made hereunder may be delivered or mailed by prepaid registered mail addressed:

(a) To Gams:

Dr. Howard G. Gams ← 780 Millwood Drive, Barrie Ont L4X 2Y7

(b) To Podoba

Dr. Walter Podoba ← 7942 Queen Mary Crescent, Orillia Ont L6Z 9M1

8.00 GENERAL

8.02 The parties hereto agree to do all such further and other acts, and to execute all such further ~~deeds~~ documents and assurances as may be necessary to carry out this agreement.

8.01 This agreement may not be assigned by Podoba without the prior written consent of Gams.

IN WITNESS WHEREOF etc....

5. STATUTORY DECLARATION

Peter Grant has drafted a statutory declaration that is shown below. Prepare on legal-size paper to be sworn in your city later this week. Refer to Precedent 7.6.

CANADA	)	IN THE MATTER OF the title to part of
	)	Lot 297, Plan BR-324, City of
Province of Ontario	)	Brampton, Reg. Muni. of Peel
	)	municipally known as 478 Elliot Street,
TO WIT:	)	Brampton

WE, PETER GAUDIER and NICOLE GAUDIER, both of the City of Brampton, in the Reg. Muni. of Peel, SEVERALLY SOLEMNLY DELCARE, that:

1. We have been tenants at 478 Elliott Streeet, Brampton, for over 25 years and as such have knowledge of the matters hereinafter deposed to.
2. We originally moved into the premises known as 478 Elliott Street, Brampton, in Oct. of 1980 and have occupied the premises continuously since that time.
3. Since prior to 1980, the premises have always been used as a multi-residential building with 6 separate apartment units and this use of the premises has been continuous
4. The building located on the lands has been in its present location and form without exterior alterations or additions since prior to 1980.

AND WE make this solemn Declaration etc...

6. NOTARIAL CERTIFICATE

Michael Colucci (his middle name is Dominic and he lives in Toronto or in your city) has requested that you prepare a notarial certificate for his signature for the agreement between Drs. Gams and Podoba which was executed this morning. Refer to Precedent 7.8.

7. RELEASE

Prepare a draft release using the following information. Refer to Precedent 7.9.

release to be given by Jason Mark Fisher, Law Clerk, (he lives in Barrie)...
in consideration of the settlement of the claim for damages for personal injuries by me against Arthur Raul Hawchukwood and in consideration of the monies paid thereunder...
relating to personal injuries sustained as a result of an accident on the property of the said Arthur Raul Hawchukwood

C. LEGAL TERMINOLOGY

After completing this exercise you should be able to spell and define the following legal terms. Read the definitions shown below. Then select the correct term and match it with the words or phrase that best matches it in meaning, and write the correct term in the space provided. There are more terms than definitions.

Legal Terms

attest	jurat	release
notarial certificate	testimonium	county
affidavit	clause	definitions
duplicate original	consideration	preamble
deponent	recitals	town

Definitions

1. introductory clauses in an agreement _____

2. copy of document that is considered also an original _____

3. final clause of a commercial document _____

4. document relinquishing rights or interests _____

5. person who swears an affidavit _____

6. the return given for act or promise of another _____

7. an example of an upper-tier municipality _____

8. to witness the signature of parties to an agreement _____

9. an example of a lower-tier municipality _____

10. ending of affidavit attesting where and when sworn _____

11. written statement of facts sworn under oath _____

12. document that certifies authenticity of document to which is attached _____

13. words or phrases in an agreement stated to have a specific meaning and/or format _____

CHAPTER 8 – ASSIGNMENTS
Introduction to Civil Litigation

A. LEGAL OFFICE PROCEDURES

1. COURT STRUCTURE

In the space provided, indicate the appropriate word or phrase that matches the definition.

1. the language(s) of the courts in your province	
2. the highest court in Canada	
3. the highest court of first instance in your province	
4. the court in your province that hears traffic offences	
5. the court in your province that hears applications for judicial review	
6. the court in your province that hears claims for small amounts as specified by the rules	

B. LEGAL DOCUMENT PRODUCTION

1. FILE OPENING RECORDS, RETAINER AND TICKLERS – EAST v. EAST FILE

Peter Grant has just seen Peter and Leslie East and gives you some handwritten notes he has made during the appointment. He asks that you prepare a retainer, the new matter form/label and the required tickler slips. He also gives you Peter East's cheque for $500.00 as a retainer.

> *New File:* East v. East
> *Our clients:* East, Peter Bruce
> East, Leslie Margaret
> R.R. #7, Brock ON L2C 5P4
> Tel: 905-233-6435
> Reg. Municipality of Durham
> No business address

AGAINST: Mary Ann East
 24 Albert Street
 Newcastle ON L3K 4G4

For Superior Court of Justice action for specific performance

We'll bill on a time basis - LCR & MDC will also be working on this file. John A. Hamid of Smith, Fraser, is representing Mary Ann East.

TICKLERS:
1. one month from now - get in touch with Smith, Fraser if no word on option agmt.
2. Limitation Date - 6 years from last July 31 - tickler for 1 month before - commence action if exercise of option not settled - no due date yet

2. MEMO TO FILE – EAST v. EAST FILE

Prepare the following draft memorandum to file relating to this matter. Peter Grant also gives you the copy of the lease and of the exercise of option left with him by Mr. and Mrs. East. These should be placed in the file for safekeeping.

Memo to file
Re: East v. East

LCR & I had an interview on (today's date) with Peter & Leslie East re the exercise by them of their option under an agmt. of sale to them by Mary Ann East - Mr. East aunt - of property in the Township of Brock.
 Under a lease dated the 29th of Oct/02, M-A-East leased to P-East & L-East the north half of Lot 7, 3rd Concession, Twp. of Brock, for a period of 10 years. The lease contained a proviso that PE & LE had an option to purchase the property during the term of the lease.
During the summer of 20xx (last summer) PE & LE orally advised MAE that they were exercising their option & in August of that year gave her written advice. MA East apparently now claims there was no valid lease & that she was subjected to undue influence & had no independent legal advice. PE gave me their copy of the lease & a copy of the exercise of option.
 Following the exercise of option, draft documents were drawn to complete the carrying out of the sale, but not executed.
 MAE also apparently says that she was unaware of the clause in question & that it was added without her consent and knowledge.
 We are to:
1. Pursue the matter with Smith, Fraser & verify the status of M-A-E's position
2. Commence legal proceedings if it appears M-A-East is not prepared to carry out the transactions.

TO: MARY ANN EAST

NOTICE OF EXERCISE OF OPTION

The undersigned, the Lessees in a lease dated the 29th day of October, 2002, hereby exercise the option contained in paragraph 7 of the said Lease, which provision reads as follows:

> The parties hereby covenant and agree with the other that the Lessees shall, in consideration of the agreement to pay the rent, have the option to purchase the said lands and premises at any time within the term of this lease at the price of Two Hundred and Sixty Thousand Dollars ($260,000.00), and if the Lessor shall vacate the house on the said lands at any time within the term of this lease the Lessees shall be bound to exercise the option.

This notice confirms the oral notice given by the Lessees to the Lessor on or about July 1, 20xx, that they exercised the said option to purchase.

DATED the *18th* day of August, 20xx.

WITNESS:)
)
) *Peter B. East*
) ———————————————
) Peter Bruce East
Donna Fitzgerald)
)
) *Leslie M. East*
) ———————————————
) Leslie Margaret East

Note: *In this Notice of Exercise of Option, assume the year shown as 20xx represents the year in which "last" July and August occurred.*

THIS AGREEMENT made in duplicate the 29th day of October, 2002.

B E T W E E N:

        MARY ANN EAST, of the Municipality
        of Clarington, in the Regional Municipality
        of Durham

        (herein the "Lessee")

        - and -

        PETER BRUCE EAST, and
        LESLIE MARGARET EAST, both
        of the Township of Brock, in the
        Regional Municipality of Durham

        (herein the "Lessors")

WITNESSETH that in consideration of the rents, covenants, and agreements hereinafter reserved and contained on the part of the Lessee, the Lessor doth demise and lease until the Lessee all that parcel or tract of land situate, lying and being in the north half of Lot 7, in the 3rd Concession of the Township of Brock, in the Regional Municipality of Durham.

1.   **TO HAVE AND TO HOLD** the said demised premises for the term of ten (10) years, to be computed from the 1st day of November, 2002, yielding and paying therefor yearly and every year during the said term with the Lessor, her heirs, successors, administrators, and assigns, the sum of TWENTY-FOUR THOUSAND DOLLARS ($24,000.00), to be payable in monthly payments of TWO THOUSAND DOLLARS ($2,000.00) on the 1st day of each month during the term of the said lease.

2.   The first of such payment as set out in paragraph 2 hereof shall become due and payable on the 1st day of November, 2002, and the last of such payments shall

Assume this lease contains 6 pages and a back.

3. LETTER – EAST v. EAST

At Peter Grant's request, Lynda Ritchie drafted the following letter to the Smith Fraser law firm. Peter Grant has now reviewed it and requests that you prepare it for his signature.
(Practice Files: Drafts Folder – File: Draft 9)

Smith Fraser etc.
~~Attention L.A. Blackwell~~ John A. Hamid

Dear Sirs:

East and East & Leslie   Your reference 659A/JAH

We have been consulted by Peter East, in connection with their rights under a lease dated the 29th day of October, 2002, from Mrs. Mary Ann East to our clients. We have seen your letter of the 1st to Mr. East in which you ask that all correspondence with respect to this matter be addressed to you.

We enclose herewith a copy of the notice signed by our clients stating that they exercise the option in the said lease. As you are probably aware, they exercised this option orally several months ago and draft documents to complete the carrying out of the sale were prepared at that time but were not signed by your client.

My clients require that the transaction be carried out by the giving of a transfer within a reasonable period of time. If your client is not prepared to carry out the transaction, would you be good enough to let me know, as we have instructions to commence legal proceedings immediately, but wish to clarify the status of this matter with you before doing so.

We note from your letter of the 1st that your client has instructed you that she was "unaware of the clauses in question at the end of the lease and that the same was added with out her consent and knowledge." We draw to your attention to the lease of November 18, 1992, which contained the identical provisions as that now relied upon and found in the lease of October 29, 2002.

For your convenience, we enclose a copy of the provisions as they appear in those leases.

YUT

PTG.

C. LEGAL TERMINOLOGY

After completing this exercise you should be able to spell and define the following legal terms. Read the definitions shown below. Then select the correct term and match it with the words or phrase that best matches it in meaning, and write the correct term in the space provided. There are more terms than definitions.

Legal Terms

action	plaintiff	rules of court
applicant	defendant	registrar
application	judicial regions	sheriff
appellate court	master	statutory holiday
court of first instance	respondent	settlement

Definitions

1. Canada Day is an example of this

2. person who commences an application proceeding

3. a person against whom an action is commenced

4. lawyer appointed to assist judges in carrying out their duties

5. civil proceedings that are usually adversarial

6. A court administrative area composed of several counties

7. civil proceeding requesting the advice, direction or authority of the court

8. a person who commences an action

9. a person against whom an application is commenced

10. court of original jurisdiction that hears a case for the first time

11. term used to describe a court that hear appeals

12. statutory acts, rules and regulations that set out court procedures

13. officer of the crown who may summons jurors

CHAPTER 9 – ASSIGNMENTS
Preparing Court Documents

A. LEGAL OFFICE PROCEDURES

Some court forms and court offices now require the law society membership number of the individual lawyer to be shown, usually in brackets, following their name on court documents. The membership numbers for the lawyers of Hill, Johnston & Grant are listed in the reference section. The membership number for any solicitor on the other side is obtained from the documents served on your law firm. Your instructor will advise whether you are to insert such membership numbers in the court documents you prepare.

B. LEGAL DOCUMENT PRODUCTION

1. GENERAL HEADINGS

Prepare general headings for the following two proceedings based on the information provided below. These proceedings are to be in the Ontario Superior Court of Justice unless your instructor advises otherwise. You will need to refer to these general headings as you prepare other documents in this and future assignments. Refer to Figure 9.1.

(a) The first proceeding is between James David Black and Jennifer Mary Black as Plaintiffs and Humber Tool & Dye Company Limited as Defendant. The action was commenced in Barrie and assigned Court File No. 08/CV/112311. The document is an affidavit to be sworn by the female plaintiff.

(b) The second proceeding is between Joan Catherine Cochrane, a minor, by her litigation guardian, Mary Elizabeth Cochrane as Plaintiff and Jacob Aaron White, John Gregory Waynewood and Patrick Warren Hook as Defendants. The action was commenced in Toronto and assigned Court File No. 08/CV/334556. The document is a Notice of Motion.

2. MEMORANDUM TO FILE – EAST v. EAST FILE

Peter Grant had a long telephone conversation yesterday with John A. Hamid of the Smith Fraser law firm in regard to the East action. He has now prepared a memorandum and asks you to prepare a good copy for the file.

> *East and East File*
> *John Hamid called (today's date) in response to my letter in regard to this matter.*
> *He has instructions from (MAW) that ~~the lease~~ she is not prepared to carry out the sale of the property. She alleges that the option provision was added to the latest lease without her consent*

or knowledge. She has indicated her nephew cannot exercise an option provision that she says was added to the latest lease without her consent or knowledge. She does not intend to move out of the property at this time.

I advised John Hamid that we would now proceed to issue the statement of claim. He agreed Smith, F- will accept service of the S/C on behalf of Mrs. East. Apparently, she is not in good health and they wish to relieve her of as much detail as they can.

I have discussed this file with LCR and she is to draft the statement of claim for my review.

PTG

3. AFFIDAVIT FOR YOU TO SWEAR – HARRISON v. HARRISON

You are to prepare a good copy of the following draft affidavit that is to be sworn later today in your office. The first page of the exhibit for the affidavit is provided on the following page. Be sure to mark it as an exhibit and complete the stamping. Refer to Precedent 9.4.

Court File no. 12433/08

ONTARIO
SUPERIOR COURT OF JUSTICE

BETWEEN:

GREGORY P. HARRISON

Plaintiff

- and -

PATRICIA HARRISON

Defendant

A F F I D A V I T

I, *(your name in all capitals)*, of the *(your lower tier municipality)*, in the *(your upper tier municipality)*, MAKE OATH AND SAY:

1. I am a legal assistant in the offices of H, J. & G., solicitors for the defendant, and as such have knowledge of the matters hereinafter deposed to.

2. On Friday, *(date of last Friday, in month day and year order)*, I mailed to the plaintiff a notarial copy of the marriage contract that the defendant had provided to H. J. & G.

3. Attached hereto and marked Exhibit "A" to this my affidavit is a copy of the said marriage contract.

SWORN etc.

THIS MARRIAGE CONTRACT made the 1st day of July, 2000

BETWEEN:

GREGORY P. HARRISON

(herein "the husband")

- and -

PATRICIA MACINTOSH

(herein "the wife")

WHEREAS the husband and the wife intend to marry and enter into this contract freely and under no undue influence or duress

AND WHEREAS the husband and the wife wish to enter into this contract setting out the mutual promises hereinafter set forth and for other good and valuable consideration, the receipt and sufficiency of which is hereby acknowledged.

NOW THEREFORE the husband and the wife agree as follows:

1.00 INTERPRETATION

1.01 In this contract:

(a) "husband" means Gregory P. Harrison who is a party to this contract

(b) "wife" means Patricia Macintosh who is a party to this contract

(c) "*Family Law Act*" means the *Family Law Act*, R.S.O. 1990, as amended

(d) "property" has the meaning set out in the *Family Law Act*

(e) "matrimonial home" has the meaning set out in the *Family Law Act*

(f) "breakdown of the marriage" means:

(i) the separation of the parties with no reasonable prospect that they will resume cohabitation

4. CORRESPONDENCE – PALMER v. ROSE

Michael Colucci has drafted a letter to Marylynn Palmer and asks you to let him have it for his signature as soon as possible.

Dear ~~Miss~~ Mrs. Palmer

Re: Palmer and Rose

Further to our recent telephone conversation I have had further discussions with Smith Fraser, the solicitors for Gerald Rose It would appear the likelihood of our settling this matter could be expedited if we took some steps to indicate that we are concerned about the delay in settling this matter. As a result, I have arranged to have the statement of claim issued & Smith F- have been advised that we will be doing this within the next few days.

By issuing the s/c we commence the action in the courts but we do not have to serve it immediately. We have 6 months within which we can serve Mr. Rose.

I strongly believe that by taking this step we will receive some form of offer to settle from the Δ. If we do not, we will serve the Δ with the s/c shortly to commence the proceeding.

In order to prepare & issue the s/c we require an affidavit sworn by your husband so that we may bring a claim for him under the Family Law Act. Please have him call my assistant & arrange a time within the next few days to come in to swear this affidavit.

I will keep you advised of what occurs once the s/c has been issued.

Yours very truly,

MDC

C. LEGAL TERMINOLOGY

After completing this exercise you should be able to spell and define the following legal terms. Read the definitions shown below. Then select the correct term and match it with the words or phrase that best matches it in meaning, and write the correct term in the space provided. There are more terms than definitions.

Legal Terms

prescribed form	style of cause	deponent
short title of proceeding	v.	commissioner
et al.	jurat	notary public
backsheet	issued	ats
exhibit	general heading	affidavit

Definitions

1. material referred to that support facts stated in an affidavit

2. court file number, court name and title of proceeding

3. person before whom affidavit is sworn

4. and others

5. ending of affidavit stating where, when and before whom sworn

6. title of proceeding

7. sworn statement of fact

8. versus

9. last page of court document

10. legal document that has its form and basic content established by act or regulation

11. court document that has been signed, sealed and assigned a court file number

12. person swearing to certain facts stated in an affidavit

13. description of parties used on backsheet of court documents

CHAPTER 10 – ASSIGNMENTS
The Originating Process

A. LEGAL OFFICE PROCEDURES

There are no legal office procedures exercises for this chapter

B. LEGAL DOCUMENT PRODUCTION

**1. NOTICE OF ACTION – SIMPLIFIED PROCEDURE
ANDERSON v. PENMAR SERVICES**

Lynda Ritchie has provided the information on the following page to assist you in preparing a notice of action in the Anderson v. Penmar matter. This action will be under the rules of simplified procedure. Refer to Precedent 10.3.

An Information Form for Court Use will also need to be prepared for this notice of action and the statements of claim below. None of these proceedings will be under case management and the "standard track" should be selected for all these actions. Refer to Precedent 10.5..

**2. STATEMENT OF CLAIM – GENERAL
EAST v. EAST**

Peter Grant has drafted the body of the statement of claim to originate this matter shown on page 61. You have been asked to prepare it in good form and to do a memorandum to Jason Fisher asking him to attend at the court office in Whitby to have it issued. Refer to Precedent 10.1.

**3. STATEMENT OF CLAIM – MONEY ONLY, SIMPLIFIED PROCEDURE
GENERAL FOOD EQUIPMENT v. 1853222 ONTARIO LIMITED**

Michael Colucci drafted the statement of claim shown on page 63 for this action and asks you prepare it in final form. Refer to Precedent 10.2.

**4. STATEMENT OF CLAIM – GENERAL
PALMER v. ROSE**

Peter Grant has reviewed the body of the statement of claim (shown on page 63) which was drafted by Howard Podoba, an articling student. He has made several revisions and also drafted an affidavit (shown on page 65) that must accompany the statement of claim when it is issued since Mr. Palmer is making a claim under the provisions of the Family Law Act. You have been asked to retrieve these drafts and prepare them in good form. Refer to Precedent 10.1.
(Practice Files: Drafts Folder – Files: Draft 10 and Draft 11)

Court File No.

ONTARIO
SUPERIOR COURT OF JUSTICE

Kevin John Anderson

- and -

Penmar Services of Canada Limited

NOTICE OF ACTION

TO: Penmar Services etc.
4509 University Ave
Suite 1600
Toronto ON M2K 3V2

// PAGE 2:

(SIMPLIFIED PROCEDURE)

1. The plaintiff's claim is for:

   (a) damages in the amount of $40,000.00 for breach of contract for ~~his~~ employment of the plaintiff as a designer/~~checker~~ with the defendant.

   (b) prejudgment interest on the amount described in paragraph (a) herein from September 15, 20xx to the date of the order herein, pursuant to the provisions of section 128(1) of the courts of Justice Act;

   (c) his costs of this action; and

   (d) postjudgment interest on amount described in paragraph (a) form the date of the order to the date of payment pursuant to the provisions of section 129(1) of the CJA

Proceeding to be tried at Toronto
Information for Court Use Form required.

s/c General

Peter Bruce East and
Leslie Margaret East

πs

- and -

Mary Ann East

Δ

To: Mary Ann East
24 Albert Street Newcastle ON L3K 4G4

Page 2:
1. The plaintiffs claim:
   (a) specific performance of an agmt. for sale to them of the premises known as the north half of Lot 7, 3rd Concession, Township of Brock, which said agmt. was constituted by an option to purchase granted to the πs by the Δ in a lease the 29th day of October, 2002, which said option was duly exercised by the πs
   (b) their costs of this action; and
   (c) such further and other relief as this court may deem just
2. The plaintiff Peter Bruce East is a farmer, residing in the Twp. of Brock, in the Regional Municipality of Durham; the plaintiff Leslie Margaret East is the wife of Peter Bruce East.
3. The Δ is a widow residing in the Municipality of Clarington in the Reg. Muni. of Durham.
4. By leased dated the 29th day of October, 2002, the Δ leased to the πs the said land & premises for a term of ten years from the first day of November, 2002, reserving to the Δ the use of the house and certain facilities. The lease contained the following provision:

(Copy provision from Notice of Exercise of Option - should be in the file)

5. In the summer of 20xx, the πs orally notified the Δ that they exercised the said option to purchase and on or about the 18th day of August, 20xx, the πs notified the Δ in writing of such exercise of the said option.
6. The Δ refuses to carry out the sale of the said lands & premises to the πs.
7. The πs have indicated to the Δ that they are ready & willing, as is the fact, to carry out the said purchase & to pay the purchase of $260,000.00.

The plaintiffs propose that this action be tried at Whitby

HILL, JOHNSTON & GRANT etc.....

ONTARIO
SUPERIOR COURT OF JUSTICE

Court File No.

B E T W E E N:

GENERAL FOOD EQUIPMENT LIMITED

- and -

185322 ONTARIO LIMITED
c.o.b. as EILEEN'S COFFEE SHOP

STATEMENT OF CLAIM (Note - money only – allow $750 for costs)

TO: 185322 ONTARIO LIMTIED
67 Maxwell Court, Brampton ON L6T 4T9

Page 2.

1. The plaintiff claims:
   (a) the sum of $27,390.02 being the amount of outstanding invoices rendered by the plaintiff to the defendant.
   (b) prejudgment interest from October 1, 20xx at the rate of 2% per month or 26.8% per year as specified in the invoices;
   (c) postjudgment interest from the date of judgment herein at the rate of 2% per month or 26.8% per year as specified on the plaintiff's invoices;
   (d) the costs of this action; and
   (e) such further and other relief as this Honourable Court may deem just;

2. The plaintiff is a corporation incorporated under the laws of the Province of Ontario, and carries on business in the City of Mississauga in the Regional Municipality of Peel, as a supplier of food equipment.

3. The defendant is a corporation incorporated under the laws of the Province of Ontario, and carries on business as a coffee shop at 983 Palacewood Drive, Brampton, Ontario.

4. By purchase orders dated June 10, 20xx, and August 14, 20xx, the defendant ordered various pieces of food equipment as set out in those purchase orders.

5. Between June 10, 20xx, and August 14, 20xx, the plaintiffs delivered food equipment to the defendant pursuant to the said purchase orders. The following is a summary of what is due and owing to the plaintiff

Invoice No.	Date	Amount	Payment	Balance
7941	June 10, 20xx	$4,802.68	Nil	$14,803.68
8361	August 24, 20xx	$2,512.67	Nil	$12,586.34
	TOTAL BALANCE OUTSTANDING			$27,390.02

6. The plaintiff has sent numerous requests to the defendant for payment. To date the defendant has failed and refused to make any payment and the full amount of the invoices together with interest thereon remains unpaid and outstanding.

The plaintiff proposes . . . Brampton

H J & G
Michael D. Colucci etc.

Please do a memo to Jason asking him to issue this & arrange for Dover Process Servers to serve it.

Also do a tickler slip for 20 days from date of issue - if no s/d filed, proceed with default judgment.
PTG

s/c - general

Marylynn Palmer and
Robert Samuel Palmer *π's*

and

Gerald Rose *Δ*

To: Gerald Rose
8637 Kayside drive
Mississauga Ontario L9K 4G2

Page 2:

(To be tried at Brampton)

1. The plaintiffs claims:

    (a) as to the plaintiff Marylynn Palmer, damages in the amount of $75,000.00

    (b) as to the plaintiff Robert Samuel Palmer, damages in the amount of $25,000.00

    (c) their costs of this action;

    (d) prejudgment interest pursuant to the provisions of the Courts of Justice Act;

    (e) such further and other relief as ~~to the~~ this Honourable Court may deem just.

2. The plaintiff Marylynn Palmer resides in the City of Mississauga, in the Reg. Muni. of Peel, and at all material times was the owner and rider of a horse known as Thunderbolt (herein "the horse").

3. The plaintiff Robert Samuel Palmer (herein "Robert Palmer") resides in the City of Mississauga, in the Reg. Muni. of Peel and is the spouse of the plaintiff Marylynn Palmer. The ~~said~~ π Robert Palmer brings this action pursuant to the provisions of the Family Law Act, R.S.O. 1990, as amended (herein the "Family Law Act") on his own behalf and on behalf of all persons who are entitled to claim to be entitled to damages pursuant to the said provisions of the said Family Law Act.

4. The π Palmer only Robert ~~Samuel Parker~~ is the person who is entitled to or who claims to be entitled to the benefits of the within action pursuant to the ~~said~~ Family Law Act. 5. The defendant Gerald Rose (herein "Rose")

resides in the City of Mississauga, in the Regional Municipality of Peel, and was at all material times the owner of a german shepherd dog (herein "the dog").

6. On or about the 1st day of (last month), 20xx, the plaintiff Marylynn Palmer was riding her horse on a riding path located on premises owned by the Hodgson Riding School, in the Town of Caledon, in the Regional Municipality of Peel.

7. At the same time, the defendant was walking the dog on the same riding path and allowed the dog to run free on the riding path and the dog attacked the horse Marylynn Palmer was riding.

8. The plaintiffs allege that the dog's attack on the horse was caused solely by the negligence of the defendant in that he failed to keep the dog under proper control at the material time.

9. As a result of the attack, the plaintiff Palmer was thrown from the horse and landed in a rocky area adjacent to the riding path; the horse ran onto the road and was struck by a passing motor vehicle and suffered injuries of such severity that it was subsequently humanely destroyed.

10. As a result of being thrown from the horse, the plaintiff Marylynn Palmer has sustained serious, lasting, and permanent personal injuries including soft tissue injuries to her neck, shoulders and back, an injury to her left elbow, a deep gash to her right hand, multiple lacerations and contusions, and nervous, emotional, and physical upset and trauma. These injuries have been accompanied by great pain, suffering and profound shock. This plaintiff's enjoyment of life has been lessened and her ability to earn her livelihood as a costume designer has been and remains impaired. As well, this plaintiff has been put to medical, hospital and other out-of-pocket expenses, the full details of which are not available at the time of delivery of this s/c. As well, this plaintiff's horse has been destroyed and she has lost the use thereof. The plaintiff Marylynn Palmer undertakes to provide full particulars of the out-of-pocket expenses claimed prior to the trial of this action.

11. As a further result of the damages and injuries to the plaintiff Marylynn Palmer, the plaintiff Robert Palmer has been deprived of the benefit of the support, care, service, comfort, guidance, and companioship normally provided by the plaintiff Marylynn Palmer. The plaintiff Robert Palmer claims damages for

the loss of this past and future support, care, service, comfort, guidance and companionship pursuant to the provisions of the *Family Law Act*.

12. As a further result of the damages and injuries suffered by the Plaintiff Marylynn Palmer, the Plaintiff Robert Samuel Palmer has necessarily provided nursing, housekeeping and other services to the Plaintiff Marylynn Palmer and, in consequence, has lost income and is entitled to compensation for the value of these services performed and the income lost. The Plaintiff Palmer undertakes to provide the full particulars of these claims herein prior to the trial of this action.

The plaintiff proposes that this action be tried at Brampton.

Court file no.

General Heading of Palmer v. Rose

AFFIDAVIT
of
ROBERT SAMUEL PALMER

I, Robert Samuel Palmer, of the City of Mississauga, (etc...) MAKE OATH AND SAY:

1. I am a plaintiff in this action and as such have knowledge of the facts and matters hereinafter deposed to.

2. This action arises out of a personal injury accident that occurred on or about the (get date from s/c), 200x on a riding path located on premises owned by the Hodgson Riding School, in the Town of Caledon, (etc...)

3. I bring this action for damages on behalf of myself only.

4. To the best of my knowledge, information & belief, the persons named in the s/c are the only persons who are entitled to or who claim to be entitled to damages pursuant to the Family Law Act RSO 1990 c.F.3 as amended — cite properly

SWORN ... at the offices of Hill, Johnston & Grant

C. LEGAL TERMINOLOGY

After completing this exercise you should be able to spell and define the following legal terms. Read the definitions shown below. Then select the correct term and match it with the words or phrase that best matches it in meaning, and write the correct term in the space provided. There are more terms than definitions.

Legal Terms

originating process	postjudgment interest	limitation date
trial management	prejudgment interest	action
litigation guardian	unliquidated damages	pleadings
mediation	simplified procedure	case management
general damages	special damages	liquidated damages

Definitions

1. statements by the parties of their positions in the action

2. type of proceeding for claims between $10,000 and $50,000

3. damages that are certain and are determined to the penny

4. method of settling legal disputes through a neutral third party

5. interest calculated from date of judgment to date of payment of damages

6. individual who represents interest of party under a disability

7. damages for pain and suffering awarded in round amounts

8. damages to compensate for loss of wages or repairs

9. procedural system to save time and money through efficient processing of cases.

10. A statement of claim is an example of this

11. interest calculated from date of cause of action to date of judgment

12. the date by which something must be done or the right to do so is lost

CHAPTER 11 – ASSIGNMENTS
Serving and Filing Court Documents

A. LEGAL OFFICE PROCEDURES

1. SERVICE OF ORIGINATING PROCESS DOCUMENTS
   EAST v. EAST – STATEMENT OF CLAIM

The statement of claim in the East action has now been issued and assigned court file no. 89413. Key or stamp the acceptance of service in the large blank space on the left side of the back as shown in Figure 11.9B of your text. Assume you served the statement of claim today on Smith, Fraser Hamid & Lee LLP and complete the acceptance of service stamp.

2. SERVICE OF DOCUMENTS OTHER THAN ORIGINATING DOCUMENTS

From the information provided, complete the admission of service stamping for each of the following actions. Assume you are doing this today.

(a) Hill, Johnston & Grant act for all defendants.

Service of a copy of this document admitted

this ……. day of ………………… , 20……

………………………………………………
Solicitor(s) for

(b) There are three defendants; Hill, Johnston & Grant act only for the defendant Jacob Aaron Roe

Service of a copy of this document admitted

this ……. day of …………………, 20……

………………………………………………
Solicitor(s) for

(c) Hill, Johnston & Grant act for the plaintiffs

Service of a copy of this document admitted

this ……. day of …………………, 20……

………………………………………………
Solicitor(s) for

(d) There are three respondents; Hill, Johnston & Grant act for the respondents Rajit Khan and Kalida Awali

Service of a copy of this document admitted

this ……. day of …………………, 20……

………………………………………………
Solicitor(s) for

B. LEGAL DOCUMENT PRODUCTION

1. AFFIDAVIT OF SERVICE – FARRIER et al. v. WYERS

Yesterday, Jason Fisher, a law clerk at Hill, Johnston & Grant, tried to serve the statement of claim shown below on the defendant, but he was not at home. He tried again today and left a copy of the document at 9:40 a.m. with the defendant's mother, Joan Grace Wyers. On his return to the office he mailed a copy of the statement of claim by registered mail. Jason confirmed with Mrs. Wyers that she is the defendant's mother and that she resides at that address. Prepare an affidavit of service at place of residence for Jason to swear today. Jason lives in Barrie. Refer to Precedent 11.4.

Court file no. **42289**

ONTARIO
SUPERIOR COURT OF JUSTICE

BETWEEN:

THOMAS SAMUEL FARRIER
and MARY JEAN FARRIER

PLAINTIFFS

and

ALEXANDER JOHN WYERS

DEFENDANT

STATEMENT OF CLAIM

TO THE DEFENDANT

A LEGAL PROCEEDING HAS BEEN COMMENCED AGAINST YOU by the plaintiff(s). The claim made against you is set out in the following pages.

IF YOU WISH TO DEFEND THIS PROCEEDING, you or an Ontario lawyer acting for you must prepare a statement of defence in Form 18A prescribed by the Rules of Civil Procedure, serve it on the plaintiff(s) lawyer or, where the plaintiff(s) do(es) not have a lawyer, serve it on the plaintiff(s), and file it, with proof of service, in this court office, WITHIN TWENTY DAYS after this statement of claim is served on you, if you are served in Ontario.

If you are served in another province or territory of Canada or in the United States of America, the period for serving and filing your statement of defence is forty days. If you are served outside Canada and the United States of America, the period is sixty days.

Instead of serving and filing a statement of defence, you may serve and file a notice of intent to defend in Form 18B prescribed by the Rules of Civil Procedure. This will entitle you to ten more days within which to serve and file your statement of defence.

IF YOU FAIL TO DEFEND THIS PROCEEDING, JUDGMENT MAY BE GIVEN AGAINST YOU IN YOUR ABSENCE AND WITHOUT FURTHER NOTICE TO YOU. IF YOU WISH TO DEFEND THIS PROCEEDING BUT ARE UNABLE TO PAY LEGAL FEES, LEGAL AID MAY BE AVAILABLE TO YOU BY CONTACTING A LOCAL LEGAL AID OFFICE.

Date: *Yesterday's Date*   Issued by ____*D. Smith*____
                                               Local registrar

                              Address of court office:
                              393 University Avenue
                              Toronto ON   M5G 1E6

TO: ALEXANDER JOHN WYERS
      480 Molly Avenue, Apt. 468
      Toronto ON   M8V 6K3

2. **AFFIDAVIT OF SERVICE BY MAIL ON A SOLICITOR –
BLACK et al. v. HUMBER TOOL & DYE COMPANY LIMITED**

> Court file no. 08/CV/112311
>
> ***ONTARIO***
> **SUPERIOR COURT OF JUSTICE**
>
> BETWEEN:
>
> **JAMES DAVID BLACK and
> JENNIFER MARY BLACK**
>
> Plaintiffs
>
> and
>
> **HUMBER TOOL & DYE COMPANY LIMITED**
>
> Defendant

Refer to the general heading above. Michael Colucci has now prepared a notice of motion and an affidavit to be served on the solicitors for the defendant, Picov, Blair & Schmidt, in this proceeding which was commenced in Barrie. Prepare the following short letter to Cheryl S. Blair at this firm forwarding the two documents and then prepare an affidavit of service to be sworn by you. Refer to Precedent 11.5.

Pursuant to rule 16.05(1)(a), we serve upon you herewith our notice of motion and affidavit in this action.

3. **AFFIDAVIT OF SERVICE BY FAX – COCHRANE v. WHITE et al.**

> Court file no. 08/CV/334566
>
> ***ONTARIO***
> **SUPERIOR COURT OF JUSTICE**
>
> BETWEEN:
>
> **JOAN CATHERINE COCHRANE, a
> minor, by her litigation guardian,
> MARY ELIZABETH COCHRANE**
>
> Plaintiff
>
> and
>
> **JACOB AARON WHITE, JOHN
> GREGORY WAYNE WOOD and
> PATRICK WARREN HOOK**
>
> Defendant

Refer to the general heading above for this proceeding which was commenced in Toronto. Assume you have prepared a jury notice (containing two pages including the back), and are now required to serve it by fax on solicitors for the plaintiff, Armstrong, Ward & Siegel (Attention: Katherine R. Siegel), and the solicitors for the other two defendants, Graham & Parker (Attention: Michael Cochrane). Prepare the necessary fax cover sheets and your affidavit of service by fax. Refer to Precedents 11.6 and 11.7.

C. LEGAL TERMINOLOGY

After completing this exercise you should be able to spell and define the following legal terms. Read the definitions shown below. Then select the correct term and match it with the words or phrase that best matches it in meaning, and write the correct term in the space provided. There are more terms than definitions.

Legal Terms

serve	admission of service	deponent
file	personal service	backsheet
perjury	substitutional service	wpos
alternative to personal service	acceptance of service	ordinary service

Definitions

1. part of a court document that is usually not required for an affidavit of service _____

2. service at place of residence is an example of this type of service _____

3. service by fax is an example of this type of service _____

4. placing a copy of the court document in the hands of one of the parties is an example of this type of service _____

5. acronym used to indicate that a document is being filed with evidence that is has been served _____

6. when a law firm agrees to allow service of a court document on their firm of an originating document _____

7. when a law firm agrees to allow service of a court document, other than an originating document, on their firm _____

8. person who swears how, when and where service was effected _____

9. providing the original court document to the appropriate court office with any support material that is required _____

10. to wilfully make a false or incomplete statement _____

11. giving a copy of a court document to all other parties in the proceeding _____

CHAPTER 12 – ASSIGNMENTS
Responses to the Originating Process

A. LEGAL OFFICE PROCEDURES

1. DOCUMENTS SERVED ON HILL, JOHNSTON & GRANT – EAST v. EAST

Smith, Fraser has now served the Hill, Johnston & Grant law firm with the statement of defence and a jury notice in this action. These documents appear as part of this assignment material. The back for each of these documents was reproduced as a two-sided document. Note that normally the backsheet would be a separate page.

Key or stamp an acceptance of service for each of these documents and then complete it on behalf of Hill, Johnston & Grant. Remove these pages and keep them with your statement of claim in this action; they will be required when you prepare the trial record.

Note: In actual litigation practice, these documents would of course be dated. Because of the difficulty in using a date that would be appropriate regardless of when students use this material, the date has been left blank. Your instructor will advise you of the date to insert in each document; it will be approximately 20 days after the date on which the statement of claim was served.

B. LEGAL DOCUMENT PRODUCTION

1. REPLY – EAST v. EAST

Peter Grant has requested that you prepare the draft reply shown below in good form. Once it has been prepared, it will be served by fax. Prepare the appropriate cover letter, fax cover sheet, and your affidavit of service.

General Heading – East v. East

REPLY

1. The plaintiffs deny the allegations contained in para. 4 & 5 of the s/d.
2. The plaintiffs deny that there was any misrepresentation of the contents of the lease as alleged in para. 5 of the s/d & allege as is the fact that the lease was drawn up by the solicitors for the defendant.
3. The plaintiffs deny that the defendant had no independent legal advise as alleged in para. 5 of the s/d & allege as is the fact that the solicitor for the defendant, Horace Z. Hermann, was present when the lease was executed.

H, J & G – etc....

TO: Smith, Fraser – etc...

2. NOTICE OF INTENT TO DEFEND –
GEORGIAN TECHNOLOGY INC. ats BAYSIDE ELECTRONICS LTD.

BAYSIDE ELECTRONICS LTD. Plaintiff	and	GEORGIAN TECHNOLOGY INC. Defendant
		Court file no. 101124
		ONTARIO **SUPERIOR COURT OF JUSTICE** Proceeding commenced at Barrie
		STATEMENT OF CLAIM
		SMITH, BROWN & BLACKWOOD Barristers & Solicitors 25 Belfast Road Toronto ON M8X 6G2 Karen P. Emond (42261E) Tel: 416-936-8870 Fax: 416-936-8871 Solicitors for the plaintiff

Michael Colucci is acting for Georgian Technology Inc. who have been served with a statement of claim, the back of which is shown above. Prepare the notice of intent to defend (refer to Precedent 12.1) and the following covering letter:

> David S. Ross
> Hare, Ross & Wilkinson
>   in Barrie
>
> Re: Georgian Technology Inc. ats Bayside Electronics Ltd.
>   We enclose herewith the original and 2 copies of our notice of intent to defend in the above proceeding. Please arrange to have this served & filed at the court office in Barrie. ¶ Please return the original with a copy of your affidavit of service or admission of service & your account.
>   Yours etc...
>   MDC

Court File No. 89413

ONTARIO
SUPERIOR COURT OF JUSTICE

BETWEEN:

**PETER BRUCE EAST and
LESLIE MARGARET EAST**

Plaintiffs

- and -

MARY ANN EAST

Defendant

STATEMENT OF DEFENCE

1. The defendant (herein "East") admits the allegations contained in paragraphs 2, 3 and 4 of the statement of claim.

2. East denies the allegations contained in paragraphs 5, 6, and 7 of the statement of claim.

4. East alleges that if there is such a lease as referred to in paragraph 5 of the statement of claim, she was subjected to undue influence by the plaintiffs to obtain the execution of said lease.

5. East alleges and the fact is that if the lease was executed by the defendant, her signature was obtained by misrepresentation of the contents of the said lease, and that she had no independent legal advice at the time of the execution of the said lease.

6. East submits that this action should be dismissed with costs.

Date: *Yesterday's Date*

SMITH, FRASER, HAMID & LEE LLP
74 Victoria Street, Suite 503
Toronto ON M5C 2B1

TO: **HILL, JOHNSTON & GRANT**
17 Princess Street South
Suite 2501
Toronto ON M8Y 3N5

Peter T. Grant (12345G)
Tel: 416-354-9900
Fax: 416-354-9909

Solicitors for the plaintiffs

John A. Hamid (53664H)
Tel: 416-233-9985
Fax: 416-233-9980

Solicitors for the defendant

PETER BRUCE EAST and LESLIE MARGARET EAST	- and -	MARY ANN EAST		
Plaintiffs		Defendant		
		Court File No. 89413		
		ONTARIO **SUPERIOR COURT OF JUSTICE** Proceeding commenced at Whitby		
		STATEMENT OF DEFENCE		
		SMITH, FRASER, HAMID & LEE LLP Barristers & Solicitors 75 Victoria Street, Suite 503 Toronto ON M5C 2B1 John A Hamid (53664H) Tel: 416-233-09980 Fax: 416-233-9983 Solicitors for the Defendant		

Court File No. 89413

ONTARIO
SUPERIOR COURT OF JUSTICE

BETWEEN:

**PETER BRUCE EAST and
LESLIE MARGARET EAST**

Plaintiffs

- and -

MARY ANN EAST

Defendant

JURY NOTICE

THE DEFENDANT requires that this action be tried with a jury.

Date: *Yesterday's Date*   **SMITH, FRASER, HAMID & LEE LLP**
                                 74 Victoria Street, Suite 503
                                 Toronto ON M5C 2B1

                                 John A. Hamid (53664H)
                                 Tel: 416-233-9985
                                 Fax: 416-233-9980

                                 Solicitors for the defendant

TO: **HILL, JOHNSTON & GRANT**
      17 Princess Street South, Suite 2501
      Toronto ON M8Y 3N5

      Peter T. Grant (12345G)
      Tel: 416-354-9900
      Fax: 416-354-9909

      Solicitors for the plaintiffs

PETER BRUCE EAST and LESLIE MARGARET EAST	- and -	MARY ANN EAST		
Plaintiffs		Defendant		
		Court File No. 89413		
		ONTARIO **SUPERIOR COURT OF JUSTICE** Proceeding commenced at Whitby	**JURY NOTICE**	**SMITH, FRASER, HAMID & LEE** LLP Barristers & Solicitors 75 Victoria Street, Suite 503 Toronto ON M5C 2B1 John A Hamid (53664H) Tel: 416-233-09980 Fax: 416-233-9983 Solicitors for the Defendant

3. STATEMENT OF DEFENCE –
1975311 ONTARIO LIMITED AND OTHERS ats PORTER BUILDINGS SUPPLIES

Prepare in good form the following statement of defence for this action which was drafted by Peter Grant for his clients 1975311 Ontario Limited and 1746292 Ontario Limited. This action was commenced in Brampton. Refer to Precedent 12.2.

Court File No. C95216

PORTER BUILDING SUPPLIES LTD.

and

1975311 ONTARIO LIMITED c.o.b. as DEES CONDOS and
1746292 ONTARIO LIMITED c.o.b. as FOUNTAIN PROPERTIES

S/D

1. The defendants 1975311 Ontario Ltd. (herein "1975311") & 1746292 Ontario Limited (herein "1746292") admit paragraph 2 & 3 of the s/c but deny each & every other allegation contained in the statement of claim except as expressly admitted herein.

2. 1746292 admits that it requested the plaintiff (herein "Porter") to deliver reinforced steel & wire mesh to a job site in Caledon, Ontario (herein "the property") in October of 2007 but states that Porter had been paid in full for all of the reinforced steel that 1746292 requested it to supply to this job site.

3. In the alternative, 1746292 states that the reinforced steel & wire mesh referred to in the statement of claim was delivered to some other site, not the one 1746292 was working on.

4. In the alternative, 1746292 states that if Porter did deliver reinforced steel & wire mesh material to this job site in Caledon that remain unpaid for, that such material was inferior and was subsequently replaced by reinforced steel and wire mesh that was of the proper specifications by another building supplier.

5. 1746292 states that Porter agreed with it on or about the 8th day of Jan. 2008, that all invoices for this job had been paid & that their were no outstanding balances owed to it by 1975311 & 1746292.

6. 1975311 states that at no time did it contract with Porter to do any work on this property and that 1975311 had no privity of contract with Porter whatsoever in respect of this matter.

7. 1975311 and 1746292 submit that this action be dismissed against them with costs payable to them by Porter.

H J & G
Solicitors for the defendants

TO: Fox, Wolfe & Lyons
    Brianna T. Wolfe

4. STATEMENT OF DEFENCE AND COUNTERCLAIM – HALCHCUK ats WALDEN AND OTHERS

Peter Grant has been acting in this action for Gregor Halchuk, and the file was opened some time ago. He accepted service of the statement of claim ten days ago. Peter Grant has now drafted the body of the statement of defence and counterclaim on his computer. Refer to Precedent 12.3. Retrieve this draft and prepare it in good form. Make sure you proofread the whole document, not just the revisions noted. (Practice Files: Drafts Folder – File: Draft 12)

Court File No. 91992

MATTHEW JOHN WALDEN and
STEPHEN DARRYL McCLAREN

– and –

GREGOR IVAN HALCHUK

DRAFT ONLY
Double Space Document

STATEMENT OF DEFENCE & COUNTERCLAIM

1. The defendant admits the allegations contained in paragraphs 2 and 3 of the s/c.
2. The defendant has no knowledge of the allegations contained in paragraphs 1, 8, 9 and 10 of the s/c.
3. The defendant denies paragraph 5 of the s/c.
4. The defendant states and the fact is in accordance with allegation 4 in the plaintiffs' s/c, the plaintiffs assigned the contract under which they took beneficial title to the land on the 17th day of October, 2007 and thus the plaintiffs' solicitor was in no position to pass title on July 2, 2008, as set out in para 10 of the s/c.
5. The defendant specifically denies paragraph 6 of the plaintiffs' s/c and states that the notice sent to the defendant's solicitor on December 2, 2007, merely set out that the application for consent was being made as of Dec 3, 2007, and further stating that he was not advised until Jan. 16/07 that the condition had been fulfilled.
6. The defendant specifically denies paragraph 7 of the s/c and states that the condition set out in paragraph 9(b):

    Vendor to submit proof that this draft plan of subdivision of said lands has been approved in principal by the Council of the Township of Georgian Bluffs within thirty (30) days from the date of acceptance.

has never been fulfilled, and that the document signed by the defendant on the 28th day of September, 2007, and referred to in paragraph 7 of the s/c, merely set out that the draft plan of subdivision has been approved in principal by the Planning Board and in no way referred to the Council of the Twp. of Georgian Bluffs.

7. The defendant alleges and the fact is that the plaintiff knew the purpose for which the defendant was purchasing the land, and they knew or ought to have known that the said plan of subdivision would not receive approval of the Ontario Municipal Board, or the Ministry of Intergovernmental Affairs, even after it had been obtained approval of the Council of the Township of Georgian Bluffs.

7. The defendant therefore asks that this action be dismissed with costs.

COUNTERCLAIM

8. The defendant and plaintiff by counterclaim claims:
   (a) damages in the amount of $~~10,000.00~~; 35,000.00
   (b) interest in accordance with sections 128 & 129 of the <u>Courts of Justice Act</u>, R.S.O. 1990, c.43;
   (c) his costs of this action; and
   (d) such further and other relief as this honourable court may deem just.

10. The plaintiff by counterclaim repeats the allegation contained in his s/d and states that under the agreement of purchase and sale the plaintiff counterclaim was required to deposit $20,000.00 which was to be forfeited and paid to the vendor should the purchaser refuse to close.

11. The plaintiff by counterclaim states that the $20,000.00 deposited was paid to the defendants to the counterclaim on or about the 28th day of September, 2007, when the agreement was signed.

13. The plaintiff by counterclaim states and the fact is that the defendants to the counterclaim are in possession of the $20,000.00 deposit, and that such deposit should be returned to the plaintiff by counterclaim as the defendants to the counterclaim are not in a position to give title, and the defendants to the cc. have breached the contract by refusing to comply with the requisites set out in the agreement

Date   Hill, Johnston & Grant   PTG etc.

             Solicitors for the plaintiff by counterclaim

TO: McCLELLAND, WYERS & CHAE etc.

 Solicitors for the defendants to the counterclaim

12. The plaintiff by counterclaim states & the fact is that the conditions set out in Schedule A as annexed to the agmt of purchase & sale herein have not been fulfilled in that the vendor did not submit proof that the draft plan of subdivision of the said lands had been approved in principle by the Council of the Twp of Georgian Bluffs within 90 days from the date of acceptance and also in fact that the vendor did not obtain a final consent from the Committee of Adjustment for the Twp of Bentinck within the 90 days specified in the agreement.

Identify this document on the backsheet as Statement of Defence and Counterclaim

C. LEGAL TERMINOLOGY

After completing this exercise you should be able to spell and define the following legal terms. Read the definitions shown below. Then select the correct term and match it with the words or phrase that best matches it in meaning, and write the correct term in the space provided. There are more terms than definitions.

Legal Terms

demand for particulars	reply	pleadings
counterclaim	statement of defence	indemnify
crossclaim	*a priori*	*intra vires*
third party claim	notice of intent to defend	*ultra vires*
allegation	*inter alia*	*in toto*

Definitions

1. document that allows a defendant additional time to file their defence document

2. document that sets out the defendant's version of the facts

3. among other things

4. a separate & distinct claim of a defendant against a plaintiff

5. written request (usually by the defendant) for specifics of a claim or statement in a pleading document

6. beyond the power

7. a claim where a defendant claims to be entitled to a contribution from a party not a party to an action,

8. a separate and distinct claim of one defendant against another defendant

9. within the power

10. optional court document that may be prepared by the plaintiff to respond to the defendant's allegations

11. to promise to compensate someone for loss as a result of another's act or default

12. from the cause to the effect

CHAPTER 13 – ASSIGNMENTS
Consents, Requisitions, Notices and Notices of Motion

A. LEGAL OFFICE PROCEDURES

There are no legal office procedures exercises for this chapter

B. LEGAL DOCUMENT PRODUCTION

NOTICES

1. JURY NOTICE – HALCHCUK ats WALDEN and others

Prepare a jury notice for this proceeding (see p. 78 of this assignment book for the general heading). This proceeding was commenced in Owen Sound. Refer to Precedent 13.1. When you have this document completed, prepare the appropriate letter to serve this document by mail and your affidavit of service by mail.

2. NOTICE OF CHANGE OF SOLICITORS – CAMPBELL v. BUTLER

Lynda Ritchie has now had an interview with Judith Campbell in connection with a legal proceeding in which she is presently involved. She had originally retained the Smith Fraser law firm to represent her in an action against Cameron Butler and the statement of claim has been issued. Pleadings are not yet closed, and she has now decided that she wishes to change her solicitors. Hill, Johnston & Grant have agreed to act for her. Prepare the following required notice of change of solicitors.

Court file no. 90046

BETWEEN:

JUDITH CAMPBELL
and
CAMERON BUTLER

NOTICE OF CHANGE OF SOLICITORS

The π, formerly represented by Smith, Fraser, Hamid & Lee LLP has appointed Hill, J- & G- as solicitors of record.

Date   *Hill, Johnston & Grant etc...*
                                                                      Lynda C. Ritchie
                                                                      Solicitors for the π

TO: *Smith, Fraser, etc.*
         Mary J. Spencer
         (no solicitors for line)

AND TO: *Armstrong, Ward & Siegel etc.*
         Roberto M. Colabresie
         Solicitors for the Δ   *Proceeding commenced in Brampton*

3. NOTICE OF PAYMENT INTO COURT – MELVILLE HOLDINGS LIMITED ats SIMPSON

HECTOR IAN SIMPSON and **IDA GLADYS SIMPSON** Plaintiff		**MELVILLE HOLDINGS LIMITED** and **WRAGG PLUMBING LIMITED** Defendant

Court file no. 428811

ONTARIO
SUPERIOR COURT OF JUSTICE
Proceeding commenced at Guelph

STATEMENT OF CLAIM
(GENERAL)

SIMPSON, STAINTON & CRAWFORD
Barristers & Solicitors
83 Suffolk Street
Guelph ON N1H 7B4

Norman A. Crawford
Tel: 519-424-6744
Fax: 519-424-5745

Solicitors for the Plaintiffs

Michael Coclucci is acting for Melville Holdings Limited, who have been served with a statement of claim, the back of which is shown above. Smith, Fraser is representing the other defendant. Prepare the following notice of payment into court for this proceeding.

Notice of Payment into Court

The defendant Melville Holdings Limited paid into court on (today's date) the sum of $20,000.00 under the offer to settle dated the 1st day of current month, year.

Hill, Johnston & Grant etc.

Michael D Colucci
Solicitors for the defendant
Melville H- L-

TO: Simpson, Stainton & Crawford etc.
   Norman A. Crawford
   Solicitors for the Plaintiff

AND TO: Smith, Fraser, etc.
   Leonard A. Blackwell
   Solicitors for the defendant Wragg P- L-

4. NOTICE OF MOTION –
BLACK v. HUMBER TOOL & DYE COMPANY LIMITED

Michael Colucci has been working for the plaintiff in this legal proceeding; you will find a specimen of the general heading on page 69 of this assignment book. He now wishes to bring a motion asking that the defendants' statement of defence be struck out. He requests that you prepare in good form the following notice of motion. Refer to Precedent 13.2. Sylvia is preparing the affidavit to be sworn by Lynda Ritchie. Note that the proceeding was commenced in Barrie.

Notice of Motion

The πs will make a motion to a judge on Monday, November 15, 20__, at 10:00 a.m. or so soon after that time as the motion can be heard at Osgoode Hall, 130 Queen Street West, Toronto.

Proposed Method of hearing -----
X in writing as an opposed motion

The motion is for the striking of the π's s/d for non-attendance at the examinations for discovery & for an order requiring the defendant to pay forthwith the πs costs needlessly expended on a solicitor & his own client's basis.

The grounds for the motion are Rule 34.15(1)(b), s. 131.1 of the Courts of Justice Act RSO 1990 c. C.43 and Rule 57(01)(1)(e).

The following documentary evidence will be used...
Affidavit of Lynda Carol Ritchie dated (today's date)
The pleadings herein

Date: HILL, JOHNSTON & GRANT etc..

                                                    Michael D. Colucci
                                                    Solicitors for the πs

TO: PICOV, BLAIR & SCHMIDT etc..

        Cheryl S. Blair
        Solicitors for the Δ

5. NOTICE OF MOTION – EAST v. EAST

Peter Grant wishes to bring a motion to strike out the jury notice served in this action. He has drafted the following notice of motion. Refer to Precedent 13.2 to correctly format this document.

General Heading - East v. East

Notice of Motion

The πs will make a motion to the court on Friday (use a date a week from next Friday) at 10:00 a.m. or as soon after that time as the motion can be heard, at 605 Rossland Road East, Whitby, Ontario

Proposed Method of Hearing ----

X in writing as an opposed motion

The motion is for an order striking out the jury notice dated (check date of jury notice) served by the defendant on the plaintiffs.

The grounds for the motion are that the action ought to be tried without a jury in accordance with Section 108(s) of the Courts of Justice Act RSO 1990

The following documentary evidence...

1. Affidavit of Lynda Carol Ritchie sworn (date you prepare it)
2. True copy of lease dated (get date from lease Agreement), Exhibit "A" to the affidavit of LCR
3. True copy of Notice of Exercise of Option (get date from Notice), Exhibit "B" to the affidavit of LCR

Date: HILL, JOHNSTON & GRANT etc.

                                Peter T. Grant

                                Solicitors for the πs

TO: SMITH, FRASER, etc.

6. SUPPORTING AFFIDAVITS WITH EXHIBITS – EAST v. EAST

Peter Grant has now revised the following draft affidavit in support of the notice of motion for this action and asks that you prepare it in good form. He reminds you that you already have the lease and the notice of exercise of the option for this file which will need to be photocopied so they may be used as exhibits to the affidavit. **(Practice Files: Drafts Folder – File: Draft 13)**

GENERAL HEADING OF EAST v. EAST

AFFIDAVIT of LCR

I, Lydia Carol Ritchie – she lives in Oakville – solicitor in the offices of H-J-&G-, solicitors for the plaintiffs, MAKE OATH AND SAY AS FOLLOWS:

1.2 This action was commenced by issuance of a statement of claim for specific performance of ~~an option exercised by them on an agreement of purchase and sale of property located in the~~ of an agreement of purchase and sale under an option exercised orally by them on – *get date from exercise of option.*

2. The plaintiffs occupy the said land under a lease dated – *see lease for date* Now produced and shown to me and marked Exhibit "A" *to this my affidavit* is a true copy of the said lease.

3. Under the provisions of the lease the plaintiffs had an option to purchase the said lands and under date of – *get date from exercise of option* gave written notice to the defendant of the exercise of such optoin. Now produced and shown to me and marked Exhibit "B" *to this my affidavit* is a true copy of the said exercise of option.

4. I am informed ~~by the plaintiffs~~ and verily believe that the defendant has refused to carry out the sale of the property.

5. On – *get date from back of jury notice*, the solicitors for the defendant served upon the solicitors for the plaintiff a jury notice *requiring that this action be tried with a jury.*

6. Section 108(2)(9) of the Courts of Justice Act specifies that an action for specific performance shall be tried without a jury.

SWORN etc.

1. *I am associated with the law firm of H-J-&G-, solicitors for the Pl's and as such have knowledge of the facts hereinafter deposed.*

7. MOTION RECORD – EAST v. EAST

When you have the notice of motion and affidavit in this action in proper form, photocopy one copy of each, omitting the backsheets; then prepare the motion record with a front or face page and a table of contents. Refer to Precedent 13.3.

In this assignment, you will prepare only one copy of the motion record; in actual litigation practice you require a minimum of three copies.

8. CONFIRMATION OF MOTION – EAST v. EAST

Peter Grant has now spoken with Leonard Blackwell at Smith, Fraser to confirm the date and time of the motion hearing in this action. You are to prepare the confirmation of motion that is drafted below. Refer to Precedent 13.5. You will also need to prepare the necessary fax cover pages to fax the confirmation to the court house and to Smith, Fraser.

General Heading – East v. East

Confirmation of Motion

I, PETER T. GRANT, with the law firm of H-, J- & G-, counsel for the moving party, confirm that the moving party has conferred with the other party and that motion to be heard on (insert date of motion hearing) will proceed on the following basis:

X for hearing of the following issues only: to strike out the jury notice served in this action

Counsel will refer the presiding judge to the following materials:

1. List the documentary evidence referred to in the notice of motion

I estimate that the time required for the motion, including costs submission, will be 15 minutes for the moving party and 15 minutes for the responding party for a total of 30 minutes.

Date: *HILL, JOHNSTON & GRANT etc..*

                                                           Peter T. Grant
                                                           Solicitors for the πs

TO: Superior Court of Justice

TO: SMITH, FRASER, etc.

9. CONSENT –
BLACK AND OTHERS v. HUMBER TOOL & DYE COMPANY LIMITED

Michael Colucci has drafted a consent that is required for use in this proceeding, for which you prepared a notice of motion earlier in this chapter. He has drafted the body of the consent to assist you in preparing this document. Refer to Figure 13.7.

General Heading - Black and others v. Humber Tool & Dye Company Limited

CONSENT

The parties by their solicitors hereby consent to an order dismissing this action without costs.

DATED at Toronto, insert today's date.

                                                        _____
                                                        Hill, Johnston & Grant etc.

                                                        Michael D. Colucci

                                                        Solicitors for the plaintiffs

                                                        _____
                                                        Picov, Blair & Schmidt etc.

                                                        Cheryl S. Blair

                                                        Solicitors for the defendant

10. REQUISITION – COCHRANE v. WHITE et al.

You have been asked to prepare a requisition to the court office at Brampton for this matter. The general heading for this proceeding is shown on page 69 of this assignment book. The requisition should request the following:

> I REQUIRE a certified copy of the order dated July 15, 2008, appointing Mary Elizabeth Cochrane as litigation guardian for Joan Catherine Cochrane.

11. MOTION FACTUM

Sylvia Sharpe prepared a motion factum for Peter Grant yesterday. She is away today and Peter Grant asks that you prepare the first and last pages of this revised factum as shown on the following two pages. Remember to format all citations correctly.

Court file no. 07-CQ-94446

ONTARIO
SUPERIOR COURT OF JUSTICE

BETWEEN:

THE ROYAL BANK OF CANADA

Plaintiff

- and -

MARGARET EMILY RUSSELL

Defendant

FACTUM OF THE MOVING PARTY
THE ROYAL BANK OF CANADA

PART I – NATURE OF THE MOTION

1. The plaintiff brings this motion for summary judgment on its claim as set out in its statement of claim.

PART II – THE FACTS

2. The Royal Bank of Canada has brought the within action against the defendant, Margaret Emily Russell, on a guarantee dated September 23, 2006, for indebtedness arising from loans made to 1898956 Ontario Ltd. (herein "1898956").

Affidavit of John Joseph Jackson, tab 2, page 5, paragraph 4

3. As security for advances made to 1898956, the plaintiff received, *inter alia*, two mortgages from 1898956, dated September 5, 2006, in the sum of $200,000.00, and January 30, 2007, in the sum of $500,000.00

Affidavit of John Joseph Jackson, tab 2, page 7, paragraph 4

7.

a mortgage is whether or not the mortgagee has fraudulently, wilfully or recklessly sacrificed the property of the mortgagor.

> Wilson v. Taylor 1913 4 OWN 1376 at page 1378
>
> Victoria and Grey Trust Company v. Promor Holdings Inc. 1983 42 OR 2d at 27 (H.C.)

22. It is respectfully submitted that where a mortgagee employs competent appraisers, has the property listed with competent real estate brokers who advertise the property and use the multiple listing services, and eventually accept an offer in the amount of the appraisal, the mortgagee can be said to have made reasonable efforts to obtain the best price in the circumstances.

> Victoria and Grey Trust Company v. Promor Holdings Inc. supra

23. The main assertion of undervalue in a power of sale proceeding is insufficient to raise a triable issue.

> Randy Construction Company Limited et al v. Highlens Building Corporation Limited et al 1980 14 RPR 187 (Ont. Div. Ct.)

All of which is respectfully submitted.

H J & G etc.
Michael D. Colucci

TO: TASKER, MATTEA, AULD & GUESS
Darcy L. Kozak

C. LEGAL TERMINOLOGY

After completing this exercise you should be able to spell and define the following legal terms. Read the definitions shown below. Then select the correct term and match it with the words or phrase that best matches it in meaning, and write the correct term in the space provided. There are more terms than definitions.

Legal Terms

notice	responding party	*ex parte*
notice of motion	factum	consent
requisition	motion record	citation
interlocutory proceeding	moving party	authorities

Definitions

1. document setting out statement of facts and law to be relied on by parties in an application and on certain motions _____

2. a reference to a decided case or matter _____

3. the party that requests a motion hearing _____

4. a request to a court official to carry out a duty _____

5. document that asks the court to order that some particular thing either be done or not done _____

6. an act or decision of a court that is made after a legal proceeding has been commenced and is complete in itself before the legal proceeding is complete _____

7. cases cited in support of a legal principle _____

8. document filed with the court in which parties to a legal proceeding mutually agree to do or not to do something _____

9. document that advises the court and the solicitors for the other party of some procedural step in a legal proceeding _____

10. without notice; on one side only; by or for one party _____

11. a person against whom a motion is made _____

CHAPTER 14 – ASSIGNMENTS
Proceeding to Trial – General Actions

A. LEGAL OFFICE PROCEDURES

1. ARRANGING APPOINTMENT FOR EXAMINATIONS FOR DISCOVERY – EAST v. EAST

Peter Grant has asked you to arrange an appointment for examination for discovery of all parties in this action; he suggests a week from next Monday would be a suitable date.

Make a note of the steps that you would take and the information that you would require from Peter Grant in order to carry out his instructions.

B. LEGAL DOCUMENT PRODUCTION

1. AFFIDAVIT OF DOCUMENTS – EAST v. EAST

Mr. Grant has listed below the productions for the affidavit of documents (individual) for this action which will be sworn by Peter Bruce East. Refer to Precedent 14.1.

Schedule A

Number	Date	Description
1	Fall 1999	Photograph of farm in question
2	Oct 29/02	Duplicate original of lease from Mary Ann East to Peter Bruce East & Leslie Margaret East
3	Aug. 18/last year	Copy of exercise of option by PBE & LME
4	Nov. 15/last year	Copy of letter to Mary Ann East from PBE & LME
5	Nov. 20/last year	Original of letter from Smith, Fraser, Hamid & Lee to PBE
6.	Jan. 17/this year	Copy of letter from PBE to Mary Ann East

Schedule B
Adapt standard wording from precedent in text.

Schedule C
1. Original of (item #3 above) which was sent to the defendant
2. Original of (item #4 above) which was sent to the defendant
3. Original of (item #6 above) which was sent to the defendant

2. AFFIDAVIT OF DOCUMENTS - GEORGIAN TECHNOLOGY INC. ats BAYSIDE ELECTRONICS LTD.

You have been asked to prepare the affidavit of documents (corporation) for this simplified procedure action for which you prepared a notice of defence in Chapter 12 assignments (page 72). The affidavit will be sworn by Ronald James McIntosh, the Secretary of Georgian Technology Inc. Mr. McIntosh lives in your city. The productions are listed below although not in chronological order. Refer to Precedent 14.2 in your text.

Schedule A
1. Copy of Patent No. 8999848004 dated 3rd July, 2008.
2. Agreement between Bayside Electronics Ltd. and Georgian Technology Inc. dated August 30, 2007.
3. Copy of letter from Georgian Technology Inc. to Strong, Rendal & Jones dated Feb. 20, 2007.
4. Copy of letter from Georgian Technology Inc. to Bayside Electronics Ltd. dated March 15, 2008.
5. Copy of letter from Georgian Technology Inc. to Strong, Rendal & Jones, dated Feb. 14, 2008
6. Schematic diagram of Patent No. 8999848004 dated July 3, 2008.
7. Photograph of model of Patent No. 8999848004.
8. Certificate of Incorporation, Georgian Technology Inc., dated 12th Jan. 2000.
9. Copy of letter from Georgian Technology Inc. to Bayside Electronics Ltd. dated Feb. 1, 2008.
10. Copy of letter from Georgian Technology Inc. to Algonquin Permanent Trust Company dated September 30, 2008.

Schedule B
Adapt standard wording from precedent in text.

Schedule C
Once you have Schedule A completed, prepare Schedule C for the following items which should also be listed in chronological order. List each item separately. Refer to the precedent for suitable wording.

1. The original of (item 1 above) which has been filed with the Ministry of Government Services.
2. The original of (items 4 and 9 above) which were mailed to the plaintiff.
3. The original of (items 3, 5 and 10 above) which were mailed to the company to whom they were addressed.

Schedule D
Ruth P. Rendal, P. Eng., Strong, Rendal & Jones, 4200 Davis Drive, Unit 400, Newmarket, Ontario, L2K 2S4

Stefan G. Kozak, Bayside Electronics Ltd., 45 Esna Park Avenue, Suite 100, Toronto, Ontario, M9B 3X3

3. NOTICE OF EXAMINATION FOR DISCOVERY – EAST v. EAST

Assume the examination for discovery for the East v. East action has been arranged to take place at 2:00 p.m. a week from next Monday, at the offices of Toronto Court Reporters. Prepare the appropriate notice of examination for discovery form for Mary Ann East. Refer to Precedent 14.3. Assume you will be serving this notice by fax today.

4. TRIAL RECORD – EAST v. EAST

You have been instructed to "prepare the record" in this action. In the RECORD subfile for this client you find the statement of claim, statement of defence, jury notice and a one-page order striking out the jury notice. Prepare one copy of the record including the Solicitor's Certificate of Trial Record. Refer to Precedents 14.4, 14.5 and 14.6 in preparing this record.

> *Note: In an actual office environment you would, or course, prepare three copies of this record, but in a classroom environment you will prepare only one.*

5. OFFER TO SETTLE – MAHARWOOD v. PENDERGAST AND OTHERS

Lynda Ritchie has prepared and revised an offer to settle for this action which is shown below and on the following page and asks that you prepare it in good form. She reminds you that each defendant has his own solicitors and as a result the offer must be addressed to both law firms. Refer to Precedent 14.8.

Court file no. 90046

ONTARIO
SUPERIOR COURT OF JUSTICE

BETWEEN:

HENRIETTA JANE MAHARWOOD
and JEFFERY BOYD MAHARWOOD

Plaintiffs

MAURICE JAMES PENDERGAST
and JOSEPH GEORGE WILLOUGHBY

Defendants

<u>Offer to Settle</u>

The plaintiffs offer to settle this proceeding on the following terms:

1. Payment by the defendants to the plaintiffs in the amount of $35,000.00 inclusive of costs.

2. In consideration of payment as aforesaid the plaintiffs will provide a release without undue delay.

3. In consideration of payment as aforesaid, the plaintiffs to discontinue their action against the defendants.

4. Upon the defendants accepting the offer, it is clearly understood that full payment by certified check will be made in one lump sum and that terms for repayment are not acceptable.

5. This offer will be open until (2 weeks from today's date) after which if not accepted it shall be deemed to be null and void.

Date

H J & G etc.
LCR
Sol. for the plaintiffs

TO: SMITH, FRASER, HAMID & LEE LLP
Leonard A. Blackwell
Solicitors for the defendant M- J- Pendergast

AND TO: ARMSTRONG, WARD & SIEGEL
Burt M. Ward
Solicitors for the defendant J- G- Willoughby

Proceeding commenced at Toronto

6. PRE-TRIAL MEMORANDUM – EAST v. EAST

Peter Grant has drafted part of his pre-trial conference memorandum in this action which is shown below and on the following page. You are to retrieve this draft and make the requested changes. Refer to Precedent 14.9. **(Practice Files: Drafts Folder – File: Draft 14)**

Court file no. ??

ONTARIO
SUPERIOR COURT OF JUSTICE

SHORT TITLE OF PROCEEDING: EAST v. EAST
PRE-TRIAL DATE: Friday, (a week from next Friday) at 2:30 p.m.
LIST NO. Sittings commencing 15th of next month
SUBMITTED BY: Plaintiffs
Counsel for the plaintiff(s): Peter T. Grant
Counsel for the defendant(s): John A. Hamid

THEORY OF THE PLAINTIFF'S CASE INCLUDING FACTUAL CONTENTIONS:

1. On October 29/02, the plaintiffs entered into a lease with the defendant providing for the lease of the north half of Lot 7, in the 3rd Concession of the Township of Brock, in the Reg. Muni. of Durham.

2. Pursuant to paragraph 7 of the lease the plaintiffs were given an option to purchase certain lands over the term of the lease at a cost of $260,000.00. Para. 7 further provided that if the defendant vacated the house at any time over the term of the lease, the plaintiffs were bound to exercise the option to purchase

3. On or about July 1, 20xx, the plaintiffs gave oral notice to the defendant exercising the option to purchase, and notice in writing of the exercise of this option was given on August 18, 20xx.

4. Following the verbal & written exercise of the option to purchase being given to the defendant, draft documents were forwarded to the defendant in order to complete the carrying out of the sale, but the defendant has refused to execute them.

5. The plaintiffs then commenced this action for specific performance.

THEORY OF THE DEFENDANT'S CASE INCLUDING FACTUAL CONTENTIONS:

1. The defendant denies that there is a lease between the defendant and the plaintiffs

2. The defendant alleges that if there is such a lease, she was subjected to duress & undue influence by the plaintiffs when she executed the lease.

3. the defendant alleges that her signature on the lease was obtained by material & fundamental misrepresentation as to the terms of the lease, and that she had no independent legal advice prior to executing the lease

THE LEGAL ISSUES RAISED IN THE PLEADINGS AND TO BE DETERMINED AT TRIAL:

1. Is there a valid lease between the plaintiffs and the defendant under which the plaintiffs may exercise the option to purchase?

PLEADINGS AND RELEVANT MATTERS:

1. Are the pleadings in order or do they require amendment?   *In order*
2. Are there any contemplated or outstanding motion?   *No*
3. Are productions complete?   *Yes*
4. Are all transcripts available?   *Yes*
5. Other: *n/a*

MOTIONS:

Will there be any motions at trial? *No*
If so, what are they? *n/a*

ADMISSIONS:

None

REPORTS:
None

BUSINESS RECORDS:

Will any be tendered under the Evidence Act and has the appropriate notice been given? *n/a*

EXPERT WITNESSES:

1. Will any be called? *No*
2. On what issues? *n/a*
3. Identity of experts? *n/a*

TRIAL DATE:

1. Are parties ready for trial? *Yes*
2. Are there any times the case cannot proceed because of witnesses or other matters? *No*
3. How long will the trial last? *2 days*

SETTLEMENT

What are the prospects? *Poor*

DAMAGES

Special Damages: Can any or all be agreed? *n/a*
If so, what are particulars? *n/a*
General Damages: *n/a*
Punitive Damages: *n/a*

IS THIS CASE WHERE IT MAY BE ADVISABLE TO DIRECT A REFERENCE?
No

WHAT PRE-TRIAL ORDERS ARE REQUESTED?
None

7. **SUMMMONS TO WITNESS – EAST v. EAST**

Norma Grace Brownlee of 135 Alexander Blvd., Toronto, M2C 4A3, is to be asked to give evidence on behalf of the plaintiffs. She will drive each day to the court house in Whitby – which is 52 km from her home. She will be required for two days, commencing a week from next Monday. Prepare the necessary summons, and requisition the cheque for attendance money (referred to the witness fees as discussed in your text). Refer to Precedent 14.11.

8. **SUMMONS TO WITNESS – HALCHUK ats WALDEN AND OTHERS**

This action is proceeding to trial in Owen Sound next month. Two witnesses are to receive a summons to give evidence on behalf of the defendant. Prepare the two summons and requisition the necessary cheques for attendance money. Refer to Precedent 14.11.

(a) George Henry, 46 Timberline Drive, Owen Sound
He will be required for one day on the 15th of next month

(b) Patricia Joan Wicks, 967 Holly Avenue, Toronto
She will be required for two days, commencing on the 15th of next month. She will be driving to the court house in Owen Sound – which is 100 km from her home. She will stay overnight in Owen Sound.

9. **BRIEF OF AUTHORITIES – GEORGIAN TECHNOLOGY ats BAYSIDE**

Sylvia has already photocopied the cases for the brief of authorities required for this action for which you prepared an affidavit of documents earlier this chapter. Michael Colucci has now drafted the following index page for the brief. Prepare the index in good form checking that all cases are cited correctly. Refer to Figure 14.10 for the format of the index.

Murphy v Welsh 1993 106 Dominion Law Reports 4th 404

Glassman v. Honda Canada Inc. 1996 28 Ont. Reports 3rd 359

Ryan v Singh 1993 19 Carswell Practice Cases 3d 41

Swiderski v Broy Engineering Ltd. 1992 11 Ont. Reports 3d 594

Dawson v. Chow 1993 27 CPC 3d 291

C. LEGAL TERMINOLOGY

After completing this exercise you should be able to spell and define the following legal terms. Read the definitions shown below. Then select the correct term and match it with the words or phrase that best matches it in meaning, and write the correct term in the space provided. There are more terms than definitions.

Legal Terms

interrogatories	trial record	settlement conference
examination for discovery	trial brief	case book
stay of proceedings	status notice	privilege
attendance money	affidavit of documents	pre-trial conference

Definitions

1. document advising plaintiff's solicitors that action may be dismissed for delay _____

2. confidential communications between a lawyer and a client are protected by this _____

3. mandatory booklet(s) containing material relevant to the proceeding for the use of the judge at the trial _____

4. term used to describe set of questions asked during discovery stage of a proceeding _____

5. funds given to a person who is called as a witness at a trial _____

6. an examination under oath of parties to a legal proceeding, held before the trial or hearing _____

7. an order of the court to temporarily halt a legal proceeding, usually a trial _____

8. brief of authorities _____

9. conference held to dispose of, shorten, or simplify the proceedings prior to trial _____

10. document prepared by all parties to a proceeding, listing all material relating to any matter or issue in the proceeding _____

11. optional booklet(s) containing material for use of lawyer at the trial _____

CHAPTER 15 – ASSIGNMENTS
Application Proceedings

A. LEGAL OFFICE PROCEDURES

There are no legal office procedures exercises for this chapter

B. LEGAL DOCUMENT PRODUCTION

1. NOTICE OF APPEARANCE – MATTHEWS and MATTHEWS

Mr. Grant has now seen a new client, John R. Matthews, who was served yesterday with a notice of application, the back of which is shown below. Refer to Precedent 15.2.

SHIRLEY ARLENE MATTHEWS APPLICANT	and	JOHN RICHARD MATTHEWS RESPONDENT
		Court file no. **M9908**

	ONTARIO **SUPERIOR COURT OF JUSTICE** Proceeding commenced at Milton
from the desk of **PETER THOMAS GRANT** *Please prepare a Notice of Appearance –* *we'll mail it to Smith, Brown* *Authority in heading –* *Family Law Act RSO 1990 c. F.3*	**NOTICE OF APPLICATION**
	SMITH, BROWN & BLACKWOOD Barristers & Solicitors 25 Belfast Road Toronto ON M8X 6G2 Karen P. Emond (42261E) Tel: (416) 490-1246 Fax: (416) 936-8871 Solicitors for the applicant

2. NOTICE OF APPLICATION AND SUPPORTING AFFIDAVIT – HUMPHRIES and HUMPHRIES

Peter Grant asks you to prepare the notice of application and supporting affidavit in an estate matter for which he has been working for some time. Our client, Carew Phillip Humphries, is one of the two executors of the estate and is coming into the office later today to swear the affidavit. The will that is to be an exhibit to this affidavit is reproduced as part of this material for this assignment. Refer to Precedent 15.1 in preparing the notice of application. The body of the affidavit is available to be retrieved and revised.
(Practice Files: Drafts Folder – File: Draft 15)

Carew Phillip Humphries

Applicant

and

Kristen Patricia Humphries
and John Peter Humphries

Respondents

Application under the Trustee Act RSO 1990

Notice of Application

To be heard – 2 weeks from next Monday at 45 Main Street East, Hamilton, Ontario

TO: K. P. Humphries
57 Prince Edward Avenue
Hamilton L5X 4T7

Court office:
45 Main Street East
Hamilton L8N 2B7

J. P. Humphries
340 Ballacaine Drive
Hamilton L9W 4R2

Page 2---

1. The applicant makes application for the opinion, advice or direction of the court upon the question arising under the last will and testament of Algernon Patrick Humphries, late of the City of Hamilton, deceased, as follows:

(a) Under the said last will does the widow, Clarissa Mary H- acquire an absolute title or simply a life estate in the northeast quarter of Lot 16 in the Sixth Concession of the City of Hamilton, in the Reg. Muni. of Hamilton?

2. The grounds for the application are:

(a) the deceased, Algernon Patrick Humphries, died on Dec. 1, 2007, leaving as his next of kin his widow, Clarissa Mary H-, his daughter Kristen Patricia H-, and his son, Carew Phillip H-.

(b) Pursuant to the terms of a will dated Jan. 10, 1999, the deceased appointed his son Carew Phillip Humphries and his cousin, John Peter Humphries, as estate trustees of his estate.

(c) Under the will, the deceased left everything he owned to his wife and stipulated that at her death what remained of his estate was to be divided equally between his son & his daughter

(d) The widow of the deceased wishes to dispose of the property but the daughter & the joint estate trustee, John Peter Humphries, have refused to enter into a conveyance to dispose of the property.

3. The following documentary evidence will be used at the hearing of the application:

(a) Affidavit of Carew Phillip H-, sworn ...

(b) Last will and testament of Algernon Patrick Humphries dated Jan. 10, 1999

Date of issue: H-, J- & G-
                                              etc.....

                                              Peter T. Grant
                                              Solicitors for the applicant

General Heading - Humphries

AFFIDAVIT ~~of~~
C- P- Humphries

I, Carew Phillip Humphries, of the ~~-~~ he lives in Mississauga

estate trustee   Patrick
one of the ~~executors~~ of the estate of Algernon Humphries, late of the City of Hamilton, deceased, MAKE OATH AND SAY:

Dec. 1/07

1. I am the son of the above-named Algernon P- H-, who died on ~~Sept. 1/92~~. He left him
   his   Mary   Kristen Patricia
surviving as ~~her~~ next kin my mother, ~~Clarissa~~ Patricia Humphries, my sister ~~Clarissa Mary~~
                         18
Humphries, and myself. We are all over ~~eighteen~~ years of age.

                                                9
2. My said father left a will dated January 10, 197/9, and by that will appointed myself and
     /   estate trustee
my cou~~s~~in John Peter Humphries ~~executor~~s. Now produced and shown to me is a true copy of the will of the said (APH) as certified by the Registrar of the Ontario Superior Court of Justice at Toronto.

                                    property,
3. The major asset of my father's estate was a farm, which is a house and farm consisting of
                                              9
the northeast quarter of Lot ~~No.~~ 16, in the Sixth Concession of the City of Hamilton, in the (Reg)(Muni) of Hamilton, containing 50 acres more or less. This property was never my parents' matrimonial home.
                                                                          a
4. It is my mother's desire to sell this property and to continue to live in the apartment in which she and my father were living at the date of his death. I am quite in agreement with
                                              Execute a transfer/deed.
this and am prepared to put the farm up for sale and to ~~sign a conveyance~~.

5. My sister has indicated an unwillingness to have this property pass out of the family. My
     joint estate trustee   refused
cousin is my ~~co-executor~~ and has consistently ~~declined or neglected~~ to join with me in conveying the property to my mother's name.

                          not   advice
6. Because the will is ~~something less than perfectly~~ clear, I request the opinion, or direction
                          or not   d   y
of the court as to whether ~~under that will~~ my mother acquire an ab solute title or simple a life estate in the said property pursuant to the terms of the will.

SWORN etc.

102

Toronto
Jan 10th 1999

I declare this my last will and testament

Everything I own goes to my wife Clarissa Mary Humphries and at her death what remains of my estate if any goes to be divided equally between my son Carew Phillips Humphries and my daughter Kristen Patricia Humphries.

I wish to appoint Carew Phillip Humphries and John Peter Humphries to be Executors

Signed

Algernon P Humphries
Hamilton, Ontario

Witness: Dorothy M. Hunter

Witness: George T. Harter

CERTIFIED

M.R. Brown

_____
Registrar

3. APPLICATION RECORD – HUMPHRIES and HUMPHRIES

*Prepare the required face page, table of contents page, and backsheet for the application record. Refer to Precedents 14.5 and 14.6 and adapt these precedents for a trial record to prepare an application record. You will need to prepare the application record in order to know what page number to insert in paragraph 3 of the accompanying factum, where you refer to the page in the record where the will may be found. This proceeding was assigned **court file no. 889554** when it was issued.*

4. FACTUM – HUMPHRIES and HUMPHRIES

Peter Grant has now drafted and revised the following applicant's factum in this application which you are asked to prepare in good form. Refer to Precedent 15.3.

GENERAL HEADING - HUMPPHRIES

THE FACTS

1. The applicant requests the opinion advice or direction of this court as to whether under the last will and testament of Algernon Patrick Humphries, deceased, his widow acquired an absolute title to certain lands & premises, or simply a life estate in the property.

2. The applicant is the son of the deceased, and an estate trustee named in the last will and testament of the deceased.

3. The respondent Kristen Patricia H - is the daughter of the deceased. The respondent John P - H - is a nephew of the deceased, & a joint estate trustee with the applicant of the estate of the deceased.

4. The will of the deceased was homemade and was executed on January 10, 1999. It reads as follows:

Key in the body of the will from "Everything.... to Executors")

Record p. ?? - fill in number on which page of the record that the will appears.

5. The property in question is the northeast quarter of Lot No. 16 in the Sixth Concession of the City of Hamilton, in the Reg. Muni. of Hamilton. The property in question had been the family home of the deceased before his marriage and was left to the deceased under the will his father in 1963. The property has never been the matrimonial home of the deceased or his widow, & over the years has been occupied various members of the Humphries family. It is presently occupied by my cousin Blair Craig Davidson, a nephew of my mother, at a monthly rental of $1,000.00.

6. The widow, Clarissa Mary H-, wishes to sell the property to the said Blair Craig Davidson, & the applicant is prepared to carry out her wishes. The joint estate trustee, John Peter H-, has declined or neglected to join in such a conveyance.

7. The respondent Kristen Patricia H- has indicated that she does not wish the property to pass out of the Humphries family.

LAW

8. It is respectfully submitted that it is clear that the widow has an absolute title to the property.

> Re Alvine 1923 DLR 614 at page 620
> Re Lamony 1946 94 Ont. Rep. at pages 96-7
> Re Marshall 1972 2 Ont. Reports 214 at p. 218
> Re Henderson 1979 26 Ont. Rep. 2d 174 at page 176

} *format citations properly*

ORDER SOUGHT

9. The applicant respectfully requests an order of this court that the widow Clarissa Mary H- acquire an absolute title to the property under the last will and testament of the said deceased;

Algernon Patrick Humphries, and has the right to dispose of the property.

ALL OF WHICH IS RESPECTFULLY SUBMITTED this   day of , 20__

Peter T. Grant

H J & G etc...

TO: GRAHAM & PARKER etc.
Michael Cochrane

5. CONFIRMATION OF APPLICATION – HUMPHRIES and HUMPRIES

Peter Grant has now spoken with Michael Cochrane at Graham & Parker to confirm the date and time of this application hearing. You are to prepare the confirmation of application that is drafted below. Refer to Precedent 15.4 in your text. You will also need to prepare the necessary fax cover pages to fax the confirmation to the court house and to Graham & Parker.

General Heading – Humphries and Humphries Application

Confirmation of Application

I, PETER T. GRANT, with the law firm of H-, J- & G-, counsel for the applicant, confirm that the application to be heard on (insert date of application hearing) will proceed on the following basis:

X for hearing of all the issues

I estimate that the time required for the motion, including costs submission, will be 30 minutes for the applicant and 30 minutes for the respondent for a total of 60 minutes.

Date: HILL, JOHNSTON & GRANT etc..
                             Peter T. Grant
                             Solicitors for the πs

TO: Superior Court of Justice etc.

TO: Graham & Parker, etc.

6. NOTICE OF APPLICATION – AGOSTO ESTATE

Michael Colucci is acting for Eterna Agosto in her claim against the estate of the late Thomas Van Brenck. He asks that you prepare the following draft notice of application in final form. The <u>body</u> of the application is available to be retrieved and revised. You will need to insert this draft document into the correct court form. Refer to Precedent 15.1.
(Practice Files: Drafts Folder – File: Draft 16)

ETERNA AGOSTO – Applicant

BEATRIX WYERS, Estate Trustee of the Estate of Thomas Van Brenck, Deceased – Respondent

APPLICATION under the Succession Law Reform Act, R.S.O. 1990

NOTICE OF APPLICATION for a hearing on Monday *(2 weeks from next Monday)* at 393 University Avenue, Toronto

TO: BEATRIX WYERS, Estate Trustee of the Estate of Thomas Van Brenck, Deceased
c/o Martin J. Brownlee

Court office: ~~145 Queen Street West~~ *393 University Ave Toronto M5G 1E6*, Toronto, ~~M5H 2N9~~

<u>Page 2:</u>

APPLICATION

1. The applicant(s) make(s) application for:

(a) An order that such provision as this Honourable Court considers proper be made out of the Estate of the deceased, for the support of the applicant;

(b) an order for periodic payments pursuant to s. 63(2) of the <u>Succession Law Reform Act</u>, R.S.O. 1990, c. S.27;

(c) an order securing the payment under a support order, *on* ~~out of~~ the property of the deceased pursuant to s. 62(2)(f) of the SLRA;

(d) an order that the payment be made retroactive to the date of death of the deceased Thomas Van Brenck *(herein "the deceased")*, in order to meet the reasonably incurred *debts* of the applicant for her own support up to the date of the application pursuant to s. 63(2)(g) of the SLRA;

(e) an order that the applicant be entitled to possession of the matrimonial home belonging to the deceased and being the premises municipally known a 46 Grandlake Court, in the City of Toronto, during her life time *pursuant to s. 63(d) of the S-L-R-A*;

(f) an order suspending in whole or in part the administration of the estate of ~~Thomas Van Brenck~~ *the* deceased, pending the return of the application herein pursuant to *s. 59 of the S-L-R-A*

line up

(i) such further other order as seems just.

(g) an interim order for the relief claim pending the disposition of the application herein, pursuant to s. 64 of the SLRA

(h) costs of this application on a solicitor and client basis;

2. the grounds for the application are:

(a) the deceased ~~Thomas Van Brenck~~ did not make adequate provision in his last will and testament; dated the 15th of July 1986, for the support of the applicant;

(b) the applicant is a dependent within the meaning of the SLRA

(c) the applicant who is 62 years of age, is in need of and entitled to provision for her support out of the estate of the deceased ~~Thomas Van Brenck~~ pursuant to the provisions of Part V of the SLRA

(d) The applicant resided with the ~~late Thomas Van Brenck~~ deceased for a period of ~~twelve~~ 12 years and cohabited as husband and wife during the last ~~ten~~ 10 years up to the time of the deceased's death;

(e) during cohabitation the applicant was ~~totally and~~ entirely dependant upon the deceased, ~~Thomas Van Brenck~~, for her support, as she did not and does not have any other income, assets or resources in order to be self-sufficient.

(f) During cohabitation, the applicant lived with the deceased, ~~Thomas Van Brenck~~, in his house located at 46 Grandlake Court, Toronto, Ontario. During this ~~ten~~ 10-year period, the applicant shopped, cooked, cleaned, did laundry, ~~and ironing~~, and performed any other duties as were necessary from time to time ~~in~~ to maintain the household,

(g) during the last ~~two~~ 5 years of his life, the deceased, ~~Thomas Van Brenck~~, was disabled with arthritis and depended increasingly on the applicant to help look after him. The applicant was his constant companion.

(h) On numerous occasions, the deceased, ~~Thomas Van Brenck~~, during his lifetime had told the applicant and others that he intended to leave his estate to the applicant and had looked after her in his will, and

3. The following documentary evidence will be used at the hearing of the application:

(a) The affidavit of Eterna Agosto sworn ~~(insert date)~~ leave date blank, 200x, and the exhibits therein referred to;

(b) financial statement of Eterna Agosto sworn ~~(insert date)~~ leave date blank

(c) such further + other material as counsel may advise

Date of issue:

C. LEGAL TERMINOLOGY

After completing this exercise you should be able to spell and define the following legal terms. Read the definitions shown below. Then select the correct term and match it with the words or phrase that best matches it in meaning, and write the correct term in the space provided. There are more terms than definitions.

Legal Terms

application	list of authorities	regulations
applicant	estate	transcript
respondent	affidavit	notice of appearance
factum	statute	notice of application

Definitions

1. a written record of an examination of a witness _____

2. a law enacted by the legislative branch of a government _____

3. document that originates an application _____

4. the real and personal property owned by a person as of the date of his or her death _____

5. written statement of facts sworn under oath _____

6. civil proceeding requesting the advice, direction or authority of the court _____

7. rules outlining how the provisions of an act are to be carried out or administered _____

8. concise statement of the facts and the law relied on in an application hearing _____

9. document filed by the respondent in an application proceeding _____

10. the person who makes the application to the court _____

11. the personal against whom an application is made _____

CHAPTER 16 – ASSIGNMENTS
Orders, Judgments and Costs

A. LEGAL OFFICE PROCEDURES

There are no legal office procedures exercises for this chapter.

B. LEGAL DOCUMENT PRODUCTION

1. **ORDER – BLACK v. HUMBER TOOL & DYE**

Michael Colucci has reviewed a draft order prepared by Kim Chae and has asked you to prepare it in final form. You will find a specimen of the general heading in this action on page 69 of this assignment book for which you also prepared the consent in Chapter 13 Assignments. Refer to Precedent 16.3 for the format of the order.

ONTARIO
SUPERIOR COURT OF JUSTICE

Master P. R. Irvine   )   Order made today
*   )*

Title of Proceeding of Black v. Humber Tool & Dye

THIS MOTION made by the πs for an order dismissing this action without costs heard this day at Toronto.

UPON READING the consent of the parties hereto, filed;

1. THIS COURT ORDERS that this action be & the same is hereby dismissed without costs.

———————————————

Do a memo to Kim asking her to have this order signed & entered.

Thanks
MDC

2. ORDER – EAST v. EAST

Peter Grant asks you to prepare the order in the East action to strike out the jury notice. He gives you his handwritten draft of this order. Refer to Precedent 16.3.

General Heading – East v. East

The Honourable   Date in Notice of Motion
Mr. Justice Almond

THIS MOTION made by the πs for an order striking out the jury notice, was heard this day at Whitby.

On reading the affidavit of Lynda Carol Ritchie & the exhibits thereto & on hearing the submissions of council for the πs, no one appearing for the Δ although properly served as appears from the admission of service,

1. This court orders that the jury notice be & the same is hereby struck out.

_____

Also do a memo to Jennifer Stauffer –

Please arrange to have this order signed and entered at Whitby. We will then need to provide a copy of the signed and entered order to Smith, Fraser.

PTG

3. JUDGMENT FOLLOWING TRIAL – WEBSTER et al v. HOLLAND et al.

Peter Grant was counsel for the plaintiffs in a recent action that proceeded to trial. Judgment has now been handed down and was drafted by Thomas Hussain. Peter Grant has now reviewed and revised the order shown on the following page and asks that you prepare the revised judgment in final form along with the following letter to the solicitors for the defendants. The body of the order is available to be retrieved and edited. Refer to Precedent 16.1.
(Practice File: Drafts Folder – File: Draft 17)

Henry P. Green
Re: Webster et al. v. Holland et al.

I enclose a copy of the draft judgment in this action. Please return this to me with your comments or approved as to form as soon as conveniently possible.

Court File No. C9784

The Honourable } *Friday, (last Friday's date)*
Mr. Justice Dees

JOHN HARVEY WEBSTER, PETER MARK THORNDYKE and GRACE ~~John~~ *JOAN* THORNDYKE

– *and* – *Ms*

ROBERT HOWARD HOLLAND, WILLIAM JONES and INTERESTED INVESTMENTS INC.

As
JUDGMENT
~~ORDER~~

THIS ACTION heard on the *12th, 13th, 14th and 17th of last month*, 200x, without a jury at Milton, in the presence of counsel for all parties *and the*

ON READING THE PLEADINGS AND HEARING the evidence *submissions* of counsel for the parties, and on reading the minutes of settlement, filed, with respect to the plaintiff*s J-H-W-, P-M-T and G-J-T-*,

1. This court orders and adjudges that the plaintiff Peter Mark Thorndyke do*es* recover from the defendants the sum of $5,217.95 for claims together with interest in the sum of $2,556.80 for a total of $7,774.75.

2. THIS COURT*s* ORDERS AND ADJUDGES that the plaintiff ~~Peter Mark~~ *Grace Joan* Thorndyke do*es* rec*o*ver from the defendants the sum of ~~$5,217.95~~ *$13,570.50* for *all* claims together with interest in the sum of $6,159.55 *for a total of $?*

3. This court orders and adjudges that the defendants do *see* pay to the plaintiffs (PMT) and (GJT) *names in full* their costs of this action fixed in the sum of $2,500.00, together with costs of the reports of experts in the sum of $7*5*00.00

4. This court orders and adjudges that the plaintiff John Harvey Webster do*es* recover from the defendants the sum of $*7*,250.00 for all claims together with interest in the sum of $3,075.20 for a total of ~~$9,125.20~~ *?*.

5. THIS COURT ORDERS AND ADJUDGES that the defendants do *tel* pay to the plaintiff John Harvey Webster his costs of this action.

THIS JUDGMENT BEARS INTEREST at the rate of (insert proper rate) percent per year commencing on (date of judgment).

4. JUDGMENT – EAST v. EAST

Judgment following trial has now been handed down in this action and Peter Grant has drafted the judgment shown below that you are to prepare in final form. Refer to Precedent 16.1.

General Heading – East v. East

The Honourable Mr. Justice Hook	)))	Yesterday's date

JUDGMENT

THIS ACTION was heard on the 26th and 27th of (current month), (current year), without a jury at Whitby in the presence of counsel for all parties,

ON READING ……. the submissions of counsel for the parties,

1. THIS COURT DECLARES that the plaintiffs are entitled to specific performance of the agreement for purchase & sale of the lands and premises being composed of the north half of Lot 7, in the 3rd Concession of the Township of Brock, in the Regional Municipality of Durham, at the price of $260,000.00, subject to the usual adjustments.

2. THIS COURT ORDERS AND ADJUDGES that in the event of the party being unable to agree upon the carrying out of such purchase & sale, then upon appointment applied for by either party, there shall be a reference to the Master at Whitby so that all necessary inquiries may be had, accounts taken, & the said sale may be carried out under the supervision of the courts.

3. THIS COURT DOES NOT see fit to make any order as to costs.

_____

5. BILL OF COSTS FOLLOWING TRIAL – DURHAM TECHNOLOGY INC.

Peter Grant was involved in a trial that was completed several months ago. Judgment was reserved and has just recently been handed down. The plaintiff was awarded costs on a partial indemnity basis. Peter Grant has now drafted the bill of costs and asks you to prepare it in final form. Note that, unlike in an account, disbursements are not separated into those subject or not subject to GST. Instead an asterisk is keyed after those disbursements subject to GST. Refer to Precedent 16.4.

Court file no. 941699

ONTARIO
SUPERIOR COURT OF JUSTICE

BETWEEN:

DURHAM TECHNOLOGY INC.

Plaintiff
(Defendant
to the Counterclaim)

and

MARKHAM ENTERPRISES LTD.

Defendant
(Plaintiff
by Counterclaim)

BILL OF COSTS OF THE PLAINTIFF

Partial Indemnity Costs	Fees	Disbursements
1. Pleadings		
Drafting, issuing and serving the s/c herein, and drafting and serving the reply and the defence to the counterclaim herein		
Peter T. Grant – 15 hours Christopher Dubois – 10 hours	$3,625.00	

Paid to file statement of claim	$ 181.00
Transaction levy surcharge	50.00*
Paid to file reply & defence to counterclaim	144.00
Photocopies	45.00*

2. Discovery of Documents

Review of documents & preparation of affidavit of documents

Peter T. Grant – 10 hours
Christopher Dubois – 5 hours
Jennifer Stauffer – 2 hours   2,550.00

Photocopies   45.00*

3. Examinations

Examination for discovery on March 6 and 7, 20xx, including preparation and counsel
    of the plaintiff
    of the defendant

Peter T. Grant – 20 hours   3,500.00

Paid to Court Reporting Services   850.00*
Paid for transcripts of examinations   350.00*

4. Pre-trial conference

Preparation of pre-trial memorandum, memorandum of law and trial brief

Peter T. Grant – 5 hours
Christopher Dubois – 5 hours   1,375.00

Photocopies 36.00*
Quicklaw Legal Research 500.00*
Expert Report – Matlock Forensic
    Accounting Services 250.00*

5. Trial before Mr. Justice Brownleigh
September 8, 9, 10 and 11, 200x

Peter T. Grant – 40 hours
Christopher Dubois – 15 hours   8,500.00

Paid to file trial record 337.00
Photocopies 148.00*
Paid witness fees
    Healthcliffe King – 1 day 53.00
    Joyce Newman – 1 day 53.00
    Margaret Cochrane – 2 days 106.00
Ontario Court Agents 175.00*

Total Fees $?.??
GST on Fees   ?.??

Total Disbursements $?.??
*GST on Disbursements   ?.??

TOTAL PARTIAL INDEMNITY COSTS $?.00

Statement of Experience   Rate

Peter T. Grant, Year of Call 1990 $175.00

Christopher Dubois, Year of Call 2000 $100.00

Jennifer Stauffer – Law Clerk $70.00

C. LEGAL TERMINOLOGY

After completing this exercise you should be able to spell and define the following legal terms. Read the definitions shown below. Then select the correct term and match it with the words or phrase that best matches it in meaning, and write the correct term in the space provided. There are more terms than definitions.

Legal Terms

pro rata	bill of costs	entered
judgment	assessment of costs	tariff
substantial indemnity costs	prejudgment interest	costs
partial indemnity costs	postjudgment interest	order

Definitions

1. interest calculated from date of cause of action to date of judgment

2. hearing to determine the amount of money to be paid as costs to the successful parties in legal proceedings

3. costs awarded in legal proceedings to compensate a party for their legal costs at a considerably higher rate than normally awarded in extraordinary circumstances

4. the final decision of a court in a legal proceeding

5. costs awarded in legal proceedings to partly compensate a party for their legal costs

6. a decision of the court that does not finally dispose of a legal proceeding.

7. a schedule of fees that may be charged to perform specified legal services

8. reimbursement to the successful party for expenses of a litigation proceeding

9. interest calculated from date of judgment to date of payment of damages

10. a document in legal proceedings that sets out in detail the claim for costs in an action or application

11. according to specified rate, share or proportion

CHAPTER 17 – ASSIGNMENTS
Disposition of Actions Without Trial

A. LEGAL OFFICE PROCEDURES

There are no legal office procedures exercises for this chapter.

B. LEGAL DOCUMENT PRODUCTION

1. NOTICE OF DISCONTINUANCE – PALMER v. ROSE

Peter Grant have now been able to settle the claim in this action, for which you prepared the statement of claim in Chapter 10 Assignments. When the statement of claim was issued, it was given court file no. C84631.

You are instructed to prepare a notice of discontinuance, and are reminded that because the statement of claim was never served on the defendant, the notice is addressed to the local registrar at the court office where the statement of claim was issued.

2. LETTER & ACCOUNT – PALMER v. ROSE

The Palmers have signed a release and the settlement cheque from Mr. Rose has now been given to the Accounting Department for deposit in the trust account. The rough drafts of the covering letter and account to the Palmers are shown below and on the following page. You are to prepare these in good form and requisition the necessary cheques.

Letter to Mrs. Marylynn Palmer

Re: Palmer and Rose

The settlement of this matter has now been completed on the terms we discussed with you. ¶ Your release was forwarded to Smith Fraser to be held until we received the settlement funds. We have now received Mr. Rose cheque for $26,784.67, representing a payment to you of $25,284.67 and $1,500 for costs.
I am now enclosing our firm's cheques for:
1. $25,284.67 being the settlement amount from Gerald Rose
2. $(fill in this amount after you calculate the account) being the excess funds rec'd from you to cover our fees & disbursements as set out in our account.
I am enclosing our account marked PAID, as well as some material you left with us at our first interview. As this appears to complete this matter we are closing our file.

Marylynn Palmer – Account

To Professional......
(from file opening date to today's date)

To receiving instructions on your behalf in the above matter; to requesting & receiving Dr's reports & accounts therefore; to drafting, issuing & holding s/c; to correspondence with solicitors for the defendant; to effecting settlement of the claim for $25,284.67 plus costs; to all other relevant telephone conversations and correspondence, in all;

			Our Fee	$1,200.00
			GST	?
Disb'ts				
Subject to GST				
Paid account of Dr. J. Bragna	$ 150.00			
Paid account of Dr. I. Harrison	100.00			
Transaction Levy Surcharge	50.00			
Photocopying	8.70			
	?			
GST	?			?
Not Subject to GST				
Paid to issue s/c	181.00			181.00
Subtotal				?
Less:				
Retainer received from you	$ 500.00			
Costs received on settlement	1,500.00			$2,000.00
Cheque payable to you				?
				PAID

HILL, JOHNSTON & GRANT etc......

Requisition the 2 cheques to Marylynn Palmer

PTG

3. **DEFAULT JUDGMENT –**
   GENERAL FOOD EQUIPMENT LIMITED v. 1853222 ONTARIO LIMITED

Assume that the statement of claim that you prepared in Chapter 10 assignments was served 20 days ago and no statement of defence has been delivered. Michael Colucci has advised you that a requisition for default judgment and the draft judgment are to be prepared. He provides the following information to assist you. Refer to Precedents 17.2 and 17.3.

1. Court file no. C84589
2. No statement of defence delivered
3. Claim in statement of claim is for a debt.
4. No payment on account.
5. Part A of requisition – not applicable.
6. Principal sum claimed – see statement of claim
7. Prejudgment interest – see statement of claim
8. Interest calculation:

    Principal sum: see statement of claim
    Start date: see statement of claim
    End date: today's date
    Interest rate: see statement of claim
    No. of days: start date to today's date

9. Interest amount:

    $$\frac{\text{No. days} \times \text{interest rate} \times \text{principal sum}}{365}$$

10. Postjudgment interest: as claimed in statement of claim.
11. Costs: to be fixed by local registrar.

4. **NOTICE OF WITHDRAWAL –**
   1975311 ONTARIO LIMITED ET AL. ats PORTER BUILDING SUPPLIES LTD.

The defendants in this action wish to withdraw paragraph 6 of their statement of defence. You are asked to prepare the appropriate notice of withdrawal. You prepared a statement of defence for this proceeding in Chapter 12 Assignments. Refer to Precedent 17.1.

C. LEGAL TERMINOLOGY

After completing this exercise you should be able to spell and define the following legal terms. Read the definitions shown below. Then select the correct term and match it with the words or phrase that best matches it in meaning, and write the correct term in the space provided. There are more terms than definitions.

Legal Terms

notice of discontinuance	writ of seizure and sale	judgment debtor
dismissed	foreclosure	de facto
default judgment	execution	default
summary judgment	judgment creditor	final judgment

Definitions

1. a document directed to the sheriff to reduce a judgment debtor's property to money in the amount of the judgment _____

2. a judgment against a party who does not enter any response to a legal proceeding against them _____

3. a person ordered by the court in a judgment to make payment to another person _____

4. legal proceedings when a mortgage is in default to transfer title to the lender _____

5. in fact, actually _____

6. a person to whom a judgment of the court orders that payment be made _____

7. if the defendant pays the amount of the claim against them, the action against them may be _____

8. if the plaintiff decides to not pursue their claim against one of the several defendants, this document would be prepared _____

9. failure to fulfill a financial obligation or the terms of an agreement _____

10. a judgment of the court without a trial _____

CHAPTER 18 – ASSIGNMENTS
Introduction to Family Law

A. LEGAL OFFICE PROCEDURES

1. OPENING NEW MATTER – ELVIDGE and ELVIDGE

Peter Grant will be acting for Susan Elvidge, who separated from her husband Jason Elvidge last August. She has instructed Peter Grant to apply for custody and support of their daughter and an equal division of the family property. Information on her address and the file number is located in the reference section. This application will be commenced in Family Court of Superior Court of Justice at Brampton. You are to prepare the new matter form/label and a retainer for this client. Susan Elvidge provided Peter Grant with a cheque for $500 as a retainer. Brianna T. Wolfe at the law firm of Fox, Wolfe & Lyons is acting for Jason Elvidge. Jason Elvidge's address is 9292 Morrison Blvd. Mississauga, Ontario, L5Y 1G8, Tel: 905-682-9001.

B. LEGAL DOCUMENT PRODUCTION

1. MARRIAGE CONTRACT – MARTIN and HANSON

Peter Grant has been consulted by Mara Martin in connection with a marriage contract. Peter Grant agreed to represent Mara Martin and advised Harvey Hanson to get independent legal advice, which he declined to do. Peter Grant provides you with the first two and the last page of the draft marriage contract and an acknowledgement to be prepared in good form by you.

THIS MARRIAGE CONTRACT made the 1st day of current month, year.
Harvey Herman Hanson
(herein "the husband")
- and -
Mara Martha Martin
(herein "the wife")

Whereas the husband & the wife intend to marry and enter into this contract freely and under no undue influence or duress

And whereas the husband & the wife wish to enter into this contract setting out the mutual promises hereinafter set forth and for other good and valuable consideration, the receipt and sufficiency of which is hereby acknowledged.

Now therefor the husband & the wife agree as follows:

1.00   INTERPRETATION
1.01   In this contract:
(a) "husband" means Harvey Herman Hanson who is a party to this contract;
(b) "wife" means Mara Martha Martin who is a party to this contract;

(c) "Family Law Act" means the <u>Family Law Act</u>, RSO 1990, as amended

(d) "property" has the meaning set out in the Family Law Act

(e) "family residence" means the buildings and lot located at 765 Kimberbank Road, Halton, Ontario, but does not include any other buildings or lands acquired in addition to this property

(f) "breakdown of the marriage" means:

   (i) the separation of the parties with no reasonable prospect that they will resume cohabitation

   (ii) the dissolution of their marriage; or

   (iii) the annulment of their marriage.

1.02 An act of the legislature or parliament referred to by name will mean that act in force at the material time and include any amendment or any successor Act which replaces it.

2.00 FACTS UPON WHICH CONTRACT IS BASED

2.01 This contract is based upon the following facts:

(a) the husband is a widower

(b) the wife has never been married

(c) the husband & the wife intend to marry each other on the 25th of (next month, current year)

(d) the husband and the wife intend to live in the family residence

(e) Jason Stephen Hanson is the child of the husband from a previous marriage

(f) the child Jason S. H. lives with the husband in the family residence & will continue to do so after the marriage of the husband & the wife

(g) the wife will treat the child Jason S. H. as a child of her family for financial support and as a child of the family made with the husband in all other respects

(h) the husband & the wife intend to have more children

(i) the husband & the wife intend that the wife will devote her full time to the care of their family

---

24.00 GOVERNING LAW

The law governing the procedures and the substance of the arbitration will be the law of the Province of Ontario.

25.00 EXECUTION

25.01 TO EVIDENCE their agreement the husband and the wife have each signed this contract before a witness.

SIGNED, SEALED AND DELIVERED etc.

ACKNOWLEDGEMENT

IN THE MATTER OF the intended execution of a

MARRIAGE CONTRACT between

HARVEY HERMAN HANSON and MARA MARTHA MARTIN

I, HARVEY HERMAN HANSON, hereby acknowledge that I have been advised by Peter T. Grant, a solicitor in the law firm of Hill, Johnston & Grant, to obtain my own solicitor to negotiate on my behalf in this matter

I understand that I have a right to independent legal counsel and in fact have been advised of these rights by the said Peter T. Grant, who also advised that I seek independent legal counsel. I acknowledge that I have refused to do so and I understand that the said Peter T. Grant is only acting on behalf of Mara Martha Martin.

I have read the Marriage Contract herein and hereby acknowledge that I am fully capable of understanding its contents and do in fact understand each and every provision contained therein. I acknowledge further that my signature on the Marriage Contract herein dated the 1st day of next month, current year, is freely given and I am under no duress or any improper influence of any kind.

DATED at Toronto, this _____ day of current month, current year.

_____ _____
Witness   H. H. H.

2. CERTIFICATE AND AFFIDAVIT OF SOLICITOR – LEWIS and LEWIS

Peter Grant prepared and witnessed a separation agreement for Walter Lewis and his wife Karen Lewis. You are asked to prepare the certificate and affidavit of solicitor to be attached to this separation agreement. Refer to Precedent 18.3.

3. SEPARATION AGREEMENT – QUADRINI and HALL

Peter Grant has drafted the following agreement to amend a separation agreement he drafted for his client Rob Connacher several years ago. You are asked to prepare it in final form. Refer to Precedent 18.2

THIS AGREEMENT made as of the 1st day of (current month, year)

BETWEEN:

> ROBERT JOHN QUADRINI
> (herein "the husband")
> - and -
> JESSICA LYNN HALL
> (herein "the wife")

WHEREAS the husband and the wife were married on July 15, 1995 & separated on May 15, 2001, & entered into a separation agreement on September 15, 2001 (the "Separation Agreement");

And whereas under the Separation Agmt the wife had full custody of the child of the marriage, Christopher John Quadrini born August 15, 1997 (the "child"), with the husband to have reasonable access on reasonable notice and to pay child support of $750.00 per month.

Now therefore this agreement witnesseth that the husband & the wife have agreed to amend the separation agmt as follows:

1. The husband is to have full custody of the child commencing on the 1st day of (current month, year) with the wife to have reasonable access on reasonable notice.

2. The wife shall not pay child support to the husband & the husband agrees to waive all present and future rights to claim any child support to be payable by the wife to the husband.

3. In all other respects the Separation Agreement shall remain in full force and effect.

4. The husband & the wife acknowledge that each has received independent legal advice from his or her own solicitor regarding his or her respective legal rights as related to this Separation agmt.

TO EVIDENCE THEIR AGREEMENT the husband and the wife have signed this agreement before a witness.

SIGNED, SEALED & DELIVERED etc....

4. FINANCIAL STATEMENT – ELVIDGE and ELVIDGE

Peter Grant provides you with the following notes from his interview with Susan Elvidge to prepare the first draft of the financial statement (property and support claims) for this proceeding. Note that all income and expense amounts must be shown as a monthly calculation. To get a monthly figure multiply any weekly income by 4.33 or divide any yearly amount by 12. Refer to Precedent 18.4.

Date of Marriage: May 15, 2000
Date of Separation: August 1, (last year)
Child of Marriage: Jennifer Susan Elvidge, born Jan. 3/04, living with mother

Valuation Date: August 1, (last year)
Statement Date: today's date

Income:
Annual Salary - $36,000 and Child Tax Benefit - $1200 yearly

Deductions:
Income Tax - $492 monthly; CPP - $125 monthly; EI - $50 monthly

Expenses:

Housing:
Rent - $850 monthly
Electricity - $35 monthly
Telephone - $60 monthly
Cable - $50 monthly
Home Insurance - $240 yearly

Food, etc:
Groceries - $340 monthly
Meals outside home - $15 weekly
Gen. Household - $25 monthly
Hairdresser - $50 monthly
Laundry - $25 monthly
Clothing - $1800 yearly
Public transit - $100 monthly
Taxi - $10 monthly

Susan's Health & Medical:
Regular dental - $240 yearly
Eye glasses - $360 yearly
Life Insurance - $600 yearly

Children:
Day care - $150 weekly
Regular dental - $240 yearly
Medicine & Drugs - $20 monthly

Misc:
Books, etc. - $10 weekly
Gifts $360 yearly
Alcohol & tobacco - $20 monthly
Entertainment - $240 yearly
Vacation - $480 yearly
Credit Card - $50 monthly

Susan's Employer:
Federal Courier Services, 600 Mavis Rd. Mississauga L1H 9C9
Susan will attach copies of last 3 years taxation information & current pay stub.

Assets
No land
Household - describe as contents - $5,000 at date of marriage, valuation date and today which are NOT in her possession

Bank Accounts:
Joint Savings, Royal Bank of Canada, Acct. #14002 - value on date of marriage $5,000.00, on v-date and today - $1,000.00
Joint Chequing, Royal Bank of Canada, Acct. #20012 - $500.00 on date of marriage, v-date and today.
GIC - Royal Bank - #44992 - value on v-date and today - $25,000
Life & Disability Insurance:
Sun Life, Life Policy, applicant is owner, daughter is beneficiary, face amount: $25,000, cash surrender value on v-date and today: $1,100.00

No business interests, money owed or other property

Debts:
Credit Card - Royal Bank VISA - $500.00 date of marriage and $1,000 on v-date and today
Legal Fees - family law proceedings - $1500 on v-date and today

Excluded Property:
Gift - Inheritance from father - Royal Bank GIC #44992 - value - $25,000

5. NET FAMILY PROPERTY STATEMENT – ELVIDGE and ELVIDGE

Using the information below and from the financial statement that you prepared, you are now to prepare the necessary net family property statement for this proceeding. Our client will be the applicant. Refer to Precedent 18.6.

Contents - $5,000 for each of applicant and respondent
Car - 2006 Honda Accord - $20,000 to respondent
Joint Savings - $1,000 to each of applicant and respondent
Joint Chequing - $500 to each of applicant and respondent
GIC & Life Insurance (as in financial statement) to applicant
Debts - Credit Card Debt - Applicant (as in financial statement);
Respondent $2,000 American Express;
Legal fees $1500 for both applicant and respondent
General Household on Date of Marriage -
$5,000 to each of applicant and respondent
Bank Account on Date of Marriage -
$5,500 to each of applicant and respondent
Excluded Property -
Inheritance from applicant's father (as in financial statement).

6. SUPPORT DEDUCTION ORDER INFORMATION FORM & ORDER – ELVIDGE

Because Susan Elvidge is applying for child support, it will be necessary to complete the support deduction order information form and order. Refer to the notes below and the previous documents prepared for this file to obtain the information to complete these forms. Leave the name of the judge and the date of the order blank. Refer to Precedents 18.7 and 18.8.

Payor: Jason Elvidge, born Aug. 3/75
social insurance number - 234 778 990
Mother's maiden name - Cosentino
Employer:
Queen Anne Hotel, 76 Courtney Dr., Mississauga, L6M 2Z9
Home Telephone: 905-682-9001
Work Telephone: 905-664-9300

Recipient: Susan Elvidge, born Feb. 27/78
social insurance number - 442 668 321
Mother's maiden name - Watson

7. NET FAMILY PROPERTY STATEMENT – LEWIS and LEWIS

Walter Lewis provided Peter Grant with the following information about his and his wife's assets and debts. You are asked to prepare a draft net family property statement in order to calculate the equalization payment. The valuation date is the 1st of this month and Walter is the applicant.

Joint Assets & Debts of Walter and Karen Lewis as of v-date
Matrimonial Home – 185 Timothy Drive, Toronto Ontario M2K 4C9 - $550,000
Household Contents – Total Value: $30,000
Jewellery and Art. – Total Value: $15,000
Joint Savings – CIBC – Total Amount: $30,000
Joint Chequing – CIBC – Total Amount: $20,000
Joint Life Insurance Policy – Spouses as beneficiaries - $100,000 face amount –
$30,00 surrender value
GICs – CIBC – Total Amount: $80,000
Mortgage on Matrimonial Home – CIBC – $150,000
Line of Credit – CIBC – $60,000

Individual Assets & Debts as of v-date

Walter Lewis	**Karen Lewis**
Car – Lincoln Navigator - $60,000	Car – BMW - $55,000
Stock – IBM Canada Ltd. - $250,000	Canada Savings Bonds - $40,000
Stock – Bell Canada – $150,000 – Inherited from parents after marriage	Art & Jewellery – $300,000 – Inherited from parents after marriage
Credit Card Debt – CIBC VISA - $1500	Credit Card Debt – CIBC VISA - $2500
Credit Card Debt – AMEX - $3500	
Date of Marriage - $20,000 in savings	Date of Marriage - $5,000 student loan debt

C. LEGAL TERMINOLOGY

After completing this exercise you should be able to spell and define the following legal terms. Read the definitions shown below. Then select the correct term and match it with the words or phrase that best matches it in meaning, and write the correct term in the space provided. There are more terms than definitions.

Legal Terms

net family property statement   excluded property   marriage contract
separation agreement   matrimonial home   support payments
breakdown of the marriage   financial statement   valuation date
net family property   equalization payment   support deduction order

Definitions

1. property of a spouse that does not form part of the spouse's net family property, such as an inheritance

2. document required if there is any claim for support, property, or exclusive possession of matrimonial home

3. value of all of a spouse's property, less allowed deductions

4. grounds for divorce

5. property that was at the time of separation, ordinarily occupied by the spouses as their family residence

6. contract between people who are married or intend to marry

7. a payment that may be required in order for there to be an equal division of all family property

8. contract between people who were married and now live apart

9. document required if there is any claim for division of property

10. date that spouses separate with no expectation to reunite

11. document required if there is any claim for support or variation of support

CHAPTER 19 – ASSIGNMENTS
Family Law Proceedings

A. LEGAL OFFICE PROCEDURES

There are no legal office procedures exercises for this chapter

B. LEGAL DOCUMENT PRODUCTION

1. **APPLICATION (GENERAL) – ELVIDGE and ELVIDGE**

Peter Grant has now asked that you prepare the application (general) to commence this case. Refer to the financial and net family property statements you prepared in Chapter 18 assignments and to Peter Grant's notes below to prepare this document. Our client will be providing a copy of her marriage certificate to file with the application. Refer to Precedent 19.3.

> *Case will be on the standard track and will include a claim for property*
>
> | Family History: | Susan Elvidge | Jason Elvidge |
> |---|---|---|
> | Birthdate | Feb. 27, 1978 | Aug. 3, 1975 |
> | Surname at birth | Jackson | Elvidge |
> | Surname before marriage | Jackson | Elvidge |
> | Divorced before | No | No |
>
> *Both spouses resident in Mississauga since DOB*
> *Married – May 15, 2000   Separated – August 1, (last year)*
> *One child – Jennifer Susan Elvidge*
> *DOB Jan. 3, 2004, living with mother*
> *No previous court cases or written agreements*
> *Claims for support (table amount), custody of child, equalization of NFP and costs*
>
> *Orders requested:*
> 1. *Custody of the child J. S. Elvidge born ---*
> 2. *Support for the child J. S. Elvidge in accordance with Child Support Guidelines in the amount of $367 per month*
> 3. *Equalization of the NFP of the marriage*
> 4. *Costs.*
>
> *Claim for Divorce based on separation – no reconciliation attempts*

Facts in Support
1. *The child J-S-E- has always lived with me and I have always been primary caregiver.*
2. *The child J-S-E- is settled in her home, community and daycare.*
3. *The respondent has been erratic in exercising access to the child J-S-E-*
4. *The respondent is employed as a chef and earns an annual salary of $40,000*
5. *The applicant left the matrimonial home at the time of separation and there has been no financial disclosure or division of the family assets.*

2. AFFIDAVIT OF SERVICE – ELVIDGE and ELVIDGE

Assume that the application has now been filed and assigned **Court File Number 44229** *and that you have as of today's date served the application, financial statement and net family property statement on the respondent by delivering it in person to Jason Elvidge's lawyer (Brianna T. Wolfe, Fox, Wolfe & Lyons). Prepare your affidavit of service. Assume you travelled 25 km and that the fee is $30. Refer to Precedent 19.4.*

3. CONTINUING RECORD – ELVIDGE and ELVIDGE

The continuing record must now be prepared for this case. You will need to prepare an endorsements volume containing the table of contents, an endorsements section (with three blank pages of paper) and an orders section. You also need to prepare a documents volume containing the documents prepared to date: application (and affidavit of service), financial statement of applicant, and net family property statement of the applicant. These documents should be listed in the cumulative table of contents. Refer to Precedent 19.3.

Note that in the classroom environment you will prepare only one containing record; however, in practice a minimum of two would be prepared. One for filing with the court and one to be maintained in the law firm as a duplicate. Additionally, a third copy of the table of contents would be required to be served on the respondent with the application.

4. NOTICE OF MOTION – ELVIDGE and ELVIDGE

Peter Grant has requested a motion hearing on behalf of Susan Elvidge to request an order for interim custody and support. He provides you with his notes below for preparing the notice of motion. Refer to Precedent 19.8.

<u>*Notice of Motion*</u>

Motion to be heard on (2 weeks from today's date) at 10:00 a.m.
Motion made on behalf of S- Elvidge

Copy of the affidavit in support will be filed with the notice
Documents in support:
1. Application dated (insert date)
2. Financial Statement of S- Elvidge dated (insert date)
3. Financial Statement of J- Elvidge dated (yesterday's date)
Orders requested:
1. An order for temporary custody of the child J- S- Elvidge born (insert DOB) to the applicant S- Elvidge
2. An order for temporary child support for $367 per month in accordance with the Child Support Guidelines payable by the respondent J- Elvidge to the applicant S- Elvidge

5. AFFIDAVIT IN SUPPORT – ELVIDGE and ELVIDGE

Prepare the following affidavit to be filed in support of the notice of motion for this case.

Affidavit of Susan Elvidge

1. I am the applicant herein and as such have knowledge of the matters hereinafter deposed.
2. I was married to the respondent on ---
3. There was one child of the marriage, Jennifer Susan Elvidge, born ---.
4. I separated from my husband on ---. It was necessary to separate due to a general incompatibility between my husband and me.
5. When we separated, I left our former matrimonial home, which was a rental unit, and I took Jennifer with me as I have always been the primary caregiver. I have continued to have custody of Jennifer since that time. My husband has never made request for custody of Jennifer. I believe that he is content that it is in the best interests of Jennifer that she resides with me.
6. Since the date of our separation, my husband has been very erratic in exercising access to Jennifer. I have no objection to my husband having access on alternative weekends, provided that he is regular and responsible in exercising such access.
7. Since the date of separation, my husband has not provided any payments for child support.
8. I am employed as an accounting clerk with a courier company. My financial circumstances are set out in the financial statement filed in connection with this case.
9. My husband is a chef employed at the Queen Anne Hotel on Courtney Drive in Mississauga. I believe that his annual income is approximately $40,000.

10. I make this affidavit in support of an order for interim and permanent custody of my daughter, and for interim and permanent support for my daughter

6. AFFIDAVIT OF SERVICE & UPDATED CONTINUING RECORD TABLE OF CONTENTS – ELVIDGE and ELVIDGE

Assume you have now served this notice of motion and affidavit by fax on Jason Elvidge's lawyer. Prepare your affidavit of service and the updated table of contents for the continuing record so that these documents may be filed in the court. Note that Jason Elvidge served and filed a financial statement (dated as of yesterday's date) along with his affidavit of service on your office. These documents need to be included in the updated table of contents <u>before</u> the notice of motion documents.

7. CONFIRMATION OF MOTION HEARING – ELVIDGE and ELVIDGE

Peter Grant has confirmed with Jason Elvidge's lawyer that she will attend the motion hearing for which you prepared a notice of motion. Refer to the notice of motion and Peter Grant's notes below to prepare the confirmation document. Refer to Precedent 19.7.

Case Conference has not been held;

Matter is going ahead - on all the issues

Judge should read tabs 1, 2, 4, 5 and 6 of continuing record

Time estimates: 20 minutes for each of applicant and respondent

8. ORDER – ELVIDGE and ELVIDGE

Peter Grant will need to take a copy of a draft order to the motion hearing. Refer to the notes below and to Precedent 19.10 to prepare this document.

Leave the name of the judge blank

Fill in date of order as the date of the motion hearing

Temporary order for an motion made by - Susan Elvidge

Both parties and their lawyers were in court

Evidence/submissions by Susan Elvidge and Jason Elvidge

Court orders:
1. The applicant S- Elvidge shall have temporary custody of the child J-S- Elvidge born ??
2. The respondent J- Elvidge shall have reasonable access to the child J- S- Elvidge

3. The respondent J. Elvidge shall pay temporary child support in the amount of $367.00 per month to the applicant S. Elvidge.

9. **SUMMONS TO WITNESS – ELVIDGE and ELVIDGE**

Peter Grant has requested that you prepare a summons to witness for this case which will be required when the case is heard. Refer to Precedent 19.9 in and the following notes to prepare this document.

Summons to: Karen Balsmeier, 480 Elm Rd., Oakville ON L6B 4J3

Date of Hearing: June 10, 20xx at 10:00 a.m.

Examination before: the court

Attendance Fee: 1 day of attendance, traveling 40 km each way

Documents: Financial records pertaining to the joint venture between Jason Elvidge and yourself

10. **APPLICATION (SIMPLE) – RODRIGUES and RODRIGUES**

Peter Grant has been acting for Elian Rodrigues in connection with a family law matter. Mr. Rodrigues has now decided to obtain a divorce. This will be an application (simple) as the divorce is uncontested and all custody and support issues have already been resolved under a separation agreement. This case will be commenced in the Superior Court of Justice at Newmarket. Refer to Precedent 19.11 and the information below to prepare this document.

Applicant: Elian Juan Rodrigues
7500 Yonge Street, Suite 350
Aurora ON L2K 7W3
Phone: 905-869-4522
Represented by PTG
Born: Jan 10/70
Surname at Birth: Rodrigues

Respondent: Selena Carmen Rodrigues
60 Beckett Blvd., Aurora ON L2K 4G1
Phone: 905-867-3341
Self-represented
Date of Birth: Feb. 20/73
Surname at Birth: Cortez

Married: June 25, 1995 in Orillia
Separated: June 1, 2006
Both parties have lived in Aurora since date of marriage;
Neither married before

Children: Michael Elian Rodrigues born May 28/1999
Kristina Marie Rodrigues born Nov. 14/2001
Both children live with mother
Attend Grandview Public School

Notes: claim for divorce only
no previous court cases
separation agmt. dated Oct 1, 2006 in full force
and effect
no reconciliation attempts

11. AFFIDAVIT OF SERVICE – RODRIGUES and RODRIGUES

Assume this case has now been assigned **Court File Number 38825**. *Howard Podoba, an articling student with our firm who lives in Newmarket, has now served the application by special service on the respondent today. He traveled 60 km and the fee is $50. Prepare the affidavit of service. Refer to Precedent 19.4.*

12. SUPPORT DEDUCTION INFORMATION FORM & ORDER – RODRIGUES and RODRIGUES

Prepare the necessary support deduction information order form and order for this case. Refer to Precedents 18.7 and 18.8 and the following additional information to complete these documents.

Payor: husband
social insurance number - 228 460 995
employer: Centennial Consulting Inc.
(in your address list)
mother's maiden name - Diaz

Recipient: wife
social insurance number - 889 465 350
Mother's maiden name - Cruz
Work telephone number - 905-662-4888

This is not a variation of a previous support order.

13. AFFIDAVIT FOR DIVORCE – RODRIGUES and RODRIGUES

Prepare the affidavit for divorce for this case. Refer to Precedent 19.12 and the following information to prepare this document.

> *All information in application is correct*
>
> *Certificate of Marriage was filed with the application*
>
> *Grounds for divorce are separation since June 1/06*
>
> *Divorce order to include the following sentence:*
>
> *Separation Agreement dated October 1, 2006 to remain in full force and effect*
>
> *List the children and their DOBs*
>
> *Custody and access arrangements –*
> *Custody of the children M- E- Rodrigues and K- M- Rodrigues to the wife with the husband to have access:*
> *(a) every other weekend*
> *(b) from evening of Christmas Day to evening prior to children returning to school*
> *(c) alternate March breaks commencing with the wife in 20xx*
> *(d) during the first two weeks of July*
>
> *Payor's income - $90,000;*
>
> *Child support payable by the husband in the amount of $1281 in accordance with child support guidelines*
>
> *No claim for costs*

14. DIVORCE ORDER – RODRIGUES and RODRIGUES

Prepare the draft divorce order for submission with the affidavit for divorce. Leave the name of the judge and the date of judgment blank. Strike out the paragraph about the persons in court. Remember to include the sentence about the separation agreement that you referred to in the affidavit for divorce. Refer to Precedent 19.13 and the affidavit you prepared above to complete this document.

C. LEGAL TERMINOLOGY

After completing this exercise you should be able to spell and define the following legal terms. Read the definitions shown below. Then select the correct term and match it with the words or phrase that best matches it in meaning, and write the correct term in the space provided. There are more terms than definitions.

Legal Terms

continuing record	summons	application (divorce)
regular service	orders	nee
special service	attendance fees	motion hearings
case conferences	application (general)	judgment

Definitions

1. document requiring a person to attend a hearing as a witness _____

2. document used to commence a family law case that contains any claim(s) that may be contested _____

3. at least one of these must be held before any hearings will be allowed _____

4. document used to commence a family law case for a simple or joint divorce _____

5. booklet(s) containing all court documents for a family law case organized in a prescribed manner _____

6. interlocutory proceedings to seek interim orders of the court _____

7. money given to a person who will be a witness at a hearing _____

8. born (Fr.); used to refer to a person's name at birth _____

9. serving a court document on the party's solicitor would be an example of this type of service _____

10. serving a court document by mailing the document would be an example of this type of service _____

11. decisions of the court, whether interim or final, in family law case _____

CHAPTER 20 – ASSIGNMENTS
Introduction to Real Estate

A. LEGAL OFFICE PROCEDURES

1. LAND REGISTRY OFFICES - MANUAL

Ascertain the present name and number for the land registry office or offices serving your area. Your instructor will discuss with you the names by which such land registry offices may have been previously identified.

2. LEGAL DESCRIPTION FROM OLD TRANSFER/DEED FORMS – MANUAL

You have been given a number of transfer/deeds prepared prior to 1985 and asked to prepare the legal descriptions in the form in which they should appear in a new real estate document. You will encounter these "old" forms in many real estate transactions since people often live in real property they purchased before 1985. You will need to check the current status and name of the lower and upper tier municipalities.

> THOSE lands and premises located in the following municipality, namely,
> in the Town of Kincardine, in the County of Bruce,
> and being composed of the whole of Lot 153, according to a plan registered in the Land Registry Office for the Registry Division of Bruce (No. 3) as Number 99340

> **ALL AND SINGULAR** that certain parcel or tract of land and premises situate lying and being in the Town of Lindsay, in the County of Victoria,
> and being composed of the west half of Lot 18 on the south side of Dundas Street, according to a plan registered in the Land Registry Office for the Registry Division of Victoria (No. 57) as Number 78982.

> **ALL AND SINGULAR** that certain parcel or tract of land and premises situate lying and being in the Township of Kingston, in the County of Frontenac,
> and being composed of the whole of Lot Number 4 according to Plan Number 5447 registered in the Registry Office for the Registry Division of Frontenac (No. 13).
> SUBJECT to an easement to the Bell Telephone Company over the rear four feet (4') from side to side, of the lot hereby conveyed, for normal line installation and servicing.

3. E-REG SYSTEM – INTRODUCTION

In learning the Teraview electronic system, you will be accessing the training environment. This environment replicates the records of an actual part of Ontario that has been converted to Teraview. The records are "frozen in time," meaning that what you will see are the actual property records as they existed at the time the area was converted several years ago. The training system is fully functional for almost all activities, including searching, document creation and registration. The environment is exactly as it is in the "real" system, however, you should note that Teranet regularly resets the training environment to its original status thus removing any dockets and documents that have been created and registered by persons using the training system. The following table lists the available PINs for use in the training environment.

Land Titles Absolute & Land Titles Conversion Qualified Properties		
07001-0001	to	07001-0675
07014-0001	to	07014-0600
07181-0001	to	07181-0500
07184-0001	to	07184-0700
24910-0001	to	24910-0200
24911-0001	to	24911-0275
24924-0001	to	24924-0900
24925-0001	to	24925-2000
Condominium Properties		
07982-0001	to	07982-0500
08013-0001	to	08013-0450
25473-0001	to	25473-0450

You should become familiar with the Teranet website (www.teranet.ca) as it provides information on using the software and provides regular updates of any changes to the electronic registration system. You should also become familiar with logging on, creating a docket, and correctly exiting the system. Refer to Precedent 20.1 in your text.

B. LEGAL DOCUMENT PRODUCTION

1. ARTICLE FROM DRAFT LEASE AGREEMENT

Lynda Ritchie has drafted the following article from a lengthy lease contract for you to prepare. Refer to Chapter 7 of your text for guidelines and precedents on preparing agreements.

ARTICLE TEN

MAINTENANCE

10.01 MAINTENANCE BY TENANT. Tenant shall at Tenant's own expense, keep & maintain all interior portions of Tenant's leased premises in good condition and repair and in as clean and safe a condition as when Tenant first takes possession of the leased premises, excepting reasonable use, acts of nature & normal wear and tear. Such obligations shall include maintenance of exterior entrances, plumbing, electrical, lighting, heating & cooling systems which extend into the leased premises. Tenant shall at Tenant's own expense replace and repair the glass in any display window on the premises that become scratched or broken, regardless of cause. If Tenant refuses or neglects to repair items properly required under this para as soon as reasonably possible after any written demand by Landlord, then Landlord may make any such repairs without any liability by Landlord to Tenant for any damages or losses that may occur to Tenant's merchandise, fixtures, or other property or the Tenants business by reason thereof, and upon completion, Tenant shall pay Landlord's costs for making any such repairs plus fifteen (15) percent which amount shall be added to the Tenants monthly rental fee.

10.02   Maintenance by Landlord. Landlord shall maintain in good condition & repair the exterior roof, walls, floors and structural supports, and all other portions of the building in which the leased premises are situated except as provided in paragraph 10.01 hereof. There shall be no obligation for the Landlord to make any repair pursuant to this section until after the expiration of two (2) days' written notice from tenant to Landlord of the requirement for such repair. The cost thereof shall be included into the common element expenses as described in paragraph 6.02 hereof.

10.03   ALTERATIONS. Tenant shall not have the right to make any addition, alterations, improvements or other substantive changes to the leased premises without first obtaining the Landlord's written permission. Such permission shall not be unreasonably withheld. Tenant shall present to Landlord draft plans and specifications for any such alterations at the time that such consent is requested including a commencement and completion date for any such alterations. Tenant shall not allow or cause any lien to be placed on the leased premises or any part thereof by reason of any such alterations done or not done upon the leased premises by or with the permission of Tenant. All alterations, improvements additions, and fixtures, except furniture and trade fixtures, made or placed in or on the leased premises by Tenant, or any agent of Tenant, shall become the property of the landlord, and upon termination of this lease shall remain upon and be surrendered with the leased premises as a part thereof.

C. LEGAL TERMINOLOGY

After completing this exercise you should be able to spell and define the following legal terms. Read the definitions shown below. Then select the correct term and match it with the words or phrase that best matches it in meaning, and write the correct term in the space provided. There are more terms than definitions.

Legal Terms

joint tenants	lessee	lessor
chattels	condominium	contingency fund
common elements	real property	registry
tenants in common	PIN	land titles

Definitions

1. a house is an example of this kind of property

2. land registry system that requires a minimum 40 year search of previous documents

3. holding of title to real property with right of survivorship

4. areas such as halls, elevators, and grounds that are owned as tenants in common by the individual condominium owners

5. party who rents real property from another party

6. index or file number that is assigned to real property under the e-reg system

7. personal property such as furniture or appliances

8. party who rents real property to another party

9. land registry system where the province is responsible for maintaining the records and guaranteeing title

10. multi-unit building or complex in which individuals hold ownership in fee simple of a specific unit of space

11. the fund contributed to by individual unit-owners in a condominium to meet unexpected expenses or to build up a reserve for future major repairs or replacements

CHAPTER 21 – ASSIGNMENTS
Transfer/Deed

A. LEGAL OFFICE PROCEDURES

1. SPOUSAL STATUS STATEMENT

Review each of the following situations and in the space provided set out the wording that you feel should be used to complete the wording for Box 8 of the transfer/deed.

> (8) **Transferor(s)** The transferor hereby transfers the land to the transferee and certifies that the transferor is at least eighteen years old and that

1. Two spouses are the transferors as joint tenants.

2. One spouse is the transferor, and the other spouse is a party to consent to the transaction.

3. One spouse is the transferor, and the property being transferred is not their matrimonial home.

4. The transferor is not married.

5. The transferor is a spouse, but the other spouse has released all interest in the matrimonial home under a separation agreement dated January 1, this year.

B. LEGAL DOCUMENT PRODUCTION

PREPARING TRANSFER/DEEDS

Peter Grant has asked you to prepare a number of transfer/deeds. 1 and 2 are in the manual system; 3 and 4 are in the e-reg system. The "old" transfer/deed for transaction 1 appears on the following page. You are also given the following specific information for each transaction. Refer to Precedents 21.1 and 21.2 (manual) and Precedents 21.3 and 21.4 (e-reg).

1. **TRANSFER/DEED (MANUAL) - VAN BRENCK sale to LEGGE**

Purchase Price:	*$185,000 ($1,500 for chattels)*
Vendors:	*see old transfer/deed - they are spouses*
	address for service will be c/o law firm
Purchasers:	*Legge, Bruce James - DOB: Feb. 16/69*
	Legge, Sarah Jane - DOB: June 23/69
	as joint tenants; address for service - address of property
Planning Act:	*We will complete Box 13*
Closing date:	*17th of next month*

Transfer/Deed of Land
Form 1 — Land Registration Reform Act

Province of Ontario

(1) Registry ☐ Land Titles ☒ (2) Page 1 of 2 pages

(3) Property Identifier(s): Block 44996 Property 3884

(4) Consideration: ONE HUNDRED THIRTY FIVE THOUSAND Dollars $ 135,000.00

(5) Description:
Lot 10, Plan 2468
Village of Bancroft, County of Hastings
Registry Division of Hastings (No. 21)

(7) Interest/Estate Transferred: Fee Simple

(8) Transferor(s): The transferor hereby transfers the land to the transferee and certifies that the transferor is at least eighteen years old and that **I am not a spouse.**

Name(s)	Signature(s)	Date of Signature Y / M / D
BARKER, Ian Derek		1990 / 08 / 10

(10) Transferor(s) Address for Service: 40 Lake Street, Peterborough ON K2J 4L9

(11) Transferee(s):

Name	Date of Birth Y / M / D
VAN BRENCK, John Jacob	1962 / 09 / 04
VAN BRENCK, Marion Ruth	1966 / 05 / 24

as joint tenants

(12) Transferee(s) Address for Service: P.O. Box 30, 16 Glen Road, Hastings ON K4Y 6G2

(13) Transferor(s): The transferor verifies that to the best of the transferor's knowledge and belief, this transfer does not contravene section 50 of the Planning Act.
Date of Signature: 1995 / 08 / 10

Solicitor for Transferor(s): I have explained the effect of section 50 of the Planning Act to the transferor and I have made inquiries of the transferor to determine that this transfer does not contravene that section and based on the information supplied by the transferor, to the best of my knowledge and belief, this transfer does not contravene that section. I am an Ontario solicitor in good standing.

Name and Address of Solicitor: Michael J. Picov, 480 Water Street, Peterborough ON K9H 8G7
Date of Signature: 1995 / 08 / 10

(14) Solicitor for Transferee(s): I have investigated the title to this land and to abutting land where relevant and I am satisfied that the title records reveal no contravention as set out in subclause 50 (22) (c) (ii) of the Planning Act and that to the best of my knowledge and belief this transfer does not contravene section 50 of the Planning Act. I act independently of the solicitor for the transferor(s) and I am an Ontario solicitor in good standing.

Name and Address of Solicitor: Henry J. Carmichael, 9754 Bloor Street West, Toronto ON M3K 5H2
Date of Signature: 1995 / 08 / 10

(15) Assessment Roll Number of Property: Cty. 16 / Mun. 02 / Map 420 / Sub. 102 / Par. 102 / 00000

(16) Municipal Address of Property:
16 Glen Road
Hastings ON K4Y 6G2

(17) Document Prepared by:
Michael J. Picov
PICOV, BLAIR & SCHMIDT
480 Water Street
Peterborough ON K9H 8G7

2. TRANSFER/DEED (MANUAL) - GREGLON ESTATES sale to VENERACION

PIN: 42886 7224
Purchase price: $169,500 inclusive of GST
Legal Description: Property is in the land titles system and described as:
Parcel 5-2, Section M-4276
being Part of Lot 4, Plan M-4276
designated as Parts 14 and 15 on Plan 65R-7091
Town of Parry Sound, District of Parry Sound
Vendor(s): Greglon Estates Inc. - transfer/deed will be executed by its president, Gregory Paul Dizon, no corporate seal
address for service will be c/o PTG, Hill, Johnston & Grant
Purchaser(s): Veneracion, Adam David - Sept. 24/70 - not married
address for service will be address of property
Planning Act: We will not complete boxes 13 and 14
Assessment roll no: leave blank
Property address: 736 Burwell Crescent, Parry Sound, Ontario P2A 1B9
Closing date: January 15, 20xx

3. TRANSFER (E-REG) – GUEST sale to WANG

PIN: 24925-1800
Purchase price: $275,000 (no chattels)
Property Address: 2099 Summer Heights Trail, Oakville
Vendor(s): Guest, Ronald William and Sueann - they are spouses
address for service - 46 Belmont Court, Oakville L4T 2P1
Purchaser(s): Wang, Tak Keung - DOB: Aug 12/70
Wang, Mei-Ling - DOB: Nov. 10/72
as joint tenants - address of property - address for service
Planning Act: statements are to be completed
LTT Statement: completed by both transferees who are Roman Catholics

4. TRANSFER (E-REG) – PHAM sale to GARDENWOOD/HENNING

Purchase price: $450,000 (no chattels)
PIN: 25473-0250
Property Address: 1000 Halton Place, Unit 132, Halton Hills ON
Vendor(s): Hoa Xuan Pham. He is separated from his spouse who has relinquished all rights under a separation agmt;
Address for service - 40 Elm Road, Newmarket L6V 4J3
Purchaser(s): Gardenwood, Ryan Graham - DOB: June 9/56
Henning, Jennifer Lynn - DOB: April 3/58
as tenants in common - 50% interest each
address of property will be address for service
Planning Act: statements will not be completed
LTT Statement: Single family residence; transferees English-Public

C. LEGAL TERMINOLOGY

After completing this exercise you should be able to spell and define the following legal terms. Read the definitions shown below. Then select the correct term and match it with the words or phrase that best matches it in meaning, and write the correct term in the space provided. There are more terms than definitions.

Legal Terms

transfer/deed	severances	easement
transferor	consolidations	nominal consideration
transferee	life estate	spousal status
consideration	fee simple	address for service

Definitions

1. statements regarding this are required by the Family Law Act for all real estate transactions

2. real property held by a person during their lifetime only

3. term used to describe the division of a parcel of land into two or more parcels

4. A legal instrument by which title to real property is transferred from one party to another

5. term used to described absolute ownership of land

6. A right of way over real property which is owned by another person is an example of this

7. term used to describe the combining of one parcel of land with another adjoining parcel of land

8. in real estate practice, the amount of money paid to be paid the purchase of real property

9. the party who receives title to real property under a transfer/deed

10. an amount paid for real property that does not reflect the actual market value of the property

11. the party who gives title to real property under a transfer/deed

CHAPTER 22 – ASSIGNMENTS
Charge/Mortgage

A. LEGAL OFFICE PROCEDURES

There are no legal office procedures exercises for this chapter

B. LEGAL DOCUMENT PRODUCTION

1. **CHARGE/MORTGAGE (MANUAL) –**
   MORSILLO to ABC MORTGAGE LENDERS & DAVIS, 44 Kee Street, Woodstock

Michael Colucci is acting for Antony and Rosemary Morsillo who are purchasing property from Kenneth and Catherine Preston. They have arranged a new first mortgage with ABC Mortgage Lenders and have also arranged a mortgage loan from Mrs. Morsillo's aunt and uncle, Barry and Sarah Davis, as a second mortgage. All funds will be received on the 30th of next month which is the closing date. Michael Colucci asks that you prepare both of these mortgages and provides you with the draft transfer/deed that appears on the following page as well as the information below. Refer to Precedent 22.1 and Figures 22.2 and 22.3.

(a) **First Mortgage**

Principal Amount:	*$100,000.00*
Term of mortgage:	*3 years (amortized over 25 years)*
Mortgagee:	*ABC Mortgage Lenders Inc. (in your address book)*
Repayment:	*$763.21 monthly, interest at 8% calculated half-yearly, not in advance*
Special provisions:	*right of renewal upon 30 days' notice for 5 years*
Standard charge terms:	*9320*
Insurance:	*full replacement value*

(b) **Second Mortgage**

Principal Amount:	*$25,000.00*
Term of mortgage:	*5 years (amortized over 10 years)*
Mortgagees:	*Barry Peter Davis and Sarah Jean Davis mortgage to be held jointly address for service: 843 Mayfair Street Toronto Ontario M9V 4D2*
Repayment:	*$246.41 monthly, interest at 8.5% calculated half-yearly, not in advance*
Special provisions:	*post-dated cheques*
Standard charge terms:	*9320*
Insurance:	*full replacement value*

Transfer/Deed of Land
Form 1 — Land Registration Reform Act

Province of Ontario

(1) Registry [X] Land Titles [ ]   (2) Page 1 of 2 pages

(3) Property Identifier(s):
- Block: 33451
- Property: 2806

(4) Consideration: **TWO HUNDRED TEN THOUSAND FIVE HUNDRED** Dollars $ 210,500.00

(5) Description: This is a: Property Division [ ] Property Consolidation [ ]

Easterly half Lot 17, Plan 483
City of Woodstock, County of Oxford
Registry Division of Woodstock (No. 41)

(6) This Document Contains: (a) Redescription New Easement Plan/Sketch [ ] (b) Schedule for: Description [ ] Additional Parties [ ] Other [ ]

(7) Interest/Estate Transferred: Fee Simple

(8) Transferor(s): The transferor hereby transfers the land to the transferee and certifies that the transferor is at least eighteen years old and that **we are spouses of one another.**

Name(s):
- PRESTON, Kenneth James
- PRESTON, Catherine Jane
- as joint tenants

(9) Spouse(s) of Transferor(s) I hereby consent to this transaction

(10) Transferor(s) Address for Service: 689 Prince Henry Blvd., Peterborough ON K7V 4F8

(11) Transferee(s):

Name	Date of Birth Y M D
MORSILLO, Antony Stephen	1980 10 04
MORSILLO, Rosemary Jean	1982 02 14
as joint tenants	

(12) Transferee(s) Address for Service: 44 Kee Street, Woodstock ON N4A 6J5

(13) Transferor(s): The transferor verifies that to the best of the transferor's knowledge and belief, this transfer does not contravene section 50 of the Planning Act.

Solicitor for Transferor(s): I have explained the effect of section 50 of the Planning Act to the transferor and I have made inquiries of the transferor to determine that this transfer does not contravene that section and based on the information supplied by the transferor, to the best of my knowledge and belief, this transfer does not contravene that section. I am an Ontario solicitor in good standing.

(14) Solicitor for Transferee(s): I have investigated the title to this land and to abutting land where relevant and I am satisfied that the title records reveal no contravention as set out in subclause 50 (22) (c) (ii) of the Planning Act and that to the best of my knowledge and belief this transfer does not contravene section 50 of the Planning Act. I act independently of the solicitor for the transferor(s) and I am an Ontario solicitor in good standing.

(15) Assessment Roll Number of Property

(16) Municipal Address of Property:
44 Kee Street
Woodstock ON N4A 6J5

(17) Document Prepared by:
Donald L. Guess
Tasker, Mattea, Auld & Guess
185 Ladybrooke Crescent
London ON N6H 3D2

Fees and Tax:
- Registration Fee
- Land Transfer Tax
- Total

2. CHARGE (E-REG) – VAN DYK to ABC MORTGAGE LENDERS INC.

Jessica and Stephen Van Dyk have decided to do some major renovations on the home they have lived in for many years. In order to finance the renovations, they have decided to place a mortgage for $50,000.00 on the property. Peter Grant asks you to prepare the draft electronic charge document and provides you with the following information. Refer to Precedent 22.4 and Figure 22.3 in your text.

PIN:	07184 0600
Address:	5182 Blue Spruce Avenue, Burlington ON L3N 4S9
Standard charge terms:	9320
Term of mortgage:	5 years
Interest rate:	6% calculated half yearly, not in advance
Repayment:	$299.78 on the 1st day of each month
Closing date:	1st of next month
Insurance:	full replacement value
Chargor's address:	address of property
Chargee:	ABC Mortgage Lenders Inc. (in your address book)
Special provisions:	right of open prepayments without notice or bonus

3. CHARGE (E-REG) – LINDBLAD to ALGONQUIN PERMANENT TRUST

Mary Lindblad (who is not married) is purchasing a condominium and has arranged to obtain mortgage financing from Algonquin Permanent Trust Company. You have been asked to prepare the draft electronic charge document using the following information. Refer to Precedent 22.4 and Figure 22.3.

PIN:	08013 0333
Address:	5090 Pinedale Avenue, Unit 322, Burlington, Ontario L7R 2D7
Standard charge terms:	9320
Term of mortgage:	5 years
Interest rate:	5.5% calculated half yearly, not in advance
Repayment:	$422.06 on the 1st and 15th day of each month
Closing date:	15th of next month
Insurance:	full replacement value
Chargor's address:	address of property
Chargee:	Algonquin Permanent Trust Company (in your address book)
Special provisions:	right of renewal upon 60 days' notice for a further 5 years

C. LEGAL TERMINOLOGY

After completing this exercise you should be able to spell and define the following legal terms. Read the definitions shown below. Then select the correct term and match it with the words or phrase that best matches it in meaning, and write the correct term in the space provided. There are more terms than definitions.

Legal Terms

amortized	principal	term
charge/mortgage	first mortgage	terms
charger/mortgagor	second mortgage	maturity date
chargee/mortgagee	mortgage back	first payment date
interest adjustment date	standard charge terms	interest

Definitions

1. the amount of the charge/mortgage _____

2. the conditions of repayment of the charge/mortgage _____

3. the date on which all monies secured by the charge/mortgage are due _____

4. the number of years over which payment will be made a specified interest rate _____

5. the party giving the charge/mortgage; the borrower _____

6. special provisions relating to the charge/mortgage that may be registered with the director of land registration _____

7. a type of mortgage that provides for the gradual repayment of the debt by set, periodic payments, at a rate calculated to pay the debt in a given number of years _____

8. a legal instrument used to formalize the claim upon title to real property that is security for a debt or loan _____

9. fee charged by the chargee/mortgagee for the use of money _____

10. the party to whom the property is mortgaged; the lender _____

11. the holder of this charge/mortgage will have their claim paid before the holder of any other charge/mortgage _____

CHAPTER 23 – ASSIGNMENTS
Discharge of Charge/Mortgage

A. LEGAL OFFICE PROCEDURES

There are no legal office procedures exercises for this chapter

B. LEGAL DOCUMENT PRODUCTION

1. DISCHARGE (MANUAL) – MORRISON mortgage to SIMPSON

Percival Morrison has given Peter Grant the charge/mortgage set out on the next page of this assignment book. The mortgage has now been paid off and Peter Grant asks you to prepare a discharge for this charge/mortgage. This charge/mortgage was never assigned. Refer to Precedent 23.1.

2. DISCHARGE (MANUAL) – MARTINEZ mortgage to HUMMINGDALE

Mr. and Mrs. Martinez have now fully paid the charge/mortgage that they originally gave to the Harveys in July 1997. You have now been asked to prepare the complete discharge of this charge/mortgage. Refer to Precedent 23.1 and the following information:

1. The PIN number is 82134 4553 and the legal description of the property is:

   Lot 5, Plan 40N-3801
   Being Parcel 5-1, Section 40N-3801
   Town of Cobourg
   County of Northumberland

   Land Titles Division of Northumberland (No. 39)

2. The original charge was registered as No. 97542 on July 16, 1997.

3. The charge/mortgage was transferred by a transfer of charge which was registered as Instrument No. 98642 on July 15, 1998, to Peter Allan Hummingdale. His address for service is 97 Pennway Park Crescent, Cobourg ON K9A 9Y4.

4. The charge was renewed by an agreement extending charge/mortgage registered by a document general as Instrument No. 99356 on July 15, 2003, and was renewed a second time by an agreement extending mortgage registered by a document general as Instrument No. 10458 on July 15, 2006.

5. This is a complete discharge.

Charge/Mortgage of Land
Form 2 — Land Registration Reform Act

Province of Ontario

REGISTERED No. LI9138621 AUGUST 10, 2003

(1) Registry [X] **Land Titles** [ ] **(2) Page** 1 **of** 1 **pages**

(3) Property Identifier(s)
- Block: 58766
- Property: 4532

(4) Principal Amount: FIFTY THOUSAND — Dollars $ 50,000.00

(5) Description:
Parts of Lots 436 and 437
Plan 74310
City of Brockville, United Counties of Leeds and Grenville
Registry Division of Leeds (No. 28)

New Property Identifiers: (none)

Executions: (none)

(6) This Document Contains:
- (a) Redescription New Easement Plan/Sketch [ ]
- (b) Schedule for: Description [ ] Additional Parties [ ] Other [ ]

(7) Interest/Estate Charged: Fee Simple

(8) Standard Charge Terms — The parties agree to be bound by the provisions in Standard Charge Terms filed as number **8505** and the Chargor(s) hereby acknowledge(s) receipt of a copy of these terms.

(9) Payment Provisions
- (a) Principal Amount: $ 50,000.00
- (b) Interest Rate: 10.00 % per annum
- (c) Calculation Period: half-yearly
- (d) Interest Adjustment Date: 2003 08 10
- (e) Payment Date and Period: 10th monthly
- (f) First Payment Date: 2003 09 10
- (g) Last Payment Date: 2008 08 10
- (h) Amount of Each Payment: Six Hundred Fifty Five — 17/100 Dollars $ 655.17
- (i) Balance Due Date: 2008 08 10
- (j) Insurance: Full Insurable Value Dollars $

(10) Additional Provisions

Provided that the chargors when not in default shall have the privilege of prepaying the whole or any amount of the principal hereby secured at any time or times without notice of bonus.

(11) Chargor(s) The chargor hereby charges the land to the chargee and certifies that the chargor is at least eighteen years old and that **the person consenting below is my spouse.**

The chargor(s) acknowledge(s) receipt of a true copy of this charge.

Name(s)	Signature(s)	Date of Signature (Y M D)
MORRISON, Percival Herbert	*Percival Morrison*	2003 08 09

(12) Spouse(s) of Chargor(s) I hereby consent to this transaction.

Name(s)	Signature(s)	Date of Signature (Y M D)
MORRISON, Estelle Marion	*Estelle Morrison*	2003 08 09

(13) Chargor(s) Address for Service: 135 Berry Road, Brockville ON K8Z 4G2

(14) Chargee(s):
SIMPSON, Ralph Peter
SIMPSON, Mary Ruth
on joint account with right of survivorship

(15) Chargee(s) Address for Service: 948 Glenaden Avenue South, Toronto ON M3R 7G4

(16) Assessment Roll Number of Property:

(17) Municipal Address of Property:
135 Berry Road
Brockville ON K8Z 4G2

(18) Document Prepared by:
Peter T. Grant
Hill, Johnston & Grant
17 Princess Street South, Suite 2501
Toronto ON M8Y 3N5

3. CORRESPONDENCE – MARTINEZ mortgage to HUMMINGDALE

Peter Grant has asked you to prepare the following letter in connection with this file.

Send by courier

Susan A Kublick
Steeb & Kublick

Dear Susan

Further to our telephone conversation today I confirm that your firm will be acting as our agent in the above matter.
Enclosed are two copies of the discharge of mortgage and of the insurance release to be signed by Peter Hummingdale. I understand he will be attending at your office later this week to do this. Please then arrange to have the discharge of mortgage registered at the Land Titles Office and return the duplicate original discharge, both copies the executed insurance release and your account as your earliest convenience..
Thank you for your assistance with this matter.

4. DISCHARGE (E-REG) – LAFFERTY mortgage to BANK OF MONTREAL

Robert and Teresa Lafferty have now fully paid the mortgage on their home at 33 Lauchlin Crescent, Halton Hills, Ontario and wish a discharge to be registered on title. You have been asked to prepare a complete discharge for this mortgage. Refer to Precedent 23.2 and the following information to prepare this electronic discharge:

1. The original mortgage was registered as Instrument No. H646145.
2. This is a full discharge
3. The PIN number of the property is 25043-0285
4. The mortgagee is Bank of Montreal, 100 Main Street, Milton ON L2J 4L9

5. DISCHARGE (E-REG) – ALLARD MORTGAGE TO BANK OF MONTREAL

Christianne Allard has now fully paid the mortgage on her property at 426 Maple Avenue, Oakville and wishes a discharge to be registered on title. Refer to Precedent 23.2 and the following information in order to prepare the electronic discharge document:

1. The original mortgage was registered as Instrument No. H646152
2. This is a full discharge
3. The PIN number of the property is 24806-0191
4. The mortgagee is Bank of Montreal, 400 High Street, Oakville L5M 2K9

C. LEGAL TERMINOLOGY

After completing this exercise you should be able to spell and define the following legal terms. Read the definitions shown below. Then select the correct term and match it with the words or phrase that best matches it in meaning, and write the correct term in the space provided. There are more terms than definitions.

Legal Terms

discharge of charge/mortgage	complete discharge	charger/mortgagor
assigned	final partial discharge	guarantor
assumed	mortgage back	charge/mortgage
renewed	partial discharge	open mortgage

Definitions

1. charge/mortgage given as part of the purchase price to the vendor; vendor take back mortgage _____

2. charge/mortgage that is taken over from the original chargor/mortgagor by another party _____

3. a discharge of charge/mortgage, preceded by partial discharges, that represents the last discharge of the property or debt _____

4. charge/mortgage that may be paid off or renegotiated at any time without penalty _____

5. a discharge of charge/mortgage for part of the property or debt _____

6. charge/mortgage that is sold by the original chargee/mortgagee to another party _____

7. a discharge of charge/mortgage for all the property and debt _____

8. charge/mortgage that is extended for a further period of time _____

9. a individual or company that promises to answer for the debt or default of another _____

10. a legal document used to formally acknowledge that the debt covered by a charge/mortgage has been paid and that the charge/mortgage is to removed from title to the property _____

CHAPTER 24 – ASSIGNMENTS
Commencing the Real Estate Transaction

A. LEGAL OFFICE PROCEDURES

There are no legal office procedures exercises for this chapter

B. LEGAL DOCUMENT PRODUCTION

Peter Grant has been retained to act in connection with several residential real estate transactions and provides you with the agreement of purchase and sale for each of these transactions which are shown on pages 157 to 164 of this assignment book. You are to review these agreements and his notes below and then open the files and prepare the necessary tickler slips for these transactions.

1. **FILE OPENING RECORDS – HOWARD sale to SINGH (MANUAL)**
   45 Keelesdale Avenue, Bracebridge, Ontario P1L 4B7

   Telephone: *Res: 905-570-8426*
   Bus: 416-595-9947 (Mr. Howard)
   Address after closing: *590 Timothy Drive, Apt. 704, Richmond Hill ON L4V 8S2*
   Fee: *$800* File No. *05602/1149*

2. **FILE OPENING RECORDS – ARGUS PROPERTIES sale to CHANG (E-REG)**
   Unit 3, Level A, Halton Condominium Plan No. 114
   Penthouse 3, 100 South Dundas Street, Oakville ON L2V 6R5

   PIN *08013 0175*
   Contact: *Brian Argus, President*
   Telephone: *Res: 905-864-9003*
   Bus: 905-295-5942
   Address after closing: *800 Sanderling Crescent, Mississauga ON L4N 8F3*
   Fee: *$800* File No. *05603/1328*

3. **FILE OPENING RECORDS – HARTWOOD purchase from HARVEY (MANUAL)**
   Part Lot 65, 2nd Concession, Twp. of Georgian Bluffs

   This transaction is for the purchase of a summer cottage. Thus the Hartwood's home address will be used for all correspondence and for their address after closing.

   Address: *531 Stephen Drive, Windsor ON N8Y 4T3*
   Telephone: *Res: 519-456-7409*
   Bus: 519-288-7775 (Mr. Hartwood)
   Fee: *$950.00* File No. *05604/1329*

4. **FILE OPENING RECORDS – ROUSSEAU purchase from SHAFER (E-REG)**
   Townhouse 5, 200 Bayside Way, Burlington ON L8L 4G4

PIN	*25473 0005*
Current Address:	*444 Carmichael Road, Apt. 607, Aurora ON L4G 6M9*
	Address after closing will be new property address
Telephone:	*Res: 905-750-8752*
	Bus: 416-542-9638 (Mr. Rousseau)
	Bus: 905-663-8224 (Mrs. Rousseau)
Fee:	*950.00* File No. *05605/1330*

   ### Legal Terms

   After completing this exercise you should be able to spell and define the following legal terms. Read the definitions shown below. Then select the correct term and match it with the words or phrase that best matches it in meaning, and write the correct term in the space provided. There are more terms than definitions.

   ### Definitions

offer to purchase	acknowledgement and direction
agreement of purchase and sale	requisition date
document general	closing date
conditional offer	document registration agreement

   ### Definitions

   1. purchase contract that has one or more items that must be satisfied before the contract becomes final   _____

   2. document put forward by the purchaser to the vendor in negotiating the purchase of property   _____

   3. document authorizing the law firm to enter into an escrow closing for electronic registration purposes   _____

   4. the date on which a real estate transaction is to be finalized   _____

   5. the date by which a purchaser must submit any questions to the vendor about the validity of title   _____

   6. document executed by all parties accepting the offer put forward by the purchaser   _____

   7. document setting out the terms and conditions of the electronic registration process   _____

OREA Ontario Real Estate Association

Agreement of Purchase and Sale

Form 100
for use in the Province of Ontario

This Agreement of Purchase and Sale dated this **4th** day of **March** 20**XX**

BUYER, **AMAR RAJIT SINGH and MINEERA JAYRA SINGH**, agrees to purchase from
(Full legal names of all Buyers)

SELLER, **ERNEST BRUCE HOWARD and JANE PENELOPE HOWARD**, the following
(Full legal names of all Sellers)

REAL PROPERTY:

Address **45 Keelesdale Avenue** fronting on the **North** side

of **Keelesdale Avenue** in the **Town of Bracebridge**

and having a frontage of **100 feet** more or less by a depth of **200 feet** more or less

and legally described as **Lot 135, Plan 1900, Town of Bracebridge, District Municipality of Muskoka**

(Legal description of land including easements not described elsewhere) (the "property").

PURCHASE PRICE: Dollars (CDN$) **$275,000.00**

---**TWO HUNDRED AND SEVENTY FIVE THOUSAND**--- Dollars

DEPOSIT: Buyer submits **Herewith**
(Herewith/Upon Acceptance/as otherwise described in this Agreement)

---**THIRTY THOUSAND**--- Dollars (CDN$) **$30,000.00**

by negotiable cheque payable to **Royal Real Estate Services Limited** "Deposit Holder"
to be held in trust pending completion or other termination of this Agreement and to be credited toward the Purchase Price on completion. For the purposes of this Agreement, "Upon Acceptance" shall mean that the Buyer is required to deliver the deposit to the Deposit Holder within 24 hours of the acceptance of this Agreement. The parties to this Agreement hereby acknowledge that, unless otherwise provided for in this Agreement, the Deposit Holder shall place the deposit in trust in the Deposit Holder's non-interest bearing Real Estate Trust Account and no interest shall be earned, received or paid on the deposit.

Buyer agrees to pay the balance as more particularly set out in Schedule A attached.

SCHEDULE(S) A attached hereto form(s) part of this Agreement.

1. **IRREVOCABILITY:** This Offer shall be irrevocable by **Buyer** until **6:00 p.m.** a.m./p.m. on
(Seller/Buyer)
the **4th** day of **March** 20**XX**, after which time, if not accepted, this Offer shall be null and void and the deposit shall be returned to the Buyer in full without interest.

2. **COMPLETION DATE:** This Agreement shall be completed by no later than 6:00 p.m. on the **30th** day of **June**, 20**XX**. Upon completion, vacant possession of the property shall be given to the Buyer unless otherwise provided for in this Agreement.

3. **NOTICES:** Seller hereby appoints the Listing Brokerage as Agent for the purpose of giving and receiving notices pursuant to this Agreement. **Only if the Co-operating Brokerage represents the interests of the Buyer in this transaction,** the Buyer hereby appoints the Co-operating Brokerage as Agent for the purpose of giving and receiving notices pursuant to this Agreement. Any notice relating hereto or provided for herein shall be in writing. This offer, any counter offer, notice of acceptance thereof, or any notice shall be deemed given and received, when hand delivered to the address for service provided in the Acknowledgement below, or where a facsimile number is provided herein, when transmitted electronically to that facsimile number.

FAX No. **(905) 882-4980** (For delivery of notices to Seller) FAX No. **(416) 834-5675** (For delivery of notices to Buyer)

INITIALS OF BUYER(S): ( ) **INITIALS OF SELLER(S):** ( )

OREA Ontario Real Estate Association

Schedule A
Agreement of Purchase and Sale

Form 100
for use in the Province of Ontario

This Schedule is attached to and forms part of the Agreement of Purchase and Sale between:

BUYER, AMAR RAJIT SINGH and MINEERA JAYRA SINGH, and

SELLER, ERNEST BRUCE HOWARD and JANE PENELOPE HOWARD

for the purchase and sale of 45 Keelesdale Avenue, Bracebridge

dated the 4th day of March, 20xx.

Buyer agrees to pay the balance as follows:

1. BUYER agrees to pay the balance of the purchase price in the amount of TWO HUNDRED AND FORTY-FIVE THOUSAND DOLLARS ($245,000.00) in cash or by certified cheque to the Seller on closing, subject to the usual adjustments.

2. THE BUYER AND THE SELLER hereby direct the real estate agent holding the deposit in this transaction to place same into an interest bearing account or term deposit with any accrued interest to be paid to the buyer as soon as possible after closing or other termination of this Agreement. In the event the closing is advanced or conditions not met, the Buyer agrees to accept the short-term rate allowed for deposits withdrawn before maturity. Prior to that payment the Buyer agrees to provide his Social Insurance Number for the required Revenue Canada T5 forms.

Page 2 of this agreement states

    Requisition Date is the 24th day of April, 20xx

    Chattels included in purchase price - broadloom where laid and existing light fixture

Page 4 of this agreement states

    Offer was accepted on the 4th day of March, 20xx

    Seller's Lawyer is Peter T. Grant, Hill, Johnston & Grant

    Buyer's Lawyer is Paul G. Shaw, Little, Bell, Shaw & Robinson

This form must be initialed by all parties to the Agreement of Purchase and Sale.

INITIALS OF BUYER(S): ( )   **INITIALS OF SELLER(S):** ( )

© 2008, Ontario Real Estate Association ("OREA"). All rights reserved. This form was developed by OREA for the use and reproduction of its members and licensees only. Any other use or reproduction is prohibited except with prior written consent of OREA.

Form 100   2008   

OREA Ontario Real Estate Association

Agreement of Purchase and Sale
Condominium Resale

Form 101
for use in the Province of Ontario

This Agreement of Purchase and Sale dated this **23rd** day of **November** 20**xx**.

BUYER: **DANIEL MING CHANG and MEI-LING CHANG**, agrees to purchase from
(Full legal names of all Buyers)

SELLER: **ARGUS PROPERTIES LIMITED**, the following
(Full legal names of all Sellers)

PROPERTY:
a unit in the condominium property located at **100 South Dundas Street**
in the **Town of Oakville, Regional Municipality of Halton** being
Unit No. **3** Level No. **A** Condominium Plan No. **114**
Building No. **N/A** known as **Penthouse** No. **3** together with ownership
(Apartment/Townhouse/Suite/Unit)
or exclusive use of Parking Space(s) **30 and 31**, together with ownership or exclusive use of
(Number(s), Level(s))
Locker(s) **N/A**, together with Seller's proportionate undivided tenancy-in-common interest
(Number(s), Level(s))
in the common elements appurtenant to the Unit as described in the Declaration and Description including the exclusive right to use such other parts of the common elements appurtenant to the Unit as may be specified in the Declaration and Description: the Unit, the proportionate interest in the common elements appurtenant thereto, and the exclusive use portions of the common elements, being herein called the "Property".

PURCHASE PRICE: Dollars (CDN$) **405,000.00**

-----------------**FOUR HUNDRED AND FIVE THOUSAND**----------------- Dollars

DEPOSIT: Buyer submits **herewith**
(Herewith/Upon Acceptance/as otherwise described in this Agreement)

-----------------**FORTY THOUSAND**----------------- Dollars (CDN$) **40,000.00**

by negotiable cheque payable to **Royal Real Estate Services Limited** "Deposit Holder" to be held in trust pending completion or other termination of this Agreement and to be credited toward the Purchase Price on completion. For the purposes of this Agreement, "Upon Acceptance" shall mean that the Buyer is required to deliver the deposit to the Deposit Holder within 24 hours of the acceptance of this Agreement. The parties to this Agreement hereby acknowledge that, unless otherwise provided for in this Agreement, the Deposit Holder shall place the deposit in trust in the Deposit Holder's non-interest bearing Real Estate Trust Account and no interest shall be earned, received or paid on the deposit.

Buyer agrees to pay the balance as more particularly set out in Schedule A attached.

SCHEDULE(S) A attached hereto form(s) part of this Agreement.

1. **IRREVOCABILITY:** This Offer shall be irrevocable by **Buyer** until **8:00 p.m.** a.m./p.m. on
(Seller/Buyer)
the **23rd** day of **November** 20**xx**, after which time, if not accepted, this Offer shall be null and void and the deposit shall be returned to the Buyer in full without interest.

2. **COMPLETION DATE:** This Agreement shall be completed by no later than 6:00 p.m. on the **15th** day of **March**, 20**xx**. Upon completion, vacant possession of the property shall be given to the Buyer unless otherwise provided for in this Agreement.

3. **NOTICES:** Seller hereby appoints the Listing Brokerage as Agent for the purpose of giving and receiving notices pursuant to this Agreement. **Only if the Co-operating Brokerage represents the interests of the Buyer in this transaction,** the Buyer hereby appoints the Co-operating Brokerage as Agent for the purpose of giving and receiving notices pursuant to this Agreement. Any notice relating hereto or provided for herein shall be in writing. This offer, any counter offer, notice of acceptance thereof, or any notice shall be deemed given and received, when hand delivered to the address for service provided in the Acknowledgement below, or where a facsimile number is provided herein, when transmitted electronically to that facsimile number.

FAX No. **416-228-4480** (For delivery of notices to Seller) FAX No. **416-249-3390** (For delivery of notices to Buyer)

INITIALS OF BUYER(S): ( ) **INITIALS OF SELLER(S):** ( )

© 2008, Ontario Real Estate Association ("OREA"). All rights reserved. This form was developed by OREA for the use and reproduction of its members and licensees only. Any other use or reproduction is prohibited except with prior written consent of OREA. Form 101 2008 Page 1 of 5

OREA Ontario Real Estate Association

Schedule A
Agreement of Purchase and Sale – Condominium Resale

Form 101
for use in the Province of Ontario

This Schedule is attached to and forms part of the Agreement of Purchase and Sale between:

BUYER, DANIEL MING CHANG and MEI-LING CHANG, and

SELLER, ARGUS PROPERTIES LIMITED

for the purchase and sale of Penthouse 3, 100 South Dundas Street, Oakville

dated the 23rd day of November, 20xx.

Buyer agrees to pay the balance as follows:

1. BUYER agrees to pay the balance of the purchase price in the amount of THREE HUNDRED AND SIXTY-FIVE THOUSAND DOLLARS ($365,000.00) in cash or by certified cheque to the Seller on closing, subject to the usual adjustments.

2. THE BUYER AND THE SELLER hereby direct the real estate agent holding the deposit in this transaction to place same into an interest bearing account or term deposit with any accrued interest to be paid to the buyer as soon as possible after closing or other termination of this Agreement. In the event the closing is advanced or conditions not met, the Buyer agrees to accept the short-term rate allowed for deposits withdrawn before maturity. Prior to that payment the Buyer agrees to provide his Social Insurance Number for the required Revenue Canada T5 forms.

Page 2 of this agreement states

    Requisition Date is the 22nd day of December, 20xx.

    Chattels included in purchase price - dishwasher and wide screen plasma television

    Common Expenses - $275.00 per month

Page 4 of this agreement states

    Offer was accepted on the 23rd day of November, 20xx

    Seller's Lawyer is Peter T. Grant, Hill, Johnston & Grant

    Buyer's Lawyer is Brianna T. Wolfe, Fox, Wolfe & Lyons

This form must be initialed by all parties to the Agreement of Purchase and Sale.

INITIALS OF BUYER(S):   **INITIALS OF SELLER(S):**

© 2008, Ontario Real Estate Association ("OREA"). All rights reserved. This form was developed by OREA for the use and reproduction of its members and licensees only. Any other use or reproduction is prohibited except with prior written consent of OREA.

Form 101   2008

OREA Agreement of Purchase and Sale

Form 100 for use in the Province of Ontario

This Agreement of Purchase and Sale dated this **9th** day of **October** 20**xx**

BUYER, PHILLIP ANDREW HARTWOOD and GRACE NORAH HARTWOOD, agrees to purchase from
(Full legal names of all Buyers)

SELLER, GARRY HARVEY and PATRICIA HARVEY, the following
(Full legal names of all Sellers)

REAL PROPERTY:
Address .... fronting on the **South** side of **Darwin Road** in the **Township of Georgian Bluffs**

and having a frontage of **680'6" lakefront** more or less by a depth of **520 feet** more or less

and legally described as **Southerly six hundred and eighty feet six inches, (680'6") of Lot 65, Second Concession, Township of Georgian Bluffs, County of Grey** (the "property").
(Legal description of land including easements not described elsewhere)

PURCHASE PRICE: Dollars (CDN$) **$190,000.00**

-----------------ONE HUNDRED AND NINETY THOUSAND----------------- Dollars

DEPOSIT: Buyer submits **herewith**
(Herewith/Upon Acceptance/as otherwise described in this Agreement)

-----------------TWENTY-FIVE THOUSAND----------------- Dollars (CDN$) **$25,000.00**

by negotiable cheque payable to **Martin-Harris Realty Limited** "Deposit Holder" to be held in trust pending completion or other termination of this Agreement and to be credited toward the Purchase Price on completion. For the purposes of this Agreement, "Upon Acceptance" shall mean that the Buyer is required to deliver the deposit to the Deposit Holder within 24 hours of the acceptance of this Agreement. The parties to this Agreement hereby acknowledge that, unless otherwise provided for in this Agreement, the Deposit Holder shall place the deposit in trust in the Deposit Holder's non-interest bearing Real Estate Trust Account and no interest shall be earned, received or paid on the deposit.

Buyer agrees to pay the balance as more particularly set out in Schedule A attached.

SCHEDULE(S) A .... attached hereto form(s) part of this Agreement.

1. **IRREVOCABILITY:** This Offer shall be irrevocable by **Buyer** until **6:00 p.m.** a.m./p.m. on
(Seller/Buyer)
the **9th** day of **October** 20**xx**, after which time, if not accepted, this Offer shall be null and void and the deposit shall be returned to the Buyer in full without interest.

2. **COMPLETION DATE:** This Agreement shall be completed by no later than 6:00 p.m. on the **30th** day of **November**, 20**xx**. Upon completion, vacant possession of the property shall be given to the Buyer unless otherwise provided for in this Agreement.

3. **NOTICES:** Seller hereby appoints the Listing Brokerage as Agent for the purpose of giving and receiving notices pursuant to this Agreement. **Only if the Co-operating Brokerage represents the interests of the Buyer in this transaction,** the Buyer hereby appoints the Co-operating Brokerage as Agent for the purpose of giving and receiving notices pursuant to this Agreement. Any notice relating hereto or provided for herein shall be in writing. This offer, any counter offer, notice of acceptance thereof, or any notice shall be deemed given and received, when hand delivered to the address for service provided in the Acknowledgement below, or where a facsimile number is provided herein, when transmitted electronically to that facsimile number.

FAX No. **(416) 228-4480** (For delivery of notices to Seller) FAX No. **(416) 479-8933** (For delivery of notices to Buyer)

INITIALS OF BUYER(S): ( )   INITIALS OF SELLER(S): ( )

Schedule A
Agreement of Purchase and Sale

Form 100 for use in the Province of Ontario

This Schedule is attached to and forms part of the Agreement of Purchase and Sale between:

BUYER, PHILLIP ANDREW HARTWOOD and GRACE NORAH HARTWOOD, and

SELLER, GARRY HARVEY and PATRICIA HARVEY

for the purchase and sale of Part Lot 65, Second Concession, Township of Georgian Bluffs

dated the 9th day of October, 20xx.

Buyer agrees to pay the balance as follows:

1. BUYER agrees to give back to the SELLER a first mortgage in the amount of ONE HUNDRED THOUSAND DOLLARS ($100,000.00) bearing interest at the rate of 6.5% per annum, calculated semi-annually, not in advance, amortized over a 25 year period and becoming due in five years, repayable in blended monthly payments including principal and interest of SIX HUNDRED AND THIRTY-TWO DOLLARS AND SEVEN CENTS ($632.07). Said mortgage shall contain the privilege of paying all or part of the principal sum without notice or bonus on any payment date.

2. BUYER agrees to pay the balance of the purchase price in the amount of SIXTY-FIVE THOUSAND DOLLARS ($65,000.00) in cash or by certified cheque to the Seller on closing, subject to the usual adjustments.

2. BUYER and SELLER hereby direct the real estate agent holding the deposit in this transaction to place same in an interest bearing account or term deposit, with any accrued interest on the deposit to be paid to the BUYER as soon as possible after closing or other termination of this agreement.

    Page 2 of this agreement states

        Requisition Date is the 18th day of November, 20xx

        No chattels included in purchase price

    Page 4 of this agreement states

        Offer was accepted on the 9th day of October, 20xx

        Seller's Lawyer is Timothy J. Wyers, McClelland, Wyers & Chae

        Buyer's Lawyer is Peter T. Grant, Hill, Johnston & Grant

This form must be initialed by all parties to the Agreement of Purchase and Sale..

INITIALS OF BUYER(S):   **INITIALS OF SELLER(S):**

Agreement of Purchase and Sale
Condominium Resale

Form 101
for use in the Province of Ontario

OREA Ontario Real Estate Association

This Agreement of Purchase and Sale dated this **15th** day of **April** 20**xx**.

BUYER, JASON ANDREW ROUSSEAU and DOROTHY CAROL ROUSSEAU, agrees to purchase from
(Full legal names of all Buyers)

SELLER, ILSE JOSEPHINE SHAFER, the following
(Full legal names of all Sellers)

PROPERTY:
a unit in the condominium property located at **200 Bayside Way**
in the **City of Burlington, Regional Municipality of Halton** being
Unit No. **5** Level No. **1** Condominium Plan No. **174**
Building No. **N/A** known as **Townhouse** No. **5** together with ownership
(Apartment/Townhouse/Suite/Unit)

or exclusive use of Parking Space(s) **N/A**, together with ownership or exclusive use of
(Number(s), Level(s))

Locker(s) **N/A**, together with Seller's proportionate undivided tenancy-in-common interest
(Number(s), Level(s))

in the common elements appurtenant to the Unit as described in the Declaration and Description including the exclusive right to use such other parts of the common elements appurtenant to the Unit as may be specified in the Declaration and Description: the Unit, the proportionate interest in the common elements appurtenant thereto, and the exclusive use portions of the common elements, being herein called the "Property".

PURCHASE PRICE: Dollars (CDN$) **250,000.00**

-----------------**TWO HUNDRED AND FIFTY THOUSAND**----------------- Dollars

DEPOSIT: Buyer submits **Upon Acceptance**
(Herewith/Upon Acceptance/as otherwise described in this Agreement)

-----------------**TWENTY-FIVE THOUSAND**----------------- Dollars (CDN$) **25,000.00**

by negotiable cheque payable to **Royal Real Estate Services Limited** "Deposit Holder" to be held in trust pending completion or other termination of this Agreement and to be credited toward the Purchase Price on completion. For the purposes of this Agreement, "Upon Acceptance" shall mean that the Buyer is required to deliver the deposit to the Deposit Holder within 24 hours of the acceptance of this Agreement. The parties to this Agreement hereby acknowledge that, unless otherwise provided for in this Agreement, the Deposit Holder shall place the deposit in trust in the Deposit Holder's non-interest bearing Real Estate Trust Account and no interest shall be earned, received or paid on the deposit.

Buyer agrees to pay the balance as more particularly set out in Schedule A attached.

SCHEDULE(S) A attached hereto form(s) part of this Agreement.

1. **IRREVOCABILITY:** This Offer shall be irrevocable by **Buyer** until **6:00 p.m.** a.m./p.m. on
   (Seller/Buyer)
   the **15th** day of **April** 20**xx**, after which time, if not accepted, this Offer shall be null and void and the deposit shall be returned to the Buyer in full without interest.

2. **COMPLETION DATE:** This Agreement shall be completed by no later than 6:00 p.m. on the **7th** day of **June**, 20**xx**. Upon completion, vacant possession of the property shall be given to the Buyer unless otherwise provided for in this Agreement.

3. **NOTICES:** Seller hereby appoints the Listing Brokerage as Agent for the purpose of giving and receiving notices pursuant to this Agreement. **Only if the Co-operating Brokerage represents the interests of the Buyer in this transaction,** the Buyer hereby appoints the Co-operating Brokerage as Agent for the purpose of giving and receiving notices pursuant to this Agreement. Any notice relating hereto or provided for herein shall be in writing. This offer, any counter offer, notice of acceptance thereof, or any notice shall be deemed given and received, when hand delivered to the address for service provided in the Acknowledgement below, or where a facsimile number is provided herein, when transmitted electronically to that facsimile number.

   FAX No. **416-228-4480** (For delivery of notices to Seller) FAX No. **905-982-7631** (For delivery of notices to Buyer)

INITIALS OF BUYER(S): ( ) **INITIALS OF SELLER(S):** ( )

© 2008, Ontario Real Estate Association ("OREA"). All rights reserved. This form was developed by OREA for the use and reproduction of its members and licensees only. Any other use or reproduction is prohibited except with prior written consent of OREA.

Form 101 2008 Page 1 of 5

Schedule A
Agreement of Purchase and Sale – Condominium Resale

Form 101
for use in the Province of Ontario

This Schedule is attached to and forms part of the Agreement of Purchase and Sale between:

BUYER, JASON ANDREW ROUSSEAU and DOROTHY CAROL ROUSSEAU, and

SELLER, ILSE JOSEPHINE SHAFER

for the purchase and sale of Townhouse 5, 200 Bayside Way, Burlington

dated the 15th day of April, 20xx.

Buyer agrees to pay the balance as follows:

1. BUYER agrees to pay the balance of the purchase price in the amount of TWO HUNDRED AND TWENTY-FIVE THOUSAND DOLLARS ($225,000.00) in cash or by certified cheque to the Seller on closing, subject to the usual adjustments.

2. THE BUYER AND THE SELLER hereby direct the real estate agent holding the deposit in this transaction to place same into an interest bearing account or term deposit with any accrued interest to be paid to the buyer as soon as possible after closing or other termination of this Agreement. In the event the closing is advanced or conditions not met, the Buyer agrees to accept the short-term rate allowed for deposits withdrawn before maturity. Prior to that payment the Buyer agrees to provide his Social Insurance Number for the required Revenue Canada T5 forms.

Page 2 of this agreement states

Requisition Date is the 15th day of May, 20xx.

Chattels included in purchase price - all existing broadloom, electric light fixtures, refrigerator, stove, dishwasher, washing machine and dryer

Common Expenses - $164.00 per month

Page 4 of this agreement states

Offer was accepted on the 15th day of April, 20xx

Seller's Lawyer is Michael Cochrane, Graham & Parker

Buyer's Lawyer is Peter T. Grant, Hill, Johnston & Grant

This form must be initialed by all parties to the Agreement of Purchase and Sale.

INITIALS OF BUYER(S): ( )   INITIALS OF SELLER(S): ( )

© 2008, Ontario Real Estate Association ("OREA"). All rights reserved. This form was developed by OREA for the use and reproduction of its members and licensees only. Any other use or reproduction is prohibited except with prior written consent of OREA.

Form 101   2008

CHAPTER 25 – ASSIGNMENTS
Acting for the Vendor

A. LEGAL OFFICE PROCEDURES

1. CALCULATING INDIVIDUAL ITEMS ON A STATEMENT OF ADJUSTMENTS

Set out below are many individual items for which an adjustment or allowance will be required on the statement of adjustments. In the space provided, indicate the party – that is the vendor or the purchaser – to whom an allowance would be made and indicate the amount of any such allowance.

(a) The purchase price for the new real property is $215,000.00 exclusive of GST.

(b) Deposit of $20,000.00 by purchaser

(c) The vendor is taking back a second mortgage for 75,000.00

(d) The purchaser is assuming an existing first mortgage for $35,671.96. The last payment was made on September 10; the per diem interest rate is $9.06. The mortgage is amortized. Closing date: September 15

(e) Realty taxes for current year of $2,786.94 have been paid in full. Closing date: May 10

(f) Realty taxes for current year are $3,268.16. Vendor has paid three installments totalling $2,517.68. Closing date: November 15

(g) Realty taxes for current year have been assessed at $2,715.48. There is a credit to the vendor in his mortgage tax account of $1,200.00. Closing Date: June 5

(h) Realty taxes for **last year** were $1,950.00. Vendor has paid one intallment of $450.00. Closing date: March 21

(i) Condominium common expenses of $225.00 have been paid for the month of August. Closing date: August 17.

(j) 200 litre oil tank @ $2.46 per litre.

B. LEGAL DOCUMENT PRODUCTION

1. CORRESPONDENCE – HOWARD sale to SINGH

You have been asked to prepare the following correspondence for this file.

(a) Prepare a letter to the solicitors for the purchasers, to request information on how the purchasers wish to take title. Enclose a copy of the survey of the property prepared by Gelfi & Associates, O.L.S. dated May 17, 1984. Refer to Precedent 25.2.

(b) Prepare a letter to Algonquin Permanent Trust Company, requesting a mortgage statement for discharge purposes. The mortgage account number is 98765-246. Refer to Precedent 25.3.

2. TRANSFER/DEED & LETTER – HOWARD sale to SINGH

The vendors have now provided the "old" transfer/deed which is shown on the following page. A letter from the purchasers' solicitors and the mortgage discharge statement has also been received and are shown on page 167. Using these documents, you are to prepare the following:

(a) Draft the new transfer/deed. You will need to refer to the agreement of purchase and sale as well as to the "old" transfer/deed. We will use the full purchase price of the property as the consideration. We will not be completing boxes 13 and 14.

(b) Prepare the following letter to the solicitors for the purchasers.

> *As requested, we enclose our draft transfer/deed for your review. We will forward our statement of adjustments shortly.*

3. DISCHARGE OF CHARGE/MORTGAGE & LETTER – HOWARD sale to SINGH

The vendors cannot locate the duplicate original charge of their mortgage. You will therefore prepare the discharge of charge/mortgage based on the information in the transfer/deed and the discharge statement.

(a) Draft the discharge of charge/mortgage. In Box 7 state – The duplicate registered charge/mortgage has been lost or misplaced. For Box 8, note that Algonquin Permanent Trust Company has a corporate seal with which to execute the document and that the person who signed the discharge statement will execute the discharge.

(b) Prepare the following letter to forward the draft discharge to the mortgagee which should be sent by courier.

> *Enclosed are two copies of the draft discharge of charge/mortgage. Please arrange to have this discharge executed & returned to our office at your earliest convenience. We will hold the discharge document in escrow until the closing of this transaction on June 30/20xx when we will forward the discharge funds to you by courier.*

Transfer/Deed of Land
Form 1 — Land Registration Reform Act

Province of Ontario

REGISTERED
AUGUST 10, 1990
No. B24691

(1) Registry [X] Land Titles [ ]
(2) Page 1 of 2 pages

(3) Property Identifier(s): Block 45532 Property 2389

(4) Consideration: TWO HUNDRED THOUSAND — Dollars $200,000.00

(5) Description:
Lot 135, Plan 1900
Town of Bracebridge
District Municipality of Muskoka
Registry Division of Muskoka (No. 35)

(6) This Document Contains: (a) Redescription New Easement Plan/Sketch [ ] (b) Schedule for: Description [ ] Additional Parties [ ] Other [ ]

(7) Interest/Estate Transferred: Fee Simple

(8) Transferor(s) The transferor hereby transfers the land to the transferee and certifies that the transferor is at least eighteen years old and that **the person consenting below is my spouse**

Name(s): SHAPIRO, Barry Ronald
Signature: Barry R. Shapiro
Date of Signature: 1990 08 06

(9) Spouse(s) of Transferor(s) I hereby consent to this transaction
Name(s): SHAPIRO, Michelle Angelina
Signature: Michelle A. Shapiro
Date of Signature: 1990 08 06

(10) Transferor(s) Address for Service: 50 Fairway Blvd., Hamilton ON L8P 4K3

(11) Transferee(s):
HOWARD, Ernest Bruce — Date of Birth: 1960 03 10
HOWARD, Jane Penelope — Date of Birth: 1963 01 14
as joint tenants

(12) Transferee(s) Address for Service: 45 Keelesdale Avenue, Bracebridge ON P1L 4B7

(13) Transferor(s) The transferor verifies that to the best of the transferor's knowledge and belief, this transfer does not contravene section 50 of the Planning Act.

Solicitor for Transferor(s) I have explained the effect of section 50 of the Planning Act to the transferor and I have made inquiries of the transferor to determine that this transfer does not contravene that section and based on the information supplied by the transferor, to the best of my knowledge and belief, this transfer does not contravene that section. I am an Ontario solicitor in good standing.

(14) Solicitor for Transferee(s) I have investigated the title to this land and to abutting land where relevant and I am satisfied that the title records reveal no contravention as set out in subclause 50 (22) (c) (ii) of the Planning Act and that to the best of my knowledge and belief this transfer does not contravene section 50 of the Planning Act. I act independently of the solicitor for the transferor(s) and I am an Ontario solicitor in good standing.

(15) Assessment Roll Number of Property

(16) Municipal Address of Property:
45 Keelesdale Avenue
Bracebridge ON P1L 4B7

(17) Document Prepared by:
David S. Ross
Hare, Ross & Wilkinson
94 Wimbleton Crescent, Suite 405
Barrie ON L4V 8X2

Fees and Tax: Registration Fee / Land Transfer Tax / Total

LITTLE, BELL, SHAW & ROBINSON
Barristers & Solicitors

410 University Avenue *Telephone: (613) 654-9889*
Bracebridge Ontario P1L 2V6 *Facsimile: (613) 654-9881*

Yesterday's Date

Mr. Peter T. Grant, Q.C.
Hill, Johnston & Grant
Barristers & Solicitors
17 Princess Sreet South, Suite 2501
Toronto ON M8Y 3N5

Dear Mr. Grant:

Singh purchase form Howard
<u>45 Keelesdale Avenue, Bracebridge</u>

We act for the purchasers, Amar and Mineera Singh with respect to the above transaction. We understand that you act for the vendors.

Please be advised that our clients wish the transfer/deed in this transaction engrossed as follows:

SINGH, Amar Rajit   1977 07 05
SINGH, Mineera Jayra   1981 10 17
as joint tenants

Address for service: 45 Keelesdale Avenue, Bracebridge ON P1L 4B7

Please let us have you draft transfer/deed at your earliest convenience, together with the statement of adjustments and a copy of the survey of the property.

Yours very truly,

LITTLE, BELL, SHAW & ROBINSON

Paul G. Shaw

PGW:ri

ALGONQUIN PERMANENT TRUST COMPANY
500 Tower Road
Newmarket, Ontario L6R 9V2

Telephone: 905-422-3300   **Fax:** 905-422-3380

                                     Date: June 16, 20xx

TO: Hill, Johnston & Grant
     17 Princess Street S., Suite 2501
     Toronto ON M8Y 3N5
     Attn: Peter T. Grant

Mortgage Statement as of: June 30, 20xx	Mortgage No. 98765-246
MORTGAGOR(S)	Ernest Howard and Jane Howard
PRINCIPAL AMOUNT OUTSTANDING:	$55,316.81
INTEREST RATE:	8.75%
PAYMENTS DUE DATE:	30th of each month
MATURITY:	November 30, 20xx
MONTHLY PAYMENTS: Interest & Principal	$454.51
ARREARS:	Nil
Per diem interest rate:	$13.31
Registration Information:	Instrument No. B26741 November 30, 2007

ALGONQUIN PERMANENT TRUST COMPANY

Per: _____
     Grant Ward, Manager, Mortgage Services

E. & O. E.

4. REPLY TO LETTER OF REQUISITION – HOWARD sale to SINGH

Peter Grant has received the following letter of requisition from the solicitors for the purchasers in the above file. You are asked to prepare the reply to this letter of requisition shown below as well as the draft statutory declaration for Mr. Howard to execute. Drafts of both of these documents appear on the following page.

LITTLE, BELL, SHAW & ROBINSON
Barristers & Solicitors

410 University Avenue
Bracebridge Ontario P1L 2V6

Telephone: (613) 654-9889
Facsimile: (613) 654-9881

Yesterday's Date

Mr. Peter T. Grant, Q.C.
Hill, Johnston & Grant
Barristers & Solicitors
17 Princess Street South
Suite 2501
Toronto ON M8Y 3N5

Dear Mr. Grant:

Singh purchase from Howard
45 Keelesdale Avenue, Bracebridge

I have now completed my title investigations and without prejudice to my client's rights under the agreement of purchase and sale herein, I hereby submit the following requisitions specifically reserving our right to submit further requisitions as I from time to time deem necessary:

1. Instrument No. B26741 is a mortgage registered November 30, 2007, and given by Ernest Bruce Howard and Jane Penelope Howard to Algonquin Permanent Trust Company.

    REQUIRED: On or before closing production and registration of a statutory discharge of the said mortgage.

2. Execution No. 99756, dated August 12, 2005, against one Ernest B. Howard, at the suit of Imperial Oil Limited in the amount of $759.38 plus $150.00 for costs

    REQUIRED: On or before closing, satisfaction of the execution, or satisfactory proof that Ernest B. Howard and the vendor are not the same person.

3. REQUIRED: On or before closing, that the enclosed declaration of possession be signed by your client and returned to us.

(a) Letter to purchasers' solicitors

> Paul G. Shaw
> Little, Bell, etc.
>
> Howard sale to Singh, etc.
>
> We acknowledge receipt of your letter of ---. Without prejudice to our client's rights under the agreement of purchase & sale, we reply as follows:
> 1. Will be provided on closing.
> 2. Enclosed is a copy of a statutory declaration which we will have Ernest Howard declare. It will be attached as a schedule to the transfer/deed.
> 3. Will be provided on closing.

(b) Statutory Declaration to be signed by our client. Refer to Precedent 26.10 in your text.

> Statutory Declaration
>
> In the matter of title to
> 45 Keelesdale Ave., Bracebridge
> being Lot 135, Plan 1900,
> Town of Bracebridge,
> District Municipality of Muskoka
>
> I, ERNEST BRUCE HOWARD, of the Town of Bracebridge, etc.
>
> 1. I am informed by my solicitor, Peter T. Grant, that there is registered with the Sheriff, District Municipality of Muskoka, Execution No. 99756, dated August 20/05, against a Ernest B. Howard at the suit of Union Gas Inc., in the amount of $759.38 plus $150.00 for costs.
> 2. I am not the same Ernest B. Howard as the person named in execution no. 99756 as set out above.
> 3. I do not now & never have had an account with Union Gas Inc. and my home has always been heated by oil.
> 4. There are no writs of execution registered with the Sheriff of the District Muni. of Muskoka against me.
>
> DECLARED etc.

5. STATEMENT OF ADJUSTMENTS, DIRECTION, UNDERTAKING & LETTER
   HOWARD sale to SINGH

You have been instructed to draft the statement of adjustments based on the information below and other related documents for this file. Be sure to check any figures against the material in the file. You are to prepare:

(a) statement of adjustments (refer to Precedent 25.6 and the draft below).

(b) undertaking to readjust (refer to Precedent 25.8)

(c) direction re proceeds, which are payable to Hill, Johnston & Grant, in trust (refer to Precedent 25.9)

(d) Prepare a letter to the solicitors for the purchasers, forwarding the statement of adjustments.

STATEMENT OF ADJUSTMENTS

HOWARD SALE TO SINGH
Put in short legal description & address

Adjusted as of ??

Sale Price

Deposit

Realty Taxes
Taxes for 20xx $2,746.28
Vendors have paid $1,345.00
Vendor's Share (* days)
Allow purchaser/vendor

Fuel Oil 909 L at *$2.25 per litre*
& GST

Utilities
 Final readings on closing

Balance due on closing etc....

                                                        ??
                                         _____   _____
                                                  ??   ??

E. & O.E.

6. DRAFT TRANSFER/DEED – ARGUS PROPERTIES LIMITED sale to CHANG

An e-mail from the purchasers' solicitors has been received and is shown below. You will need to refer to this e-mail along with the agreement of purchase and sale and Peter Grant's notes also shown below to prepare the electronic transfer document. Do a print out of the draft transfer instrument in progress for the file.

> To: ptgrant@hilljohngrant.com
> From: btwolfe@foxwolfelyons.ca
> Date: Today's Date
> Re: Chang p/f Argus Properties, Unit 3, Level A, Halton Condominium Plan No. 114
>
> Please be advised that our clients will take title to the above property as follows:
>
> CHANG, Daniel Ming   August 14, 1972
>
> CHANG, Mei-Ling   November 4, 1974
>
> as joint tenants
>
> Address for service: Address of property
>
> We do not require the Planning Act statements completed. A signed direction will be produced on closing.

PIN: *08013-0175*
Address: *100 South Dundas Street, Penthouse 3, Oakville*
Transferor: *Brian Argus has authority to sign for Argus Properties*
Chattels: *Allow $1,500.00 of the purchase price for chattels*
Planning Act *statements will not be completed*
LTT Statement: *completed by both transferees who are Roman Catholics*

In the actual office environment you would prepare the entire electronic document <u>except</u> the purchasers' name and dates of birth and the Land Transfer Tax Affidavit. However, your instructor will advise you how to proceed; that is, whether to complete the entire document or if you have the ability to "message" other students to complete the purchasers' portion of the electronic transfer document.

7. DISCHARGE OF CHARGE – ARGUS PROPERTIES LIMITED sale to CHANG

Peter Grant has received the requisition letter for this file. An item in that letter stated:

> 1. Instrument No. H632478 is a charge/mortgage registered May 31, 1996, by Argus Properties Limited to John Gregory.
>   REQUIRED: Discharge of said mortgage on or before closing.

You are to prepare the draft electronic discharge document. This is a full discharge of this PIN only. The mortgage has not been assigned or renewed. The mortgagee's address is 38 Huxbury Road, Burlington ON L1B 8C9. Do a print out of the draft discharge instrument in progress for the file. Refer to Precedents 23.2 and 23.3.

8. ELECTRONIC REGISTRATION DOCUMENTATION –
ARGUS PROPERTIES LIMITED sale to CHANG

Prepare the following documentation for our clients to execute before closing for this e-reg transaction. Refer to the material in your file and Peter Grant's notes below to prepare these documents the templates for which are available in the practice files. Note, however, that the Acknowledgement and Direction Report is usually required to be created in Teraview.
(Forms Folder: Acknowledgement *(Acknowledgement and Direction Report)* and **Registration Agmt** *(Document Registration Agreement)).*

    (a) Acknowledgement and Direction Report (refer to Precedents 24.4 and 24.6)

> *The consenting spouse paragraph will not be required. Brian Argus will sign as president of Argus Properties Limited. There is no corporate seal so include the statement - I have authority to bind the Corporation - beneath his name & title. Note: a copy of the draft transfer instrument in progress should be attached to this document.*

    (b) Document Registration Agreement (refer to Precedent 24.5)

> *The purchasers' solicitor will be doing the electronic registration at 11:00 am on the closing date.*

9. STATEMENT OF ADJUSTMENTS, DIRECTION & UNDERTAKING –
ARGUS PROPERTIES LIMITED sale to CHANG

You have been instructed to draft the statement of adjustments and other related documents for this file based on the Peter Grant's notes below. Be sure to check any figures against the material in the file.

    (a) statement of adjustments (refer to Precedent 25.6)

    (b) undertaking to readjust (refer to Precedent 25.8)

    (c) direction re proceeds (refer to Precedent 25.9)

> *Realty taxes*
> *Taxes for 20xx (last year) were $3,150.00*
> *Add 5% to estimate this year's taxes*
> *Vendor has paid Nil*
>
> *Condominium Common Expenses - see Agmt. of Purchase & Sale. Vendor will pay the month of closing.*
>
> *Note: Balance should be payable in two cheques of:*
>   *John Gregory $ 225,392.27*
>   *Hill, Johnston & Grant, in trust, for the remainder $??*
>
> *The direction re proceeds should reflect these amounts also.*

C. LEGAL TERMINOLOGY

After completing this exercise you should be able to spell and define the following legal terms. Read the definitions shown below. Then select the correct term and match it with the words or phrase that best matches it in meaning, and write the correct term in the space provided. There are more terms than definitions.

Legal Terms

requisitions on title	status certificate	discharge statement
undertaking	statement of adjustments	vendor
direction re proceeds	used residential property	purchaser
direction re title	new residential property	common expenses

Definitions

1. document containing information on the legal, financial and operational status of a condominium corporation _____

2. document provided by the mortgagee setting out the terms and amount required to pay of a mortgage _____

3. a detailed statement outlining the exact amount of money the purchaser must pay when the transaction is closed _____

4. a promise to take some action or provide some information at a later date. _____

5. the transferor _____

6. document authorizing to whom payment of the closing funds of a real estate transaction are to be paid _____

7. property to which GST is applied _____

8. written requests to the vendor on behalf of the purchaser, asking that defects or doubts as to the title of real property be removed or otherwise satisfied _____

9. normal costs to maintain the property, jointly shared by all owners of units in a condominium. _____

10. property that is exempt from GST _____

11. the transferee _____

CHAPTER 26 – ASSIGNMENTS
Acting for the Purchaser

A. LEGAL OFFICE PROCEDURES

1. CALCULATING LAND TRANSFER TAX

In order to determine the amount of money that the purchasers must provide to the law firm to complete the transaction, it is necessary to calculate the amount of land transfer tax and any retail sales tax that must be paid on closing. In the space provided, calculate the amount of such taxes for each of the following situations. You may assume that none of the buyers are first-time purchasers.

1. Purchase price $185,000.00. It is a single-family residence in North Bay, Ontario

2. Purchase price $275,000.00. It is a single-family residence in London, Ontario

3. Purchase price $197,500.00, of which $1,500.00 is for chattels. It is a single-family residence in Kingston, Ontario.

4. Purchase price $425,000.00 of which $3,000.00 is for chattels. It is a single-family residence in Toronto, Ontario

5. Purchase price $510,000.00 of which $6,000.00 is for chattels. The purchase involves three single-family residences, in Hamilton, Ontario.

6. Purchase price is $519,500.00. It is a single-family residence in Barrie, Ontario.

7. Purchase price is $535,000.00, of which $5,000.00 is for chattels. The property contains two single-family residences in Ottawa, Ontario.

8. Single family residence in Toronto. Purchase price $350,000.00.

B. LEGAL DOCUMENT PRODUCTION

1. **DIRECTION – HARTWOOD purchase from HARVEY**

Prepare the direction re title to be held in the file until the Hartwoods come in to sign documents. Title is to be taken in both purchasers' names as joint tenants. Mr. Hartwood's birth date is February 29, 1968; Mrs. Hartwood's birth date is October 28, 1975. Their address in Windsor will be the address for service. Refer to Precedent 26.1.

2. **CORRESPONDENCE – HARTWOOD purchase from HARVEY**

(a) Write to the vendors' solicitors advising them how our clients wish to take title (refer to the direction re title that you prepared above) and also ask how the vendors wish to take the mortgage back. Refer to Precedent 26.2.

(b) The Hartwoods have chosen not to purchase title insurance, therefore you will need to prepare the required search letters for taxes and building and work orders and requisition the necessary cheques. Use a cost of $55.00 for the tax certificate and $82.80 for the building and work order letter. Send these letters to the Township of Georgian Bluffs, 177964 Grey Road, R.R. 3, Owen Sound ON N4K 5N5 to the attention the applicable department. Refer to Precedents 26.6 and 26.7.

(c) Prepare the following letter for signature by Mr. Grant:

John R. Graham, Barrister etc., R.R. 1, Elmwood N0G 1S0

We enclose herewith a copy of the agmt. of pur. & sale in this transaction. We would ask that you search the title to the lands described below with the view of certifying title to us:

> *The southerly 686'6" of Lot 65, Second Concession, Township of Georgian Bluffs, County of Grey*

We understand the lands presently stand in the names of Garry & Patricia Harvey.

If you find the title in order, we shall arrange to provide you with the necessary documents & funds due on closing & would ask that you also attend to that matter on our behalf.

3. **MORTGAGE – HARTWOOD purchase from HARVEY**

*The letter from the vendors' solicitors has now been received. Enclosed were the draft transfer/deed and statement of adjustments which should be **reviewed carefully** for any errors. These appear on pages 177 and 178. The vendors' solicitors advised that the vendors wish to hold the mortgage back jointly. Prepare the draft mortgage. Refer to agreement of purchase and sale and the draft transfer to prepare the mortgage. The standard charge terms are number 4590. The commencement date for the mortgage is the closing date of the real estate transaction. Refer to Figures 22.2 and 22.3 and Precedents 22.1 and 22.2.*

Transfer/Deed of Land
Form 1 — Land Registration Reform Act

(1) Registry [X] Land Titles [ ] **(2)** Page 1 of 2 pages

(3) Property Identifier(s): Block / Property

(4) Consideration: ONE HUNDRED NINETY THOUSAND — Dollars $ 190,000.00

(5) Description This is a: Property Division [ ] Property Consolidation [ ]

Southerly six hundred and eighty-six feet six inches (686' 6") throughout from east to west of Lot 65, Second Concession, Township of Georgian Bluffs, County of Grey

Registry Division of Grey (No. 16)

(6) This Document Contains: (a) Redescription New Easement Plan/Sketch (b) Schedule for: Description / Additional Parties / Other

(7) Interest/Estate Transferred: Fee Simple

(8) Transferor(s) The transferor hereby transfers the land to the transferee and certifies that the transferor is at least eighteen years old and that we are spouses of one another.

Name(s):
HARVEY, Garry Derek
HARVEY, Patricia Eleanore
as joint tenants

(9) Spouse(s) of Transferor(s) I hereby consent to this transaction

(10) Transferor(s) Address for Service: 57 Hillsdown Road, North Bay ON P1B 3X9

(11) Transferee(s):

Name	Date of Birth Y/M/D
HARTWOOD, Phillip Andrew	1968 02 29
HARTWOOD, Grace Norah	1975 10 28

as joint tenants

(12) Transferee(s) Address for Service: 531 Stephen Drive, Windsor ON N8Y 4T3

(13) Transferor(s) The transferor verifies that to the best of the transferor's knowledge and belief, this transfer does not contravene section 50 of the Planning Act.

HARVEY, Garry Derek
HARVEY, Patricia Eleanore

Solicitor for Transferor(s): I have explained the effect of section 50 of the Planning Act to the transferor and I have made inquiries of the transferor to determine that this transfer does not contravene that section and based on the information supplied by the transferor, to the best of my knowledge and belief, this transfer does not contravene that section. I am an Ontario solicitor in good standing.

Name and Address of Solicitor: Timothy J. Wyers, McClelland, Wyers & Chae, 759 Main Street, Owen Sound ON N4K 5Z7

(14) Solicitor for Transferee(s) I have investigated the title to this land and to abutting land where relevant and I am satisfied that the title records reveal no contravention as set out in subclause 50 (22) (c) (ii) of the Planning Act and that to the best of my knowledge and belief this transfer does not contravene section 50 of the Planning Act. I act independently of the solicitor for the transferor(s) and I am an Ontario solicitor in good standing.

(15) Assessment Roll Number of Property: Cty. / Mun. / Map / Sub. / Par.

(16) Municipal Address of Property:
South side of Darwin Road
R.R. #1
Elmwood ON N0G 1S1

(17) Document Prepared by:
Timothy J. Wyers
McClelland, Wyers & Chae
759 Main Street
Owen Sound ON N4K 5Z7

Fees and Tax: Registration Fee / Land Transfer Tax / Total

STATEMENT OF ADJUSTMENTS

VENDORS: Garry D. Harvey
Patricia E. Harvey

PURCHASER: Phillip A. Hartwood

PROPERTY: South Part Lot 65
Second Concession, Bentinck

ADJUSTMENT DATE: November 30, 20xx

Sale Price		$190,000.00
Deposit	$ 25,000.00	
Mortgage Back	100,000.00	
Taxes 20xx taxes of $1,268.27 Paid in full Allow vendor (32 days)		111.19
All meters to be read on closing and to be paid by vendor to closing - no adjustment		
Insurance – purchaser to place own coverage		
Balance due on closing by certified cheque payable to McClelland, Wyers & Chae, in trust, as per direction	<u>$65,111.19</u>	_____
	<u>$90,111.19</u>	<u>$190,111.19</u>

E. & O.E.
November 1, 20xx
TJW/ri

4. REQUISITION LETTER – HARTWOOD purchase from HARVEY

Mr. Graham has submitted his title search and Peter Grant has now drafted the letter of requisition shown below and asks that you prepare it for his signature.

SEND LETTER BY COURIER

Timothy J. Wyers - McClelland, Wyers & Chae
Re: Hartwood etc...

Our title investigations have now been completed & without prejudice to our clients' rights under the agmt. of pur. & sale, we hereby submit the following requisitions on title & reserve the right to submit further & other requisitions.

1. Instrument No. 234968 is a mortgage registered on June 1, 2005 & given by Garry & Patricia Harvey to the Royal Bank of Canada. The principal amount was $75,000 at 6 percent due June 1, 2010.
REQUIRED: Registration of a discharge of said mortgage on or before closing.

2. REQUIRED: Satisfactory evidence that the property is a "used residential complex" within the meaning of the Excise Tax Act & is an exempt supply within the provisions of Schedule V to the said Act.

3. REQUIRED: The enclosed declaration of possession to be signed by your clients & turned over on closing

4. REQUIRED: the enclosed general undertaking to be signed by your clients and to be turned over on closing.

5. DECLARATION OF POSSESSION – HARTWOOD purchase from HARVEY

Prepare a joint declaration of possession to be signed by Mr. and Mrs. Harvey using the information in the file, Precedent 26.10 and the following:

Paragraph 1:	There is a mortgage in favour of Monarch Trust Company for $93,852.24, from the 1st day of (this month), 20xx. They have lived there since on or about the 6th day of April, 2000.
Paragraph 8:	Delete or strikeover
Paragraph 10:	Realty taxes paid up to 31st December (last year)
Paragraph 11:	Survey – prepared by Brown & Associates O.L.S. dated June 17, 1990.

6. LAND TRANSFER TAX AFFIDAVIT – HARTWOOD purchase from HARVEY

Prepare the Land Transfer Tax Affidavit for this file to be signed by both Mr. and Mrs. Harvey. The property being purchased is a single-family residence. The purchasers are not Roman Catholic and do not have French language rights. Refer to the agreement of purchase and sale, the draft transfer and Precedent 26.11 to complete this affidavit.

7. DIRECTION – ROUSSEAU purchase from SHAFER

Prepare the direction re title to be held in the file until the clients come in to sign documents. Title is to be taken in both purchasers' names as joint tenants. Mr. Rousseau's birth date is March 7, 1969; Mrs. Rousseau's birth date is September 29, 1970. The address of the property will be the address for service. Refer to Precedent 26.1.

8. CORRESPONDENCE – ROUSSEAU purchase from SHAFER

Prepare a letter to the Halton Condominium Corporation No. 174, at 200 Frontenac Drive, Burlington ON L8L 2A9, to request a condominium status certificate. The fee is $100.

9. ACKNOWLEDGEMENT AND DIRECTION – ROUSSEAU purchase from SHAFER

The Rousseaus are purchasing title insurance thus search letters will not be required, usually only verbal confirmation regarding realty taxes from the City of Burlington would be required, but your instructor will confirm this. You will need to prepare an acknowledgement and direction re title insurance to be signed by both clients. They are purchasing the title insurance from First Canadian Title. Refer to Precedent 26.8.

10. TITLE & EXECUTION SEARCHES – ROUSSEAU purchase from SHAFER

You are to do a preliminary title search by PIN for this property. Refer to Precedent 26.4. Your instructor will advise if you are to print out the parcel register, any instruments or map. You are also instructed to do a writs of execution search against the vendor. Refer to Precedent 25.5.

11. TRANSFER – ROUSSEAU purchase from SHAFER

In actual practice, the vendor's solicitor would prepare the entire electronic transfer document <u>except</u> the information on the transferees and the Land Transfer Tax affidavit and then "message" the document to the purchasers' solicitor for completion. However, this may not be possible in the classroom setting, thus you may be required to prepare the entire transfer document using the material in the file and information below. Refer to Precedent 21.3.

Purchase Price:	See Agmt. of Purchase & Sale and allow $1,000 for chattels
Vendor:	Not a spouse; address after closing 5 Elm Street Guelph L2W 4H9
Purchasers:	See instructions for direction re title above
Planning Act:	statements will not be completed
LTT Statement:	Single family residence; transferees are Roman Catholics with French language education rights

12. CHARGE – ROUSSEAU purchase from SHAFER

Mr. and Mrs. Rousseau have arranged a mortgage with ABC Mortgage Lenders Inc. for $150,000.00 at 7.5% calculated half-yearly not in advance. Repayment is to be $1,097.00 monthly, beginning the closing date of the transaction, for a term of five years. Standard Charge Terms are 4332. Prepare the draft electronic charge document. Refer to Precedent 22.4.

13. ELECTRONIC REGISTRATION DOCUMENTATION – ROUSSEAU purchase from SHAFER

Prepare the following documentation for our clients to execute before closing for this e-reg transaction. Refer to the material in your file and Peter Grant's notes below to prepare these documents the templates for which are available in the practice files. Note, however, that the Acknowledgement and Direction Report is usually required to be created in Teraview.
***(Forms Folder: Acknowledgement** (Acknowledgement and Direction Report) and*
***Registration Agmt** (Document Registration Agreement)).*

    (a) Acknowledgement and Direction (Precedents 24.4 and 24.6)

The consenting spouse paragraph will not be required as both Mr. and Mrs. Rousseau will sign. Note: a copy of the draft transfer and mortgage instruments in progress should be attached to this document.

    (b) Document Registration Agreement (Precedent 24.5)

Hill, Johnston & Grant as the purchasers' solicitor will be doing the electronic registration at 2:00 pm on the closing date.

    (c) Authorization for Withdrawal (Precedent 26.13)

Authorization Number - 599248
Amount to be withdrawn - Registration fees of $141.00
              plus LTT & PSt (which you need to calculate)
Financial Institution - Data Bank of Canada
Account Number - 4480-332902
Person Authorizing - Peter T. Grant

14. DECLARATION OF POSSESSION – ROUSSEAU purchase from SHAFER

Prepare a joint declaration of possession to be signed by the vendor using the information in the file and the following. Refer to Precedent 26.10.

    Paragraph 1:   There is no mortgage on the property – delete this first part of the sentence. She has lived there since on or about September 17, 1991.
    Paragraph 8:   Delete or strikeover
    Paragraph 10:   Taxes paid up to 31st December, (last year)
    Paragraph 11.   No survey – delete or strikeover

15. STATEMENT OF ADJUSTMENTS – ROUSSEAU purchase from SHAFER

*The draft statement of adjustments has now been received from the vendor's solicitor which is shown on the following page. This document should be **reviewed carefully** for any errors. You will need to refer to this document to calculate the funds required on closing.*

STATEMENT OF ADJUSTMENTS

SHAFER sale to ROUSSEAU
Townhouse 5, 200 Bayside Way
Unit 5, Halton Condominium Plan No. 174
Burlington

Adjusted as of June 7, 20xx

SALE PRICE $ 250,000.00

DEPOSIT $ 25,000.00

REALTY TAXES
20xx taxes of $2,495.10
Vendor's share (157 days) $1,073.88
Vendor has paid   858.92
ALLOW PURCHASER   241.31

CONDOMINIUM COMMON
EXPENSES of $164.00
Paid for June
ALLOW VENDOR (24 days)   131.20

UTILITIES
Meters to be read on closing

BALANCE DUE ON CLOSING
by certified cheque payable to
GRAHAM & PARKER,
as per direction $224,916.89

  $250,131.20 $250,131.20

E. & O.E.
May 15, 20xx
MC/ri

16. AMOUNTS REQUIRED TO CLOSE

Peter Grant has reviewed the dockets for both the Hartwood and Rousseau files and estimated the final amounts. He asks you to determine exactly how much money the purchasers should be asked to provide when they come in prior to closing to sign all the necessary documents.

1. **Hartwood purchase from Harvey**

Balance due on closing	$
Land Transfer Tax	
Provincial Sales Tax	
Our fees & disbursements	1,200.00
TOTAL need by certified cheque	$

2. **Rousseau purchase from Shafer**

Balance due on closing	$
Land Transfer Tax	
Provincial Sales Tax	
Our fees & disbursements	1,450.00
LESS: proceeds of mortgage	
TOTAL need by certified cheque	$

17. HANDLING CHEQUES

Assume each of the purchasers for the above files have brought in a certified cheque for the amount required and that these cheques have been deposited in Hill, Johnston & Grant's trust account.

Requisition the necessary cheques payable to the solicitors for the vendor or vendors for the balance due on closing and to the Minister of Finance for the appropriate land transfer tax and retail sales tax (if any) in each transaction.

C. LEGAL TERMINOLOGY

After completing this exercise you should be able to spell and define the following legal terms. Read the definitions shown below. Then select the correct term and match it with the words or phrase that best matches it in meaning, and write the correct term in the space provided. There are more terms than definitions.

Legal Terms

title	title insurance	title search
declaration of possession	land transfer tax	zoning
direction re title	provincial sales tax	encumbrance
direction re proceeds	nominal consideration	chattels

Definitions

1. regulations pertaining to land as to its use and the size of any buildings on the land _____

2. tax payable on the purchase of chattels _____

3. the right to ownership of property _____

4. this protects owners of real property against defects in title _____

5. document setting out details of title for real property owned by a vendor _____

6. document setting out names, birth dates and particulars of how they wish to hold the property _____

7. tax payable on the purchase of real property _____

8. anything which limits or affects the fee simple title to property _____

9. process of examining all records of a property to confirm the vendor is the legal owner and for all defects in title _____

10. moveable personal property _____

11. an amount paid for property that does not reflect to actual market value of the property _____

CHAPTER 27 – ASSIGNMENTS
Closing the Real Estate Transaction

A. LEGAL OFFICE PROCEDURES

There are no legal office procedures exercises for this chapter.

B. LEGAL DOCUMENT PRODUCTION

1. REPORTING LETTER – HOWARD sale SINGH

Hill, Johnston & Grant has a form letter for reporting on residential sale transactions which is based on Precedent 27.3 in your textbook and is available to be retrieved and completed.
(Practice Files: Forms Folder – File: Sale Report)

Using Peter Grant's notes below and the draft account and trust ledger statement on the following pages, you are asked to prepare the report to Mr. and Mrs. Howard. Some of the information required to complete this letter will be found in the material in the Howard file. Note that Peter Grant's notes are numbered to correspond to the numbered items in the form letter.

Howard s/t Singh - Reporting Letter

1. *See Stat. of Adjustments*
2. *See Discharge Statement for details of mortgage. Discharge of Mortgage was registered in Land Registry Office for Muskoka on June 30, 20xx (current year) as No. M46991*
3. *Delete*
4. *Delete references to estimated taxes and see Stat. of Adjustments for amounts*
5. *Mortgage in favour of Algonquin Permanent Trust Company*
6. *See Stat. of Adjustments for amounts*
7. *Commission fees of $11,000 plus GST of ? and see agmt. of purchase & sale for other amounts.*
8. *9 & 10 - as in form letter*

You attended at our office on June 30, 20xx to pick up our trust cheque for $190,000, and we now enclose our trust cheque for $ - get amount from trust ledger statement once you had done the calculations.

Howard sale to Singh - Account

TO PROFESSIONAL SERVICES RENDERD in connection with the above matter, including:

Acting on your behalf; preparing transfer/deed; preparing statement of adjustments; answering requisitions on title; preparation of direction with respect to balance due on closing; preparing documentation and attending to discharge of existing first mortgage; additional attendances and correspondence on your behalf; attending at Land Registry to complete the transaction and obtain funds; reporting to you;

	OUR FEE:		$ 800.00
	GST		?

DISBURSEMENTS

Subject to GST
Photocopies		$ 19.80	
Fax		7.75	
		────────	
		?	
	GST	?	?

Not Subject to GST
Paid to register discharge	60.00	?
	────────	
	Subtotal	?

LESS: Transfer from Trust, (date)   ?

BALANCE: Paid in Full

HILL, JOHNSTON & GRANT

Per:

PTG/**
E. & O.E.

TRUST LEDGER STATEMENT

*Howard sale to Singh
etc.*

RECEIVED proceeds of sale			$	?
PAID to discharge existing first mortgage	$	?		
PAID fees and disbursements as per account		?		
PAID to you on June 30, 20xx		190,000.00		
BALANCE to you, current date		?		
		-----------		-----------
		$?	$	?
		-----------		-----------

PTG/**
E. O.E.

2. REPORTING LETTER – ROUSSEAU purchase from SHAFER

Hill, Johnston & Grant has a form letter for reporting on residential purchase transactions which is based on Precedent 27.2 in your textbook and is available to be retrieved and completed.
(Practice Files: Forms Folder – File: Purchase Report)

Using Peter Grant's notes below and the draft account and trust ledger statement on the following pages, you are asked to prepare the report to Mr. and Mrs. Rousseau. Some of the information required to complete this letter will be found in the material in the Rousseau file.

Rousseau p/f Shafer - Reporting Letter

*Use enclosures for an e-reg transaction
(No 2nd mortgage and no survey)
Tax Bill is from the City of Burlington for 20xx (current year)*

Transfer/Deed - ownership is joint tenants to the - put in legal description of property - registered electronically at the Halton Land Registry Office on June 7, 20xx as Instrument No. B48832

Statement of Adjustments - put in closing date

First Mortgage - get details from mortgage (or original instructions on page 180) Mtg. application dated April 30, 20xx. Note: Put in that payments to be automatically deducted from your account at Halton Credit Union. Mortgage No. 8009-69925.

Mortage Back - delete

Discharge of Existing Mortgage - delete

Realty Taxes - delete references to estimated taxes & see statement of adjustments for amounts.

Insurance - Canadiana Insurance Company

Interest on Deposit - see agreement of purchase & sale for amount

Title - subject to the interest of ABC Mortgage Lenders Inc. as first mortgagee - delete reference to any other mortgagee.

Title insurance purchased from First Canadian Title, Policy No. 781104-6922

We are enclosing a copy of our trust ledger statement together with our receipted account and our cheque in the amount of $(balance due amount from the trust ledger statement) being the balance in our trust account to your credit.

Rousseau purchase from Shafer - Account

TO PROFESSIONAL SERVICES RENDERED in this transaction, including:

Receipt and perusal of agmt of purchase & sale and to advising you in respect of same;

Conducting preliminary searches, including search of title, executions, taxes and others particular to this matter;

Submitting letters of requisitions & reviewing draft transfer; statement of adjustments and preparation & review of other closing documentation

All matters relating to the documentation and registration of a first mortgage on title

All receipts and disbursements of funds and to attendance to completion of purchase transaction

All telephone calls and correspondence throughout; to reporting to you and to mortgage company, and to all other matters necessary herein

        OUR FEE: $ 950.00
        GST   ?

DISBURSEMENTS

Subject to GST
Search fees	$ 150.00
Photocopies	22.60
Fax Charges	14.20
Transaction Levy	50.00
Registration and Search Fees	52.00

     GST ?   ?

Not Subject to GST
Registration and Search Fees 120.00 ?

LESS: Transfer from Trust, (date)   ?

    TOTAL FEES AND DISBURSEMENTS Paid in Full

    HILL, JOHNSTON & GRANT

    Per:

PTG/**
E. & O.E.

Get amounts from file and account you prepared - Thanks PTG.

TRUST LEDGER STATEMENT
Rousseau purchase from Shafer etc.

RECEIVED from you, on June 5, 20xx		$?
RECEIVED proceeds of first mortgage on ?		?
PAID balance as per stat. of adj.	$?	
PAID Land Transfer Tax	?	
PAID Provincial Sales Tax	?	
PAID fees and disbursements as per account	?	
BALANCE to you, current date	?	
	$?	$?

PTG/**
E. & O.E.

C. LEGAL TERMINOLOGY

After completing this exercise you should be able to spell and define the following legal terms. Read the definitions shown below. Then select the correct term and match it with the words or phrase that best matches it in meaning, and write the correct term in the space provided. There are more terms than definitions.

Legal Terms

arm's length transaction	wear and tear	null and void
citation	commission	caveat

Definitions

1. a warning _____

2. of no legal validity or effect _____

3. all parties involved act in own best interest and under no undue influence from any other party _____

4. depreciation of an asset due to ordinary usage _____

5. percentage of purchase price that is paid by vendor to a real estate agent _____

CHAPTER 28 – ASSIGNMENTS
Introduction to Corporate Practice

A. LEGAL OFFICE PROCEDURES

1. OPEN FILE – HUMREX HOLDINGS LIMITED

You are to open a file for this new company. Prepare the new matter form/label. Fees will be on a time basis. This matter has been assigned file number 05125/0091. Refer to the memorandum to file below for further information.

B. LEGAL DOCUMENT PRODUCTION

1. MEMORANDUM TO FILE – HUMREX HOLDINGS LIMITED

Prepare the following memorandum to file:

I had an interview on (yesterday's date) with Ronald C. Anderson in connection with the incorporation of a new non-offering corporation with share capital.

The incorporators are to be:
  Ronald C. Anderson
  (address should be in office reference material)
  Howard A. Eng
  19 King High Street, Toronto M4B 8H2
  Res: 416-075 2162   Bus: 416-595-9625

There are to be 3 directors:
  R. C. Anderson
  H. A. Eng
  Mohamed J. Bhatt
  67 Finchbar Road, Toronto M4R 2Z9
  Res: 416-233-9344 Bus: 416-225-9747

All three are Canadian citizens and are Professional Engineers.

Mr. Bhatt will not be available to sign organizational documents for a few weeks - we'll use an office director for the third director in the articles.

There are to be unlimited common shares, restrictions on transfer requiring consent of directors, a limitation on the number of shareholders to 20 etc. and no other class of shares. They want the name Humrex Holdings Limited.

Registered office to be 17 Howard Street, Suite 960, Toronto M5K 6Z2

We should:
1. *Open file – Humrex Holdings Limited re Incorporation.*
   Note: LCR will be working on this file too.
2. *Order a NUANS search on proposed name*
3. *Draft articles*
4. *Select office director & have him/her consent to act.*

2. BROWN-GELON COMPANY LIMITED – SHAREHOLDERS' AGREEMENT

Michael Colucci has drafted several sections of a long shareholders' agreement which he asks that you prepare in good form for his review. The agreement is to be prepared doubled spaced with centred headings. Each section should begin on separate page. Refer to Chapter 7 for guidelines and precedents for preparing agreements.

SECTION 3
PURPOSE AND SCOPE

3.01   This Agreement shall come into effect and force as of the date set out above and shall continue in effect and force until the earlier of
(a) the date on which only one shareholder holds any share or shares in the Corporation; and
(b) the date on which this Agreement is terminated in writing and executed by all of the shareholders who continue to hold shares in the Corp.
3.02 In the event that any one or more of the shareholders ceases to be a shareholder of the Corporation pursuant to the terms of this Agmt, such shareholder shall have no further rights or obligations pursuant to the terms of this Agmt but, subject to the provisions of subsection 2.01 hereof, this Agmt shall continue to be binding upon the remaining shareholders who are parties hereto.
3.03   This Agmt shall apply <u>mutatis mutandis.</u>
3.04   Each shareholders shall vote his or her shares and act as a shareholder and in all other respects take all such steps as may reasonably be within his or her power so as to permit the Corporation to comply with and act in the manner contemplated by this Agmt in order to realize to there full extent the provisions of this agmt & to the extent permitted by the governing law of this agmt.

SECTION 4
Restrictions on issue and transfer of shares

4.01   The shareholders represent & warrant to the Corp. and to each other that the shares are the only issued and outstanding common shares of the Corporation & that as of the date of this agmt. there are no outstanding rights or options obligating the Corp. to issue additional shares to any other person or entity.

4.02   Except as otherwise provided for in this agmt., no shareholder shall sell, assign, transfer, convey, dispose, mortgage, pledge as security or otherwise transfer or encumber any of his or her shares without the proper written consent all of the shareholders herein who have the right of first refusal to purchase any such offered shares under the terms and conditions set out in Section 5 herein.

4.03   The Corp. shall not issue any additional shares or grant any option or other right to acquire additional shares without the prior written consent of all of the shareholders to this agmt.

4.04   All share certificates issued by the Corp. shall have printed thereon the following:

"Shares represented by this certificate are subject to the terms and conditions of a Shareholders' Agreement made the 1st day of (next month), (current year), a copy of which is retained at the registered office of the Corporation.

Section 5
Right to Purchase Shares

5.01   Any shareholder wishing to transfer or assign any of his or her shares must inform all the other shareholders in writing by providing at least twenty (20) business day's notice addressed to each of the other shareholders and to the Corporation at the addresses shown in Section 10 hereof.

5.02   Any shareholder or Shareholders, including the Corporation itself, shall have the right, exercisable at any time after receipt of a notice under section 5.01 herein from any shareholder stating his or her intention to transfer, assign or offer for sale any shares, or after the date of death of a shareholder, shall each have the right, exercisable at any time within 10 days of receipt of any such notice or within 90 days of the date of death of a shareholder, to purchase any such shares at a price for each share equal to the original purchase price (as defined in Section 2.02 herein) for each such Share provided that such number of purchased shares in addition to any shares currently held by any such purchasing *shareholder shall maintain the existing proportionate shareholding of the shareholders in the Corporation as defined in Section 7.03.*

5.03   Pursuant to the terms of Section 5.02, any such shareholder wishing to purchase any such shares, shall notify the Corp. and all other shareholders in writing of his or her intention to purchase any such shares.

5.04   If, prior to any shareholder making an offer to purchase any such shares discussed in this section, the Corp. makes an offer to purchase less than all such shares, then the remainder of any such shares shall be offered to the shareholders for purchase, provided that each shareholders' proportionate shareholding in the Corp. shall be maintained as set out in Section 7.03 herein.

C. LEGAL TERMINOLOGY

Legal Terms

corporation	sole proprietorship	partnership
limited liability	offering corporation	shareholders
non-offering corporation	directors	officers

Definitions

1. individuals appointed to administer the day to day affairs of a corporation   _____

2. a legal entity created under federal or provincial statutes that has its own rights, privileges and liabilities   _____

3. individuals elected to supervise or manage a corporation   _____

4. enterprise of two or more individuals who share in any profits and are liable for any debts   _____

5. corporation that sells shares in the corporation to the public   _____

6. protection provided to individual shareholders of a corporation   _____

7. the "owners" of the corporation   _____

8. enterprise owned by a single individual who earns all profits and is liable for all losses   _____

CHAPTER 29 – ASSIGNMENTS
Incorporating an Ontario Corporation

A. LEGAL OFFICE PROCEDURES

There are no legal office procedures exercises for this chapter.

B. LEGAL DOCUMENT PRODUCTION

1. ARTICLES OF INCORPORATION – HUMREX HOLDINGS LIMITED

As a result of Peter Grant's interview with Ronald Anderson, Lynda Ritchie secured the necessary NUANS report and completed the Hill, Johnston & Grant "Incorporation Information Sheet" that is used as the basis for drafting articles of incorporation which is shown on the following page. The new corporation is to have three directors, but only two of them will be available in the next few weeks to assist in the formal steps required to organize the new corporation; the third person who is to be a permanent director of the corporation, Mohamed J. Bhatt, is expected to be out of the city for the next three or four weeks. As a result, someone must be appointed as a first director. Peter Grant advises that YOU will be the third first director and that you will resign as soon as the organizational procedures have been carried out.

Prepare one copy of the articles of incorporation using the information on the following page. Refer to Precedent 29.1.

2. CONSENT TO ACT AS A FIRST DIRECTOR – HUMREX HOLDINGS LIMITED

You are to act as a first director and are not an incorporator; therefore, you should prepare a consent to act as a first director for yourself. Refer to Precedent 29.2.

3. FILING ARTICLES – HUMREX HOLDINGS LIMITED

The articles have now been reviewed and executed by Ronald Anderson and Howard Eng. Prepare a memorandum to Patricia Emery to attend at the Companies and Personal Property Securities Branch and file the articles. You will need to provide her with:

1. The executed articles of incorporation. (Assume you prepared them in duplicate.)
2. Your consent to act as first director. (Again, assume you prepared them in duplicate.)
3. The NUANS report. (Assume Lynda Ritchie provided these to you.)
4. A cheque for the required filing fee – you will need to requisition this.

INCORPORATION INFORMATION SHEET

1. **Name of corporation:** HUMREX HOLDINGS LIMITED

2. **Address of registered office:** 17 Howard Street, Suite 960
   Toronto ON M5K 6Z2

3. **Number of Directors** Minimum - 2   Maximum - 10

4. **First directors**
   Ronald C. Anderson
   Howard A. Eng
   You
   They will all be using the address of the registered office as their address for service

5. **Restrictions, etc.** Same as Precedent 29.1 in your text.

6. **Classes** Unlimited common shares

7. **Rights, privileges, etc.** Not applicable

8. **The issue, transfer, etc.**

   No share shall be transferred without the previous consent of the directors of the corporation expressed by resolution in writing passed by the board of directors or by an instrument in writing signed by a majority of directors.

9. **Other provisions, if any**

   (a) Liens on Shares: Subject to the B-C-Act, the corporation has a lien on any share registered in the name of the shareholder or his or her legal representative for any debt of that shareholder to the corporation.
   (b) No Public Offering: any invitation to the public to subscribe for any security of the corporation is prohibited.
   (c) Number of Shareholders: The number of shareholders of the corporation is limited to twenty (20) exclusive of employees who were shareholders while so employed and who have continued to be shareholders counting joint registered owners as one (1) shareholder.

10. **Incorporators** List RCA and HAE - They will sign the articles. You are not an incorporator.

4. CORPORATE SUPPLIES

Humex Holdings Limited will require corporate supplies including a minute book, corporate seal and a small book of share certificates.

Research the available suppliers and the cost for these corporate supplies.

5. SUBSCRIPTION FOR SHARES – HUMREX HOLDINGS LIMITED

Prepare a subscription for shares for Ronald Anderson and Howard Eng. Ronald Anderson is subscribing for 1,000 shares and Howard. Eng for 500 shares. The shares will be registered in their respective names. Peter Grant advises you that the price per share is to be $10.00. Refer to Precedent 29.4.

6. NOTARIAL CERTIFICATE FOR ARTICLES OF INCORPORATION - HUMREX HOLDINGS LIMITED

*The articles of incorporation were filed yesterday, and you have now been advised that they were accepted as submitted. Assume you have now received the certificate of incorporation numbered **19922638**.*

Prepare the notarial copy of the certificate of incorporation of Humrex Holdings Limited for Peter Grant to sign. Once you have prepared the certificate, you would usually photocopy the required number of copies for Peter Grant to sign. Refer to Precedent 29.3.

7. RESIGNATION AND CONSENT TO ACT AS DIRECTOR – HUMREX HOLDINGS LIMITED

You know that you will resign as a director of the corporation as soon as the directors have organized the corporation. Prepare a resignation for yourself. Refer to Precedent 29.5.

Prepare the consent to be signed by Mohamed J. Bhatt when he returns to the city. Refer to Precedent 29.6.

8. ARTICLES OF INCORPORATION – NUMBERED COMPANY

Michael Colucci urgently needs some articles of incorporation prepared for a new numbered company. He provides you with the Corporation Information Sheet on the following page. You are to prepare the draft articles of incorporation for electronic filing for the clients to sign this afternoon. Leave the first nine boxes blank for the corporation's name, followed by ONTARIO LTD. Refer to Precedent 29.1.

Research the available private-sectors service providers who do electronic registration, the procedure for filing, and the cost for this service.

INCORPORATION INFORMATION SHEET

1. **Name of corporation:** ONTARIO LTD.
2. **Address of registered office:** 500 Main Street, Hamilton ON L8S 3V9
3. **Number of Directors** Minimum – 1   Maximum – 5
4. **First Directors** John A. Ketchum, Mary R. Ketchum
   Both Canadian citizens & Chartered Accountants
5. **Restrictions, etc.** None
6. **Classes** Unlimited common shares
7. **Rights, privileges, etc.** Not applicable
8. **The issue, transfer, etc.** Same as precedent in your text
9. **Other provisions, if any** Same as precedent in your text
10. **Incorporators** Same as First Directors

C. LEGAL TERMINOLOGY

Legal Terms

by-laws	*Business Corporations Act*	eleemosynary
registered office	ex officio	quorum
winding-up	*Corporations Act*	non-resident

Definitions

1. a charitable organization

2. by virtue of his/her office

3. act that governs Ontario corporation with share capital

4. the minimum number of persons who must be present in order to hold a valid meeting

5. the permanent rules for the operation of a corporation

6. act that governs Ontario corporation without share capital

7. final settlement of the accounts and affairs of a corporation

8. means the location specified in the articles of incorporation or the most recent notice of change

CHAPTER 30 – ASSIGNMENTS
Corporate By-laws, Meetings, Minutes and Resolutions

A. LEGAL OFFICE PROCEDURES

There are no legal office procedures exercises for this chapter.

B. LEGAL DOCUMENT PRODUCTION

1. BY-LAWS NO. 1 AND NO. 2 – HUMREX HOLDINGS LIMITED

The standard By-laws No. 1 and No. 2 for Humrex Holdings Limited need to be prepared. Your instructor will advise you how you are to do this as most law firms have a template or software that produces the standard text for By-law No. 1 and 2. Peter Grant has provided you with the following notes to assist you. Refer to Precedents 30.1 and 30.2.

Name of Corporation:	HUMREX HOLDINGS LIMITED
Fiscal year:	ends on March 31
Execution of Documents:	any two officers or directors
Number of Directors:	a minimum of 2 and a maximum of 10
Quorum	Directors - a majority of the directors elected to office
	Shareholders - the holders of a majority of shares entitled to vote at a meeting of shareholders
Votes to Govern:	chair *has* a casting vote
Signature Page	See signature clauses in Precedent 30.2. All directors (including you) will sign sometime next week - leave day blank.

2. BY-LAW NO. 3 – HUMREX HOLDINGS LIMITED

Peter Grant has drafted the following By-law No. 3 for this corporation for you to prepare, which appears on the following page

BY-LAW NO. 3

A by-law relating generally to the remuneration of directors of

HUMREX H- L -

BE IT ENACTED AS A by-law of the Corporation as follows:

1. Each director of the Corporation shall be paid (in addition to any out-of-pocket expenses reasonably incurred in the furtherance of the business of the corporation) the sum of Five Thousand Dollars ($5,000.00) in Canadian funds per annum as remuneration in his or her capacity as director so long as he or she remains a director of the corporation, such remuneration to accrue from the date hereof or the date of his or her election or appointment, which is the later date.

2. The payment referred to in para. 1 hereof shall be made only upon a resolution of the board of directors being passed to authorize such payments.

3. The period for which such remuneration shall be paid shall terminate twenty (20) years from the date hereof.

Same ending as in By-laws 1 and 2.

3. BY-LAW NO. 3 – PRENNAN-VANCE LIMITED

Peter Grant has drafted the following by-law for Prennan-Vance Limited to provide for the quorum for meetings of the board of directors, which you have been asked to prepare.

BY-LAW NO. 3

a by-law relating generally to the quorum of directors of

PRENNAN-VANCE LIMITED

BE IT ENACTED as a by-law of P- V- L - as follows:

Section 3.06 of By-law No. 1 is repealed & the following is substituted therefor:

3.06 Quorum of Directors - Subject to section 3.08 of By-law No. 1, the quorum for the transaction of business at any meeting of the board shall consist of the greater of two-fifths (2/5th) of the directors then in office or three (3) directors

ENACTED by the board etc.....

```
                          _____
                                  President
                                                         c/s
                          _____
                                  Secretary
```

The foregoing by-law etc...... directors (see below)

In lieu of confirmation etc...... shareholders (see below)

Norman D. Prennan - Director & Shareholder
Richard A. Vance - Director & Shareholder
Kristin P. Trinh - Director
Gregory G. Lohnes - Director
Vanessa L. Aniston - Director

The directors & shareholders will be coming in at various times this week to sign this by-law.

PTG

4. **ORGANIZATIONAL RESOLUTIONS – HUMREX HOLDINGS LIMITED**

   (a) **Resolutions of Directors**

   Ronald Anderson has advised that he wishes to proceed to organize the corporation by resolutions in writing. You have therefore been asked to prepare the organizational resolutions of the directors of Humrex Holdings Limited.

   Refer to Precedent 30.8 and the notes on the following page in preparing these resolutions. It is expected that the other two directors will be coming into the office later this week to sign these resolutions. You, of course, may sign them now.

1. By-laws - No. 1, No. 2, No. 3

2. Shares - 1,500 common shares issued at $10.00 per share to - see subscription for shares that you prepared in Chapter 29

3. Same as precedent

4. Same as precedent

5. Officers: President - Ronald C. Anderson
   Secretary - Howard A. Eng
   Treasurer - You (for the time being)

6. Banking: Royal Bank of Canada

7. Records: address of Corporation

(b) **Resolutions of Shareholders**

Refer to Precedent 30.9 and the notes below in preparing these resolutions. Again, the shareholders will be coming in later this week to sign these resolutions.

1. By-laws - No. 1, No. 2 and No. 3

2. Auditor: Little & Bell, C.A.

3. Resignation and Appointment of Director

    That the resignation of (your name) as a director of the corporation is hereby accepted & that the following person is hereby elected a director of the Corp. to hold office until the first annual meting of the Corp. or until his successor has been duly elected, subject to the provisions of the Corp.'s by-laws:

    Mohamed J. Bhatt

(c) **Resolutions of Permanent Directors**

Now that Humrex Holdings Limited is organized and has shareholders, officers and permanent directors, the directors wish to elect permanent officers. Peter Grant asks you to prepare a resolution to be consented to in writing by the permanent directors.

Remember, you were a first director and have now resigned. To assist you, Peter Grant gives you the draft wording for the resolution below.

That the following persons be and are hereby appointed officers of the Corp. to hold office during the pleasure of the Board, namely:

> *President: R. C. Anderson*
> *Secretary: H. A. Eng*
> *Treasurer: M. J. Bhatt*

The foregoing resolutions etc....

5. RESOLUTIONS OF DIRECTORS and SHAREHOLDERS – PRENNAN-VANCE LIMITED

The shareholders of Prennan-Vance Limited, for whom you prepared a by-law changing the quorum requirements, wish to pass a special shareholders' resolution and a directors' resolution. Drafts of these resolutions appear below for you to prepare.

<u>Shareholders' Resolution:</u>

SPECIAL RESOLUTION OF THE SHAREHOLDERS
OF
PRENNAN-VANCE LIMITED

EMPOWERING DIRECTORS TO DETERMINE
THE NUMBER OF DIRECTORS

RESOLVED as a special resolution:
That the directors of the Corp. are empowered to determine the number of directors of the Corp. within the minimum and maximum number of directors provided for in the articles of the Corp.

The foregoing special resolution, etc. ... signed by all shareholders

<u>Directors' Resolution:</u>

RESOLVED:

That the number of directors of the Corp. is hereby determined to be five (5) directors.

The foregoing resolution etc. ... signed by all the directors

6. ANNUAL MEETING OF SHAREHOLDERS – EAST HARDWARE LIMITED

The annual meeting of the shareholders of East Hardware Limited was held yesterday. You are asked to prepare the minutes from the Michael Colucci's draft below. Refer to Precedent 30.6.

MINUTES of the Annual Meeting of shareholders of EAST HARDWARE LIMITED, held at the registered offices of the Corp. on (yesterday's date), at 11:00 am

PRESENT: Hoaln W. East
Christopher W. East
Lauren M. East

CONSTITUTION OF MEETING

With the unanimous consent of the meeting, the President Hoaln W. East, took the chair, and the Secretary, Lauren M. East, acted as secretary of the meeting. All of the shareholders being present & having waived notice of the meeting, the chair declared the meeting to be constituted for the transaction of business.

FINANCIAL STATEMENTS

The chair presented to the meeting the financial statements of the corp. for the year ended Dec. 31 (last year).

On motion made, seconded and unanimously carried, <u>It Was Resolved</u> that the financial statement of the corp. for the year ended Dec. 31 (last year) be received & approved.

ELECTION OF DIRECTORS

The chair then stated that it was in order to proceed with the election of directors & declared the meeting open for nominations. The following were nominated:

Hoaln W. East
Christopher W. East
Daniel J. Lam

There being no further nominations, the chair declared nominations closed. No shareholder having requested a ballot, on motion duly made, seconded and unanimously carried, <u>It Was</u>

Resolved that the following person be elected directors of the corporation to hold office until the next annual meeting of shareholders or until their successors are duly elected or appointed:

Same as above

APPOINTMENT OF AUDITORS

On motion duly made, seconded and carried unanimously, IT WAS RESOLVED that Walker Sheridan, Professional Corporation, be appointed & they are hereby appointed auditors of the Corp. until the next meeting of shareholders or until their successors are appointed at a remuneration to be fixed by the directors, the directors being authorized to fix such remuneration.

TERMINATION

There being no further business to transact, on motion the meeting was ~~adjourned~~/terminated.

Use ending from Precedent 30.6 in text including waiver of notice.

Please also prepare a consent to act as director for Daniel S. Lam whose address is 679 Valley Blvd. King City ON L4Y 6K7. He is a pilot and a Canadian resident.

7. INITIAL RETURN – HUMREX HOLDINGS LIMITED

Now that the Humrex Holdings Limited is fully organized (with the exception of issuing the share certificates), you are asked to complete the initial return. In listing the directors, list the permanent directors – you are not listed on this form at all. All the directors wish to use the Corporation's address as their address for service. The secretary of the corporation will sign the notice. Refer to Precedent 29.7.

8. NOTICE OF CHANGE – EAST HARDWARE LIMITED

As a result of the meeting of shareholders of East Hardware Limited, Lauren M. East is no longer a director and Daniel J. Lam is. It is therefore necessary to file a notice of change for this corporation. Refer to Precedents 29.7 and 30.8 for any additional information you require to complete this notice of change. Note that although Lauren M. East is no longer a director, she is still an officer. Mr. Lam wishes to use the Corporation's address as his address for service. Peter Grant will sign the notice of change.

C. LEGAL TERMINOLOGY

After completing this exercise you should be able to spell and define the following legal terms. Read the definitions shown below. Then select the correct term and match it with the words or phrase that best matches it in meaning, and write the correct term in the space provided. There are more terms than definitions.

Legal Terms

adjourned	bona fide	chair
dividend	mutatis mutandis	president
proxy	public	resolutions
due diligence	terminated	private
minutes	agenda	secretary

Definitions

1. decisions made by directors or shareholders at a meeting _____

2. the necessary changes being made _____

3. a list of items of business to be transacted at a meeting _____

4. the term once used to describe a corporation that does not offer its shares to the public _____

5. the term used to indicate that a meeting has ended _____

6. the summary of the business conducted at a meeting _____

7. the principal officer of a corporation _____

8. a written authorization for someone to act or vote for someone else at a corporation's meeting _____

9. the term used to describe the person who presides over a meeting _____

10. investigation and analysis done by a company in anticipation of entering into a business transaction _____

11. profits or earnings of the corporation paid out to shareholders _____

12. in good faith, honestly, without fraud _____

CHAPTER 31 – ASSIGNMENTS
Corporate Securities, Records and Changes

A. LEGAL OFFICE PROCEDURES

In order to prepare some of the assignments in this chapter, templates are provided in the practice files that may be used to prepare the following corporate registers:

    Practice Files: Forms Folder   – File: *Directors Register (Directors' Register)*
                                      – File: *Share Ledger (Shareholders' Ledger)*
                                      – File: *Share Register (Shareholders' Register)*
                                      – File: *Stock Transfer (Stock Transfer Register)*

B. LEGAL DOCUMENT PRODUCTION

1. DIRECTORS' REGISTER – EAST HARDWARE LIMITED

You recently prepared a consent to act as director for Daniel J. Lam, as well as minutes for East Hardware Limited. As you may recall, Lauren M. East was not re-elected a director and Daniel Lam was elected. At that time Peter Grant gave you Daniel Lam's address (page 205 of this assignment book). Refer to Precedent 31.25 – this is the register that you are updating.

2. DIRECTORS' REGISTER – HUMREX HOLDINGS LIMITED

Prepare the directors' register for this company. You will need to include all information from the date of incorporation to the recent election of Mohamed J. Bhatt as a director. You will need to refer to the memorandum to file (that was assigned on page 198 of this assignment book) for some of the necessary information.

3. SHARE CERTIFICATES AND REGISTERS – HUMREX HOLDINGS LIMITED

Peter Grant asks you to prepare the following in connection with this corporation. Refer to Precedents 33.1, 31.3 and 31.4 in preparing these documents

> *Issue share certificates: 1000 to R. C. Anderson; 500 to H. A. Eng, to be signed sometime this week. (your instructor will advise you of the date).*

> *Prepare the shareholders' register and ledger sheets.*

4. TRANSFER OF SHARES – HUMREX HOLDINGS LIMITED

Ronald Anderson and Howard Eng have now received their share certificates, but have decided that Ronald Anderson will transfer 500 of his shares to Mohammed J. Bhatt. You are therefore asked to prepare a number of documents to carry out this transfer.

(a) Resolution of all the directors of Humrex Holdings Limited. Refer to Precedent 30.8

> *RESOLVED:*
>
> *That the following transfer of 500 common shares in the capital of the Corp. is hereby approved:*
>
> | Transferor | Transferee |
> |---|---|
> | Ronald C. Anderson | Mohamed J. Bhatt |
>
> *The foregoing resolution etc....*

(b) Prepare the transfer register showing the transfer from Ronald C. Anderson to Mohamed J. Bhatt as transfer no. 1. Do what is necessary to cancel Ronald Anderson's share certificate. Refer to Precedent 31.7.

(c) Issue two new share certificates – one to Mohamed J. Bhatt for 500 shares, and one to Ronald C. Anderson for the shares he is retaining. Use the next consecutive certificate numbers.

(d) Bring the shareholders' register up to date.

(e) Prepare a shareholders' ledger for Mohamed J. Bhatt, who is an accountant. Update the shareholder's ledger sheet for Ronald Anderson.

5. CHANGE OF ADDRESS OF REGISTERED OFFICE – EAST HARDWARE LIMITED

East Hardware Limited is moving its registered office to another address in Toronto and Peter Grant asks you to:

(a) Prepare a resolution to be consented to in writing by the directors approving this change which is drafted for you below.

(b) Prepare the necessary notice of change to be filed with the Ministry.

> *RESOLVED:*
>
> *That the street address of the registered office within the City of Toronto is hereby changed from (present address) to 260 University Avenue, Suite 500, Toronto Ontario M6K 2G7.*

6. ARTICLES OF AMENDMENT – 590 STEPHEN DRIVE LIMITED

590 Stephen Drive Limited wishes to change its corporate name. The required NUANS name search report has been received. This corporation has one shareholder and director, Stephanie Anne Kozak, who is also the President. She is a Canadian citizen.

You are asked to prepare the articles of amendment. Refer to Precedent 31.9 and the following information:

1. Present Name: *590 Stephen Drive Limited*
1. Name changed to: *Stephen Investments Limited*
3. Date of incorporation: *June 10, 2005*
4. The articles are amended . . . *The name of the Corporation is changed from (present name) to Stephen Investments Limited*
5. As is.
6. The resolution . . . *assume resolution signed tomorrow.*

7. SPECIAL RESOLUTION OF THE SOLE SHAREHOLDER – 590 STEPHEN DRIVE LIMITED

Peter Grant asks you to prepare the special resolution to be signed by the sole shareholder. Refer to Precedent 31.8 and the following draft information:

1. The Corp. amend its articles as set out in the articles of amendment in substantially the form annexed hereto.

2. The directors & proper officers of the Corp. be & they are hereby authorized to do all things & execute all documents necessary or desirable to carry out the foregoing.

8. RESOLUTION RE CORPORATE SEAL – STEPHEN INVESTMENTS LIMITED

Because the corporate name is changing and the corporation has a corporate seal, it is necessary to pass a resolution approving the form of the new corporate seal. Peter Grant has drafted the following resolution of the sole director for you to prepare:

Resolution of Sole Director
of
Stephen Investments Limited

RESOLVED:
   That the form of corporate seal of the Corp. shall be in the form impressed hereon, until changed by the board.

   The foregoing etc. ...

C. LEGAL TERMINOLOGY

After completing this exercise you should be able to spell and define the following legal terms. Read the definitions shown below and sentences below. Then select the correct term and write it space provided for the sentence that best matches it in meaning. There are more terms than definitions.

Legal Terms

ledger	directors	escrow
notary public	NUANS	proxy
common	register	class
corporate seal	terminated	officers
quorum	treasury	first

Definitions

1. The _____ directors are those listed in the articles of incorporation.

2. We will hold the share certificates in _____ until her cheque is received.

3. Any shares issued to an original shareholder would come from _____.

4. The meeting could not proceed because there was no _____.

5. Please ask a/an _____ to authenticate a copy of the certificate of incorporation.

6. _____ is a name search report that must be filed with the articles.

7. As there is only one class of shares, they will be _____ shares.

8. At their annual meeting, the shareholders will elect _____ for the next year.

9. A corporation need not but may have a/an _____ for executing documents.

10. She has given her _____ to another shareholder for use at the meeting.

11. A corporation may have more than one _____ of shares.

12. When all the business was conducted, the meeting was _____.

13. At their meeting the directors elected the _____ of the corporation.

CHAPTER 32 – ASSIGNMENTS
Wills and Powers of Attorney

A. LEGAL OFFICE PROCEDURES

Please note that the wills and codicils presented in this chapter are for procedural and formatting practice purposes only and the content thereof should not be used as precedents in the creation of "real" wills.

B. LEGAL DOCUMENT PRODUCTION

1. **WILL PREPARATION - ZEKAS**

   (a) *Peter Grant has drafted a very simple will for this client. It appears below and he asks you to prepare this will for execution on Friday of this week. Refer to Precedent 32.4.*

   (b) *Prepare an affidavit of execution of will with yourself as the deponent. Peter Grant will be the other witness. Refer to Precedent 32.7.*

This is the last will & testament of me, Marguerite Selena Zekas, of …. Mississauga…

1. I hereby revoke all former wills or other testamentary dispositions by me at any time heretofore made & declare this to be my only last will & testament.

2. I nominate, constitute & appoint my son, Andrew Paul Zekas, to be the sole personal representative and trustee of this my said will & I authorize my said personal representative to sell & dispose of any of my real & personal estate on such terms as he may consider in the best interest of my estate & to do all things necessary for the proper management of my estate & to execute all documents incidental thereto.

3. I give, devise & bequeath my entire estate both real & personal & wheresoever found or situate, including any property over which

I may have a general power of appointment, to my said personal representative, in trust for the following purposes, namely:

   (a)   to pay my just debts, funeral and testamentary expenses as soon as conveniently possible after my death;

   (b)   to pay the sum of $5,000 to each of the following who survive me for 30 days:

      (i)   my niece, Danica Andrea Zekas;

      (ii)   my neice, Marie Jennifer Zekas; and

      (iii)   my nephew, Stephan John Zekas.

   (c)   to pay or transfer all of the rest & residue of my estate to my son Andrew Paul Zekas, for his own use absolutely, provided that if my son should predecease me leaving issue surviving, such issue shall take his or her share per stirpes.

In testimony etc...

2. WILL – JOHANNSEN

Peter Johannsen has requested that Michael Colucci prepare his will. Michael Colucci has provided you with the template that is shown on the following pages and the following notes to assist you in drafting a will for Peter Johannsen. The will should be prepared double spaced, 12 point font, with full justification, and you are reminded to make all necessary changes for gender and number in the template which may be retrieved from the practice files.
(Practice Files: Drafts Folder: Will)

You are also asked to prepare a will cover for this will. Refer to Precedent 32.3.

PETER JOHANNSEN (no middle name) – he lives in Ajax

  # 2   appoint my wife, Martine Claire Johannsen

          OR

          alternatively – my daughter, Karyn Gail Johannsen

  # (d)   transfer to my wife, M- C- J-

  # (e)   if my wife, M- C- J-, ...

         residue of my estate to my daughter, K- G- J-

  # (f)   delete

THIS IS THE LAST WILL AND TESTAMENT of me, *, of the *, in the *, and Province of Ontario.

1.   I HEREBY REVOKE all former wills and other testamentary dispositions made by me.

2.   I NOMINATE, CONSTITUTE AND APPOINT *, to be the estate trustee(s) of this my will and other testamentary dispositions made by me; if the said * shall predecease me or not survive me for thirty (30) days, I NOMINATE, CONSITUTE AND APPOINT * to be the estate trustee of this my will. I refer to my estate trustee(s) herein, whether original or substitute, as "my Trustee".

3.   I GIVE, DEVISE, AND BEQUEATH all my property of every nature and kind and wheresoever situate, including any property over which I may have a general power of appointment, to my Trustee upon the following trusts, namely:

   (a)   to pay, out of the capital of my general estate, my just debts, funeral and testamentary expenses, and all estate, legacies, succession and inheritance duties and taxes, whether imposed by or pursuant to the laws of any domestic or foreign jurisdiction whatsoever, that may be payable in connection with the property passing (or deemed to pass by any governing law) on my death, or in connection with any insurance on my life or in connection with any gift or benefit given or provided by me either in my lifetime, or by survivorship, or by this my will or by any codicil thereto, and whether such taxes and duties be payable in respect of estates or interests which fall into possession at my death or at any subsequent time;

   (b)   to use his/her/their discretion in the realization of my estate, save those items which are particularly named herein, with power to my Trustee to sell, call in, and convert into money part of my estate not consisting of money at such time or times, in such manner and upon such terms, and either for cash or credit or for part cash or part credit as my Trustee may in his/her/their uncontrolled discretion decide upon, or to postpone such conversion of my estate or any part or parts thereof for such length of time as he may think best;

   (c)   to pay out and charge to the capital of my estate my just debts, funeral and testamentary expenses and all estate inheritance and succession duties or taxes that may be payable in connection with any property passing on my death;

   (d)   to pay or transfer to *, the entire residue of my estate for his/her/their sole use and benefit absolutely;

(e) if * should predecease me or fail to survive me for a period of thirty days, I give the entire residue of my estate to *, or his/her/their surviving issue, for his/her/their sole use and benefit absolutely;

(f) in the event that * predeceases me leaving no issue surviving, I hereby give, devise, and bequeath my estate to *, or his/her/their surviving issue, for his/her/their sole use and benefit absolutely;

4. I HEREBY DECLARE that my Trustee, when making investments for my estate, shall not be limited to investments authorized by law for Trustees but may make any investment which in their uncontrolled discretion they consider advisable, and my said Trustee shall not be liable for any loss that may happen to my estate in connection with any such investment made by them in good faith.

IN TESTIMONY WHEREOF I have to this my last will and testament, written upon this and the * preceding pages, subscribed my name this   day of *, 20**.

3. CORRESPONDENCE - JOHANSSEN

You are asked to prepare the following letter for Michael Colucci's signature.

Dear Peter

I enclose your revised will for your review. I believe it reflects the instructions you gave me last week. If you have any questions or wish any changes, please do not hesitate to contact me.

If the will is satisfactory, however, please call my legal assistant to arrange an appointment so that you may execute the will. Pursuant to your instructions once this will has been executed by you we will retain the original copy at our firm for safekeeping and provide you with a photocopy of the executed will for your records.

Yours very truly,

etc.

4. CODICIL – RICHARDS

Amanda Richards, an old client of the firm, has asked that a codicil be prepared to her will dated April 17, 1995. She is expected to come in and sign this codicil later this week. You are asked to:

(a) *Prepare the following draft codicil in good form*

(b) *Prepare the necessary affidavit of execution of codicil with yourself as deponent. Peter Grant will be the other witness.*

THIS IS A CODICIL to the LAST WILL AND TESTAMENT of me, AMANDA CAROLINE RICHARDS, of the - Brampton which last will and testament bears the date the 17th day of April, 1995.

1. I REVOKE the appointment of HELEN MARY RICHARDS as an estate trustee contained in paragraph 2 of my said last will and testament, and I appoint my nephew <u>Mark Donald Baker</u> as Estate Trustee of my said last will and testament in the place and stead of the said HELEN MARY RICHARDS.

2. In all other respects I confirm my said will.

SIGNED …

5. POWER OF ATTORNEY – LAWRIE

Mary Elizabeth Lawrie, an elderly client of Hill, Johnston & Grant, has requested that Peter Grant prepare a power of attorney for property for her. She wishes her daughters, Shannon Lynn D'Souza and Heather Anne Lawrie to be appointed her power of attorney to act jointly and severally and with no restrictions. If either one of her daughters cannot act as attorney, then Mrs. Lawrie wishes her grandson Craig D'Souza to be the substitute attorney with no restrictions.

You are asked to prepare the power of attorney, which will be executed at the offices of Hill, Johnston & Grant next Monday. Refer to Precedent 32.8. The template of the power of attorney is available to be retrieved. **(Practice Files: Forms Folder – File: POA Property)**

C. LEGAL TERMINOLOGY

After completing this exercise you should be able to spell and define the following legal terms. Read the definitions shown below. Then select the correct term and match it with the words or phrase that best matches it in meaning, and write the correct term in the space provided. There are more terms than definitions.

Legal Terms

will	estate	testate
holographic	estate trustee	intestate
testator	testatrix	codicil
non compos mentis	*per stirpes*	grantor
beneficiary	next of kin	residue

Definitions

1. state of having a will

2. by (family) branch

3. a handwritten will

4. real and personal property of an individual

5. balance of estate after all specific bequests have been made

6. person who makes a will - female

7. the document that adds to or amends a will

8. not of sound mind

9. closest blood relatives of a deceased person

10. term for person who gives a power of attorney

11. person who makes a will – male

12. state of not having a will

13. personal representative appointed to administer an estate

14. a person who receives something under a will

CHAPTER 33 – ASSIGNMENTS
Administration of Estates

A. LEGAL OFFICE PROCEDURES

1. OPEN FILE – ESTATE OF PERCIVAL KENNETH BELL

You are to open a file for this estate matter. Prepare the new matter form/label. Fees will be on a time basis. This matter has been assigned file number 05058/1425. Refer to the estate information sheet shown on the following page for further information.

B. LEGAL DOCUMENT PRODUCTION

1. AFFIDAVITS OF EXECUTION – BELL ESTATE

(a) *As the will and codicil predate the requirement for affidavits of execution of will or codicil at the time they were executed, these affidavits must be prepared now. You will need to prepare an affidavit of execution for the will to be sworn by Doreen Joyce Spring; and for the codicil to be sworn by Peter T. Grant. Refer to Precedent 32.7.*

(b) *The will and the codicil will both need to be marked and attached as Exhibit "A" to the appropriate affidavit. Refer to Figure 33.2.*

In a *bona fide* application, you would, of course, have the entire original will and codicil. For purposes of this assignment, assume that the last pages of the will and codicil that are provided on pages 219 and 221 of this assignment material represent the full original documents.

2. NOTICE OF APPLICATION FOR A CERTIFICATE OF APPOINTMENT OF ESTATE TRUSTEE WITH A WILL – BELL ESTATE

Prepare the notice to be sent to all beneficiaries under the will. Refer to the estate information sheet for the required information – all beneficiaries are of legal age and mentally competent. Refer to Precedent 33.1. You would normally, of course, attach a copy of the entire will, or the pertinent paragraph(s) if there are specific bequests, to the notice of application. Note that any beneficiary who is an applicant, does not need to be sent the notice.

3. AFFIDAVIT OF SERVICE OF NOTICE – BELL ESTATE

Prepare an affidavit of service of notice of an application for a certificate of appointment of estate trustee to be sworn by Henry Albert Greer sometime next week. Refer to Precedent 33.2.

ESTATE INFORMATION SHEET

1. **Name**: Bell, Percival Kenneth

2. **Address**: 19 Merton Blvd. Toronto ON M8R 2K2

3. **Marital Status**: Widower

4. **Occupation**: Accountant

5. **SIN**: 986 123 054

6. **Date of Birth**: March 17, 1930 – Toronto

7. **Date of Death**: February 10, 20xx – Toronto

8. **Date of Will**: April 3, 1992
   Witnesses: Doreen Spring (a law clerk in our office who now lives in Mississauga)
   Alissa DeRosa (solicitor who has retired from our firm; lives in Toronto)

9. **Date of Codicil(s)**: October 28, 1994
   Witnesses: Peter T. Grant
   Ben Doverland (a former law clerk of our office; lives in Markham)

10. **Executors**: Henry Albert Green, Pharmacist
    14 Elm Street, Whitby ON L6M 2K9
    Telephone: 905-432-9860

    Gilbert John Bell, Merchant (son)
    35 Paulwood Street, Toronto ON M3R 2N1

11. **Beneficiaries**: Gilbert John Bell (son & executor) – **residue of estate**

Anne Marie Lee (not related) 400 Ellesmere Road, Apt. 600 Scarborough ON M1K 4G3 **Bequest**: $10,000	Jane Marie Greer (sister) 14 Elm Street Whitby ON L6M 2K9 **Bequest**: $25,000
John Craig Bell (nephew) 2 Water Street Pickering ON L2J 4K3 **Bequest**: $10,000	Hillcrest United Church 1400 Markham Road Scarborough ON M2S 4B2 **Bequest**: $5,000

12. **Assets**:

Description	Value
House – 19 Merton Blvd. Toronto (sole owner)	$520,000
Contents	$ 10,000
Chequing Account, Royal Bank	$ 10,000
Savings Account, Royal Bank	$ 35,000
GICs, Royal Bank	$100,000
Ontario Savings Bonds	$120,000
RRSPs	$ 70,000

7.

this will shall be read and construed as if she had predeceased me, except as to her appointment as executrix.

   IN TESTIMONY WHEREOF I have to this my last will and testament, written upon this and six preceding pages of paper, subscribed my name this *3rd* day of April, 1992.

SIGNED, PUBLISHED AND DECLARED) by the said testator, **PERCIVAL KENNETH**) **BELL**, as and for his last will and testament,) in the presence of us, both present at the same) time, who at his request, in his presence and) in the presence of each other, have hereunto) subscribed our names as witnesses.)	*Percival K. Bell*

Doreen Joyce Spring
400 Davisville Avenue, Apt. 204
Toronto Ontario M5J 4W2

Alicia DeRosa
24 Elm Street
Toronto Ontario M2S 4K9

2.

my nephew Henry Albert Greer as an executor and trustee of my said last will and testament in the place and stead of Margaret Ann Bell.

3. In all other respects I confirm my said will.

IN TESTIMONY WHEREOF I have to this codicil to my last will and testament, subscribed my name this 28th day of October, 1994.

SIGNED, PUBLISHED AND DECLARED)
by the said testator, **PERCIVAL KENNETH**)
BELL, as and for a codicil to his last will and)
testament, in the presence of us, both present)
at the same time, who at his request, in his)   *Percival K. Bell*
presence and in the presence of each other,)
have hereunto subscribed our names as)
witnesses.)
)
)
Peter T. Grant)
)
40 Parklawn Drive)
)
Toronto Ontario M3M 4G9)
)
)
Ben Doverland)
)
20 Ridley Blvd.)
)
Toronto Ontario M5N 4G3)

4. APPLICATION FOR A CERTIFICATE OF APPOINTMENT OF ESTATE TRUSTEE WITH A WILL – BELL ESTATE

You are now asked to prepare the application. Refer to Precedent 33.3, as well as the estate information sheet and the following information:

(a) Mr. Bell was a widower; he did not marry after the date of his will.
(b) No marriage had been dissolved by a divorce judgment or declared null after the date of the will.
(c) No witness to the will or codicil is beneficiary or the spouse of a beneficiary under the will or codicil.
(d) Calculate the value of the estate based on the assets listed in the estate information sheet.

The will and the codicil will both need to be appropriately marked and attached as exhibits to the application. Refer to Figure 33.2.

5. CERTIFICATE OF APPOINTMENT OF ESTATE TRUSTEE WITH A WILL – BELL ESTATE

Prepare the draft certificate to be submitted with the application. Leave the court file number and the date blank. Refer to Figure 35.7 in your text as precedent.

6. FILING APPLICATION – BELL ESTATE

The application for a certificate of appointment of estate trustee with a will is now ready for submission. Requisition the necessary cheque for the correct amount of court fees, and prepare the following letter for Peter Grant's signature:

DELIVERED
Estates Office, Superior Court of Justice, 330 University Avenue,
7th Floor, Toronto ON M5G 1R7

Please find enclosed the following in connection with the above estate:
1. Application for certificate of appointment of estate trustee with a will
2. Original will of P-K-Bell dated ??
3. Affidavit of execution of will
4. Original codicil of P-K-Bell dated ??
5. Affidavit of execution of codicil
6. Affidavit of service of notice of application
7. Draft certificate of appointment
8. Our certified trust cheque in the amount of $???

Yours truly etc...

7. **RENUNCIATION OF PRIOR RIGHT TO A CERTIFICATE OF APPOINTMENT OF ESTATE TRUSTEE WITHOUT A WILL AND CONSENT TO APPLICANT'S APPOINTMENT AS ESTATE TRUSTEE WITHOUT A WILL – JAMAL ESTATE**

Selima Jamal has consulted Peter Grant following the recent death of her husband, Nadir Jamal, who died intestate. You are now asked to prepare some of the required documents for this estate matter. The parties will be attending at Hill, Johnston & Grant's offices next week to execute all the documents.

Mrs. Jamal wishes her son, Ahmed Jamal, to be appointed as estate trustee and will not require an administration bond to be filed. Because she has a prior right to be estate trustee, you are asked to prepare the necessary renunciation and the consent. Refer to Precedents 33.7 and 33.8.

8. **APPLICATION FOR CERTIFICATE OF APPOINTMENT OF ESTATE TRUSTEE WITHOUT A WILL – JAMAL ESTATE**

You are also asked to prepare the application for certificate of appointment. Refer to Precedent 33.6 and the following information to complete this document.

Deceased: *Nadir Jamal, Retired Travel Agent*
Address: 44 Cairns Road, Newmarket ON L2N 4Y7
born August 1, 1935
died 10th of last month, 20xx, in Newmarket
There were no other marriages or divorces.

Estate Trustee to be appointed: *Ahmed Jamal (son), Teacher*
182 Halton Drive
Richmond Hill ON L1N 4J2
Telephone: 905-680-3241

Persons Entitled to Share in the Estate: *Selima Jamil (wife)*
Ahmed Jamal (son)

Assets:

Real Property:	44 Cairns Drive Newmarket held as joint tenant with spouse	$275,000
Personal Property:	Car, GICs, RRSPs in deceased's name	$ 90,000

9. **CERTIFICATE OF APPOINTMENT OF ESTATE TRUSTEE WITHOUT A WILL – JAMAL ESTATE**

Prepare the draft certificate to be forwarded with the other documents when they are filed. Adapt Precedent 33.5 – the only required change is for the appointment to be "without" a will instead of "with" a will.

10. DECLARATION & CORRESPONDENCE - NORDSTROM ESTATE

You have been asked to prepare the following letter and statutory declaration (refer to Precedent 7.6) in final form for Peter Grant's signature.

Letter to James R. Zedor, Mason & Walker
Re: Estate of Gordon Nordstrom & Graham,
Sale of Lake Erie Property

We now enclose a statutory declaration by Lisa Karen Tremont regarding the marital status of her brother Joshua Petroff and as to his possession of the above property. ¶ We have been unable to obtain any evidence regarding the death of Ruth Bradfield, the wife of the grantor in instrument 5623, but it seems that your client would be sufficiently protected by the Family Law Act & the declaration of ownership contained in the enclosed declaration. ¶ We are today sending Bond & Clarkson the death certificate & other papers herein, with instructions to deliver them to you tomorrow on receipt of a certified cheque to the order of the estate trustees of the above estate for $95,565.44. ¶ It is understood that if any payments of rent for next month are received by the vendors, they will be forwarded to you.
Yours very truly, etc.

Statutory Declaration...

IN THE MATTER OF the Estate of
GORDON NORDSTROM, late of
the City of Windsor, in the
County of Essex, deceased
AND IN THE MATTER OF title
to the property known as Lot 74,
Plan 4873, Niagara

I, LISA KAREN TREMONT, of the - she lives in Oshawa ----
1. I am the sister of the late Joshua Pitroff, late of the City of Niagara Falls, in the Regional Municipality of Niagara, who died on or about the 17th day of January, 20xx (this year).
2. My said brother was a joint owner with the late GORDON NORDSTROM of certain properties known as a Lot 74, Niagara, located on Lake Erie.
3. At the time of his death in January (this year), my said brother was an unmarried man. To the best of my knowledge my said brother never married during his lifetime.
DECLARED etc.

C. LEGAL TERMINOLOGY

After completing this exercise you should be able to spell and define the following legal terms. Read the definitions shown below. Then select the correct term and match it with the words or phrase that best matches it in meaning, and write the correct term in the space provided. There are more terms than definitions.

Legal Terms

notice of application for certificate of appointment of estate trustee with / without a will
certificate of appointment of estate trustee with / without a will
per capita
devise
administration bond
affidavit of service
surety
renunciation
bequest
consent
personal property
real property

Definitions

1. a house would be an example of this _____

2. to give up a right to something _____

3. document authorizing the personal representative to administer the estate of a deceased person _____

4. a person or company who promises to satisfy the obligation of another in event of default by that person _____

5. a car would be an example of this _____

6. document swearing to the delivery of the notice of application of estate trustee with / without a will _____

7. document served on all beneficiaries of an estate _____

8. to give permission for something _____

9. a gift of real property by a will _____

10. document required if there is no will or if the estate trustee is not named in a will _____

11. a gift of personal property by a will _____

CHAPTER 34 – ASSIGNMENTS
Settling the Estate

A. LEGAL OFFICE PROCEDURES

There are no legal office procedures exercises for this chapter.

B. LEGAL DOCUMENT PRODUCTION

1. NOTARIAL CERTIFICATE – BELL ESTATE

The certificate of appointment of estate trustee with a will has now been received in this estate. It was issued yesterday as number 344557. You are requested to prepare a notarial certificate. Refer to Precedent 34.1. Note that the actual office environment, you would prepare several copies, as many estate procedures require the submission of a notarial copy of the certificate.

2. CORRESPONDENCE – BELL ESTATE

Peter Grant has drafted a letter to one of the insurance companies in which Mr. Bell held a policy of insurance. He asks you to prepare this letter for his signature and to prepare a similar letter to the other insurance company shown on the estate information sheet following his instructions below:

Sun Life Assurance Company of Canada
P.O. Box 4018, Station A, Toronto M5W 2S4

Estate of Percival Kenneth Bell
Policy #L10201350

We act for the executors of the estate of P. K. Bell who died on ?? . The named beneficiary of this policy is his son, G. J. Bell. We would appreciate your advice as to the amount payable under this policy.

For 2nd letter to Royal Insurance, 400 Bay Street, Toronto ON M4A 3G2, (Policy # 4332-78891) add the following - and confirmation of our understanding that this policy was not registered as a retirement savings plan.

Yours very truly etc...

3. RELEASES OF ESTATE TRUSTEES – BELL ESTATE

Under the provisions of his will, Mr. Bell left $25,000 to his sister Jane Marie Greer, $10,000 to his goddaughter Anne Marie Lee, $10,000.00 to his nephew John Craig Bell, and $5,000.00 to Hillcrest United Church. You are asked to prepare the necessary releases for these bequests, to be held in the file until the middle of next month when the executors expect to be in a position to send the cheques for these bequests. Refer to Precedent 34.5.

4. REQUEST FOR DEATH CERTIFICATE - JAMAL ESTATE

Peter Grant asks you to request four copies of the death certificate for Mr. Jamal. His father's name was Rajesh Jamal; his mother's name was Amila Jamal, nee Kapoor. You may go to the following website to obtain the necessary form to order this certificate: **www.mgs.gov.on.ca**

5. NOTICE TO CREDITORS – JAMAL ESTATE

Prepare a notice to creditors. Claims are to be filed on or before the last day of next month. Refer to Figure 34.1.

6. CORRESPONDENCE & ACCOUNT – ESTATE OF ALBERT TREMBLAY

You are asked to prepare the following letter and account for this estate which has been wound up.

> *Letter to*
>
> *Deborah Riveiro*
>
> *Dear Deborah*
>
> *Further to our recent telephone conversation I confirm that our work in connection with this estate is now complete and I enclose herewith the following for your records:*
>
> 1. *Notices of Assesment for (last year)*
> 2. *Terminal Assessment for (this year)*
> 3. *Clearance Certificate from Canada Revenue Agency*
> 4. *Statement of Original Assets*
> 5. *Release of Executor*
>
> *I further enclose our account for our services which I trust you will find in order. It has been a pleasure working with you on this estate. If we can be of further assistance to you, please advise.*

Account -

Estate of Albert Tremblay
c/o Deborah Riveiro

TO LEGAL FEES in connection with administration of the above estate, including the following:

To meeting with estate trustee to obtain details of the assets of the Estate and review the terms of the Will of the late A - Tremblay; To preparation of the Affidavit of Execution of Will & attending on Dr. Welby at his office to swear same as witness; To preparing notarial copy of the Death Certificate & forwarding same to Royal Life Insurance and Canada Trust Company; To preparing schedule of assets together with Application for Certificate of Appointment of Estate Trsutee to the Superior Court of Justice To letter & direction to Royal Bank of Canada to pay court fees; To atending to the execution of court documents & filing the Application for Certificate of Appointment; To preparing Notice of Application for Certificate of Appointment of estate trustee and forwarding same to all beneficiaries; To collecting the information & material required by the accountant with respect to the filing of personal income tax returns for the deceased & arranging for the filing of all necessary personal income returns & obtaining notices of assessment and clearance certificate; To preparing Release of Executor & arranging for execution of same; To all attendances, telephone conversations, correspondence, etc., in all;

OUR FEE:	$1,250.00
GST	?

DISBURSEMENTS - you will need to separate these into which are subject to or not subject to GST

Photocopies	22.50
Courier	10.75
Photocopies	14.25
Estate Filing Fees	835.00
Facsimile	8.25

C. LEGAL TERMINOLOGY

After completing this exercise you should be able to spell and define the following legal terms. Read the definitions shown below. Then select the correct term and match it with the words or phrase that best matches it in meaning, and write the correct term in the space provided. There are more terms than definitions.

Legal Terms

wills	testate	null and void
beneficiary	pro rata	intestate
holographic	next of kin	administrator
per capita	codicils	testator
testatrix	*per stirpes*	administration bond
personal representative	trust	*non compos mentis*
trust	estate trustee	residue

Definitions

1. Was Mary a _____ under the terms of her father's will?

2. Since the children of the deceased son are to inherit his share of the estate, the testator obviously made the bequest _____.

3. Since the will was entirely in his handwriting, it as a _____ will.

4. The _____ of the estate after all bequests have been paid will be $50,000.

5. Because Johann died _____, Petra inherits since she is his only _____.

6. As a widower who died without a will, the estate trustee will need a/an _____.

7. The balance of the estate is to be divided equally or _____ among his children.

8. He amended his will several times, we found three _____.

9. In her will, the _____ named Catherine as her _____ to carry out her wishes.

10. She made a new will this week; as a result her will dated May 1, 2007 is _____.

11. The principal of _____ applies, because he was obviously mentally ill.

12. An executor or executrix is referred to as a/an _____ in court documents.

LEGAL TRANSCRIPTION

Introduction

The ability of a legal assistant to quickly and accurately produce documents is highly valued, including the transcription of material from audio files dictated by legal professionals. The transcription of material from audio files requires legal assistants to pull together and apply all of their skills and knowledge including keyboarding, formatting, general vocabulary and legal terminology, grammar, spelling, punctuation and proofreading.

In this section of the assignment book, you will have the opportunity to develop and practice the transcription of a variety of legal material from audio files in order to improve your skills and knowledge in producing legal documentation. As in any other skill, the only way to develop and improve it is by practicing.

Grammar/Punctuation

References texts such as the Gregg Reference Manual (McGraw-Hill Ryerson) or the Pitman Office Handbook (Copp Clark Pitman Ltd.) should be consulted when transcribing material for the insertion of correct punctuation, capitalization, paragraphing and to check for grammatical errors.

Word Usage

One of the challenges in transcribing audio files is deciding on correct word usage because the words are heard not written. For example, *there*, *their* and *they're* all sound the same, and thus you must decide which one is the correct word in the context of the material being dictated. Possessives and plural such as *plaintiff's* and *plaintiffs* also sound alike so again the decision must be made on the correct word to be used. Spellchecking will not catch errors in word usage. Additionally, a spellchecking program will catch most, but not necessarily all incorrectly spelled words and having to repeatedly use the spellchecking function to correct words considerably slows down the transcription of material.

For these reasons, in addition to the legal terminology exercises which are available at the end of each chapter of this assignment book, a series of lists of the some of the most commonly misused and misspelled words in the legal/business environment is provided on page 234. Some are true homonyms (words that sound like but have different meanings); others only sound similar and could be confused when listening to an audio tape; or are simply words that are commonly misspelled. You should review these words and be able to spell, define and correctly use each of them in a sentence. The more accurately you prepare material as you transcribe it, the less time you will spend in proofreading and correcting errors afterwards.

Proofreading

Look at the following sentence:

> Theis sntnce is fuill of erors but I'am sre yuu caan stil undrstnd it.

Research has shown that most people read the first and last letters of words when they read for information purposes. This explains how we so easily understand text messaging. However, in the business, and especially the legal, environment such errors may lead to a misunderstanding of a legal document and could have serious consequences.

Proofreading a document requires a different approach and there is no fast or easy way to master it. Each and every word, and each letter within each word, must be read to check for spelling, grammar and correct word usage within the context of the meaning of the sentence. This requires a concentration on the material, not just a skimming of it as may be done when the material is read for information purposes. Just like any other skill, such as keyboarding, speed will come with practice but the ability to focus and read in a different way for proofreading has to be developed gradually and may only be done through practice. The transcription and proofreading of the material in this assignment book will give you an opportunity to do this.

Proofreading Guidelines:

1. Read slowly and carefully, checking each word for spelling and word usage errors including possessives, singular/plural agreement, grammar, capitalization and punctuation. Make sure that each sentence reads sensibly. If it does not make sense it you, it does not make sense to just leave it. Make the necessary corrections in the document or if necessary ask for assistance in understanding what corrections should be made.

2. Check all addresses, telephone number, dates, file numbers, amounts, proper names, etc. against the reference or file material.

3. Once you have read the document through, look at the overall formatting. Formatting is a key component of legal document production especially in long documents such as wills or agreements. Many law firms use the styles function in word processing software in order to ensure consistent formatting. When you are reviewing for formatting, keep the following in mind:

    (a) Are the margins and page endings correct?
    (b) Has page numbering been used? Legal documents are usually numbered in the top centre in order to facilitate the use of such documents in record books which are bound on the left and have separate page numbering inserted in the top right corner.
    (c) Has spacing and any use of bold font been consistently applied?
    (d) Has capitalization been consistently applied? The find and replace function in word processing software can assist with this. For example, if the word *Children* is to have an initial capital throughout an agreement, use the find and replace function to search for each instance of the word within the document and check its capitalization and replace it if necessary.
    (e) Are there any missing components to the document such as the date, a subject line, file number, a signature clause or document identification?
    (f) Check to ensure that any legal document that has a prescribed form is consistent to the precedent.

4. The above may all be done on screen, but most experts agree that a final proofreading of a document should still be done of the hard copy. So once the document comes out of the printer, review it one more time before presenting it to your instructor or the lawyer.

Transcription

Just as in the actual law office environment, most punctuation and paragraphing is not dictated in the audio files that accompany this assignment book, nor is file information, such the spelling of proper names, inside addresses for letters or file numbers. You will need to insert necessary punctuation and to look up information in the reference material provided at the end of this assignment book. The index of transcription material contains information that might usually be found "in the file" provided by the lawyer in the legal office environment. Your instructor will advise which files you are to transcribe.

The **Document Description** section will let you know what type of document you are to transcribe including the approximate length of the document.

The **References Section** will list the applicable chapters and any relevant figures or precedents. Note that while is highly recommended that you have reviewed any chapters referred to, the ability to produce accurate documents in an area of law with which you may not be completely familiar may occur when you are working in a law office. The ability to adapt to new and different areas of legal practice and documentation is a necessary and ongoing proficiency that is essential in today's legal environment. It is, however, highly recommended that you do refer to any figures or precedents noted in the references section so you may more easily prepare documents that are accurately formatted. This also reflects what would occur in a law firm where you would use whatever resources are available, including precedents, to increase your speed and accuracy.

The **File Information/Additional Vocabulary** section will list the applicable file so you may locate any necessary addresses or file numbers in the reference material located at the end of this assignment book. Proper names and additional vocabulary will also be provided in this section.

Before you transcribe:

- Read ALL instructions and file information provided by the support material
- Assemble any reference material such as precedents and/or templates you may have created for letterhead, memorandum headings, or accounts

As you transcribe

- Concentrate on the content of what you are keying – be sure each sentence makes sense. Listen carefully so you hear every word said by the dictator especially small words such as prepositions like *a* or *and*. If something does not make sense, let the audio file play ahead a bit to see if this makes it clearer, and then go back and key in the material.
- Check figures, dates, names and addresses etc. as you transcribe.
- Refer to any references available, such as a reference manual, chapters in your text, figures, precedents, legal dictionary (hard copy or online) and the file information

When you finish transcribing

- Proofread carefully, using the guidelines discussed on page 232, both onscreen and after you print the document out.

COMMONLY MISSPELLED / MISUSED WORDS

1	2	3	4	5
accept	addition	affect	capital	assistance
except	edition	effect	capitol	assistants
deposition	envelop	hear	council	brake
disposition	envelope	here	counsel	break
device	formally	heir	disburse	to
devise	formerly	its	disperse	too
farther	presents	it's	leased	two
further	presence	there	least	quiet
overdo	personal	they're	passed	quit
overdue	personnel	their	past	quite
6	**7**	**8**	**9**	**10**
adapt	conscience	accede	acknowledgement	decent
adept	conscious	exceed	allusion	descent
citation	conscientious	emigrated	delusion	dissent
cite	convenience	immigrated	illusion	physical
sight	convenient	licence	formerly	physician
site	perception	license	formally	lose
wave	perceive	possession	precede	loose
waive	receipt	perseverance	proceed	rite
waiver	receive	weather	suspicious	writ
waver	receivables	whether	susceptible	write
11	**12**	**13**	**14**	**15**
acquire	assure	continual	access	coarse
inquire	ensure	continuous	excess	course
advice	insure	dew	separate	defendant
advise	precedence	do	separation	dependent
advisor	precedents	due	therefor	realize
liable	recommend	passed	therefore	realistically
libel	receive	past	patience	sheer
marital	receipt	so	patients	shear
marshal	reality	sew	persecuting	stationary
martial	realty	sow	prosecuting	stationery
16	**17**	**18**	**19**	**20**
absence	accommodate	allege	commission	defer
absent	accumulate	allegation	omission	differ
alleged	negligible	legislation	perspective	deference
cease	negligent	minutiae	prospective	intercede
seize	practice	minutes	suspicious	interfere
thorough	practice	privileged	susceptible	feasible
through	pursuant	recommend	rotation	indefensible
threw	prejudice	than	rote	liaison
unanimous	prejudicial	then	route	statue
unilateral	prescription	yield	wrote	statute

INDEX TO LEGAL TRANSCRIPTION FILES

No.	Document Description & Instructions	References	File Information & Additional Vocabulary
	Note: The first four transcription documents are articles that provide general information about the legal environment. These documents should be prepared double spaced with indented paragraphs and the headings should be centred, in all capitals, and in bold font.		
1	Law Office Structure & Personnel (530 words)	Chapters 1, 2, 3	sole practitioners Mailboxes, etc.
2	Areas of Legal Practice (540 words)	Chapters 1, 2, 3	intellectual property law mediation sole proprietor corporation
3	Legal Documentation (375 words)	Chapters 1, 2, 3	boiler plate text commercial document notarial certificates administrative tribunals statements of claim prescribed land registry office
4	Conflict of Interest (470 words)	Chapters 1, 2, 3	impartial

No.	Document Description & Instructions	References	File Information & Additional Vocabulary
5	Retainer (235 words)	Chapter 3 Precedent 3.1	Chan and Chan re Separation Agreement Mary Susan Chan
6	Memorandum (246 words)	Chapter 4 Precedent 4.1	Chan and Chan re Separation Agreement amicable mediation matrimonial home prejudgment interest
7	Letter (135 words)	Chapter 4 Precedent 4.4	Chan and Chan re Separation Agreement net family property questionnaire
8	Account (145 words)	Chapter 5 Precedent 5.2	General Motor Leasing and McLeod escrow **Disbursements:** **General Motor Leasing and McLeod** Photocopying $ 16.30 Courier Charges 23.14 Facsimile Charges 15.22 Long Distance Charges 28.95

No.	Document Description & Instructions	References	File Information & Additional Vocabulary
9	Account (200 words)	Chapter 5 Precedent 5.2	Centennial Consulting Inc. re Corporate Affairs Mark Walters Janice Gomez
		Disbursements: **Centennial Consulting re Corporate Affairs** Photocopying $ 74.50 Courier Charges 48.25 Facsimile Charges 39.53 Long Distance Charges 53.95	
10	Memorandum (160 words)	Chapters 4, 6 Precedent 4.1	Pindar ats Hadji discovery examinations trial record detrimental
11	Memorandum (of law) (684 words)	Chapter 2 (Quotations) Chapter 6 Precedent 6.1 Table 6.1	Pindar ats Hadji Stickney v. Trusz Mr. Justice Zuber Gillis v. Eagleson Fifth Amendment U.S. Constitution prejudgment interest
12	Agreement (465 words) Note: Mark Hall, President, has authority to bind the corporation – there is no corporate seal	Chapter 7 Precedents 7.1, 7.2, 7.3	Green and Black re Hall General Contracting Ltd. City of Orillia County of Simcoe Lots 3 and 4, Plan 789 487 and 489 Queen Anne Drive holdback *Construction Lien Act*

No.	Document Description & Instructions	References	File Information & Additional Vocabulary
13	Letter (235 words)	Chapters 4, 7	Green and Black re Hall General Contracting Ltd. Mason & Walker
14	Letter (140 words)	Chapters 4, 8	General Motor Leasing and McLeod $45,000
15	Letter (230 words)	Chapters 4, 8	Brown-Gelon Company and Matthews Alison Matthews $12,240 $734.40 $12,974.40
16	Letter (205 words)	Chapters 4, 9	Anderson v. Penmar Services of Canada Limited breach of contract
17	Affidavit (390 words) Refer to p. 60 of this assignment book for the general heading in this proceeding.	Chapter 9 Precedent 9.4	Anderson v. Penmar Services of Canada Limited Humber Construction Company Inc. Brandon Mississauga James Carlson

No.	Document Description & Instructions	References	File Information & Additional Vocabulary
18	Letter	Chapters 4, 10	Gordon's Art Gallery Inc. re Corporate Affairs ABC Heating & Air Conditioning Inc. 426 Water Street Toronto ON M1A 3P8 sculptures $24,000
19	Statement of Claim Refer to p. 60 of this assignment book for the general heading in this proceeding.	Chapter 10 Precedent 10.1	Anderson v. Penmar Services of Canada Limited $40,000 architectural designer $46.00 breach of contract
20	Letter	Chapters 4, 11	Gordon's Art Gallery Inc. re Corporate Affairs $25,000
21	Memorandum	Chapters 4, 11	Juliette's Boutiques Limited re Nancy White
22	Memorandum	Chapters 4, 12	Metha v. Levin Julie Metha Samuel Levin Provincial Mutual Quick v. MacKenzie

No.	Document Description & Instructions	References	File Information & Additional Vocabulary
23	Statement of Defence See Precedent 10.1 in your text for the general heading.	Chapter 12 Precedent 12.2	Delos-Rayes ats Williamson allegations
24	Affidavit of Peter T. Grant See p. 81 of assignment book for general heading.	Chapters 9, 13 Precedent 9.4	Campbell v. Butler verily
25	Letter (250 words)	Chapters 4, 13	Campbell v. Butler merited affirming unwarranted
26	Letter (150 words)	Chapters 4, 14	Pindar ats Hadji
27	Affidavit of William McClelland (270 words) See Precedent 15.1 in text for the general heading in this proceeding.	Chapters 9, 15 Precedent 9.4	McClelland and Holman Court File No. 96621 *Crown Administration of Estates Act*, R.S.O. 1990, c. C.47 Francis McClelland Thomas McClelland George McClelland Jeffrey Holman

No.	Document Description & Instructions	References	File Information & Additional Vocabulary
28	Order (375 words) See p. 108 of this assignment book for general heading	Chapters 15, 16 Precedent 16.2	Agosto and Wyers Court File No. 989774 Madam Justice Stellar 393 University Avenue 46 Grandlake Court, Toronto interim support *sine die*
29	Letter (150 words)	Chapters 4, 16	Trimble v. Scott King case
30	Order (150 words) Court File No. 468781	Chapter 16 Precedent 16.2	Centennial Consulting Inc. and Thompson The Honourable Mr. Justice Black Business Corporations Act, R.S.O. 1990, c. B.16 Jason Fisher
31	Letter (200 words)	Chapters 4, 16	Centennial Consulting Inc. and Thompson notarial copy, abide
32	Release (225 words)	Chapters 7, 17 Precedent 7.9	Metha v. Levin Julie Metha Mississauga, Peel Samuel Levin

No.	Document Description & Instructions	References	File Information & Additional Vocabulary
33	Settlement Agreement	Chapters 7, 17 Precedents 7.1, 7.2, 7.3	Maharwood et al. and Pendergast et al. Henrietta Jane Maharwood Jeffery Boyd Maharwood Maurice James Pendergast Joseph George Willoughby
34	Separation Agreement (1000 words)	Chapters 7, 18, 19 Precedents 7.1, 7.2, 7.3	Chan and Chan July 5, 2000 Kelly Anne Chan Patrick John Chan June 15, 2002 75 kilometres
35	Letter (160 words)	Chapters 4, 18, 19	Chan and Chan Paragraph 1.09
36	Memorandum (of law) (370 words)	Chapter 2 (Quotations) Chapters 6, 18, 19 Precedent 6.1 Table 6.1	Chan and Chan Burgess and Burgess Mr. Justice Weiler Courts of Justice Act, R.S.O. 1990, c. C.43 Millicone v. Millicone Starkman v. Starkman
37	Letter (390 words)	Chapters 4, 20-27	Drydale re Walters

No.	Document Description & Instructions	References	File Information & Additional Vocabulary
38	Option to Purchase Agreement (930 words) Sheila McFarlane, President & James Bolger, Treasurer will sign for Hawick Holdings Ltd. under the corporate seal	Chapters 7, 20-27 Precedents 7.1, 7.2, 7.3	Hawick Holdings Ltd. re Rennick Mary L. Rennick $50,000 $500,000 Land Registry Office $2,500 encumbrances
39	Letter (170 words)	Chapters 4, 20-27	Khan purchase from Smythe Unit 515, 9845 Welby Avenue Burlington Instrument No. 476089 Kenneth and Marilyn Smythe Emilio DeSanto Halton
40	Letter (165 words)	Chapters 4, 20-27	Abbas, Discharge of Mortgage Alex Wong $23,000.00 $434.50 $23,435.50
41	Letter (190 words)	Chapters 4, 20-27	Smiley, Roger re Estate of Ronald Smiley Heyer Mortgage, 431 Niagara Road, Kingston Instrument No. 644281 Boston Fire and Marine Policy No. P88764 Main & Norris O.L.S.

No.	Document Description & Instructions	References	File Information & Additional Vocabulary
42	Letter (190 words)	Chapters 4, 20-27	Hawick Holdings Ltd. re Rennick
43	Security Agreement (650 words) Bruce MacPherson, President will sign on behalf of Mohawk & Joseph Minovski, Vice-President will sign on behalf of Algonquin. Both companies have corporate seals	Chapters 7, 28-31 Precedents 7.1, 7.2, 7.3	Mohawk Industries Inc. re Algonquin Permanent Trust collateral promissory note $200,000.00 contingent unencumbered remedies successors and assigns
44	Letter (700 words)	Chapters 4, 28-31	Green, John re Paperback Publishing Joseph R. King liquidation, liquidator Business Corporations Act Markdale Inc. Ministry roundabout Mr. Richardson
45	Minutes (445 words)	Chapters 28-31 Precedent 30.6	Martin-Moore Productions Limited James Martin Kenneth Moore Jessica Moore PricewaterhouseCoopers LLP Walter Loomis

No.	Document Description & Instructions	References	File Information & Additional Vocabulary
46	Letter (120 words)	Chapters 4, 28-31	Gordon's Art Gallery Inc. re Corporate Affairs
47	Account (150 words) **Disbursements** Photocopies - $14.20 Courier - $25.00	Chapters 5, 28-31 Precedent 5.2	Gordon's Art Gallery Inc. re Corporate Affairs ABC Heating & Air Conditioning Inc.
48	Will (390 words)	Chapter 32 Precedent 32.4	Gary Martin Brooks David James Brooks Marilyn Jean Brooks Fort Erie *per stirpes*
49	Letter (150 words)	Chapters 4, 31-34	Marriot, Victoria re Lillian Vlaznezki
50	Letter (345 words)	Chapters 4, 31-34	Mayhue, Gordon re Wills predecease Christopher Lake Muskoka capital gains

REFERENCE MATERIAL

for the law firm of

Hill, Johnston & Grant

**17 Princess Street South
Suite 2501
Toronto ON M8Y 3N5**

or

| *Your:* | *City* | *Province* | *Postal Code* |

Areas of Legal Practice Codes 248

Staff List...249

Index of Forms 250

Matter/Client Numbers 251

Address List...255

Proofreader's Marks 262

AREAS OF LEGAL PRACTICE CODES

01	Administrative Law
02	Appeals – Provincial
03	Appeals – Supreme Court of Canada
04	Business Law
05	Civil Litigation
06	Civil Litigation – Small Claims Court
07	Corporate
08	Corporate – Non-Resident
09	Corporate / Commercial
10	Environmental
11	Entertainment
12	Estates Administration
13	Family Law
14	Immigration
15	Intellectual Property
16	Real Estate – Residential
17	Real Estate Commercial
18	Taxation
19	Wills
20	General

STAFF LIST

NAME	POSITION	STAFF NO.	LAW SOCIETY NO. *(if applicable)*	HOURLY RATE *(if applicable)*
BONILLA, Mitra Josie	Associate	004	67832B	$175.00
COLUCCI, Michael Dominic	Associate	007	76331C	$200.00
DUBOIS, Christopher F.	Associate	012	46682D	$175.00
GRANT, Peter Thomas	Partner	015	12345G	$350.00
HILL, Frank Patrick	Partner	002	69439H	$350.00
JOHNSTON, Edward Neil	Partner	025	12471J	$350.00
PORTER, Lauren Michelle	Associate	031	78090P	$175.00
RITCHIE, Lynda Carol	Partner	035	42212R	$275.00
RIVEIRO, Paul	Associate	038	43578R	$175.00
EMERY, Patricia Forzana	Articling Student	205		$50.00
PODOBA, Howard Gordon	Articling Student	206		$50.00
ARMSTRONG, Marie J.	Law Clerk	305		$50.00
HUSSAIN, Thomas E.	Law Clerk	310		$50.00
STAUFFER, Jennifer M.	Law Clerk	320		$50.00
FISHER, Jason	Law Clerk	401		$50.00
ASPIN, Margaret	Office Manager	440		
SHARPE, Sylvia	Legal Assistant	440		

INDEX OF FORMS

The following is a list of the common forms and templates that the Hill, Johnston & Grant law firm uses. These may be accessed at http://www.legaloffice.nelson.com website by clicking on Student Resources and selecting the Forms folder.

Form	File Name
Accounting Forms	
Cash Receipt	Cash Receipts
Cheque Requisition	Cheque
Daily Time Record	Time Record
Petty Cash	Petty Cash
Client Records Forms	
New Matter Form	Matter Form
Tickler Slips	Tickler
Document Templates	
Acknowledgement and Direction (e-reg)	Acknowledgement
Document Registration Agreement (e-reg)	Registration Agmt
Directors' Register	Directors Register
Fax Cover Page	Fax Cover
Power of Attorney (Property)	POA Property
Purchase Reporting Letter (Residential)	Purchase Report
Sale Reporting Letter (Residential)	Sale Report
Shareholders' Ledger	Share Ledger
Shareholders' Register	Share Register
Stock Transfer Ledger	Stock Transfer
Will Template	Will

MATTER / CLIENT NUMBERS

A

AGOSTO, Eterna
and Wyers　　　　　　　　　　05082/1451

ANDERSON, Kevin J.
re Penmar Services of Canada　　04955/1386

ANDERSON, C.
re Power of Atttorney　　　　　　04943/0091

ANDERSON, R.
re Peterson　　　　　　　　　　04765/0076
re Pickering　　　　　　　　　　04914/0076

APPLEGATE HOLDINGS
re Corporate Affairs　　　　　　04932/0087

ARGUS PROPERTIES
LIMITED
sale to Chang　　　　　　　　　05603/1328

ABBAS, Faisal
re Discharge of Mortgage　　　　04891/1934

B

BELL, Percival Kenneth
re Estate of　　　　　　　　　　05058/1425

BLACK and others
v. Humber Tool & Dye　　　　　04924/1027

BROWN-GELON COMPANY
re Matthews　　　　　　　　　　04951/0057
re Corporate Affairs　　　　　　05061/0057

C

CAMP　　　　　　　　　　　　04806/0614
re Miyata

CAMPBELL, Judith
v. Butler　　　　　　　　　　　05084/1452

CENTENNIAL CONSULTING
INC.
re Corporate Affairs　　　　　　04421/0891
re Thompson　　　　　　　　　09932/0891

CHAN, Mary
re Separation Agreement　　　　09125/9015

COCHRANE, J.
re White et al　　　　　　　　　04926/0719

COLLISTER
ats Dees　　　　　　　　　　　04726/1228

CRENWOOD
re Staufferdale　　　　　　　　04642/1189

D

DELOS-RAYES
ats Williamson　　　　　　　　05001/1384

DROHAN (MARTIN) LIMITED
re Alistair Cormack　　　　　　05016/0786

DRYDALE, H.
re Walters　　　　　　　　　　04817/0768

DURHAM TECHNOLOGY INC.
re Corporate Matters　　　　　　07922/4801
re Markham Enterprises Ltd.　　06811/4801

MATTER / CLIENT NUMBERS

E

EAST HARDWARE LIMITED
re Corporate Affairs — 03063/0009
re Collections — 04987/0009
re Graham — 04902/0009
re: v. Masterwood — 04999/0009

EAST, Hoaln
re General Affairs — 05047/0996
re Purchase from Woodworth — 05017/0996

EAST, Peter & Leslie
v. East — 05501/1466

ELVIDGE, S.
and Elvidge — 05036/1416

F

FARRIER
v. Wyers — 04973/1364

FISHER, Jason
Re Hawchukwood — 04928/1317

FITZGIBBONS
and Fitzgibbons — 04971/1362

590 STEPHEN DRIVE
re Corporate Affairs — 04621/0862

G

GENERAL FOOD EQUIPMENT
Re 1853222 Ontario Limited — 04978/1369

GENERAL MOTORS LEASING
re McLeod — 04979/0080

GEORGIAN TECHNOLOGY INC.
ats Bayside Electronics Ltd. — 04865/1175

GORDON'S ART GALLERY INC.
re Corporate Affairs — 09110/9002

GREEN, John S.
re Paperback Publishing Company — 04984/1301
re Hall Contracting — 04963/1301

GREGLON ESTATES
sale to Veneracion — 04984/1374

H

HAGAN, Brendan and Priscilla
purchase from O'Hearn — 05009/1391

HALCHUK, Gregor I.
ats Waldon et al. — 04855/1081

HANDEL, Hubert
re Estate — 04821/0521

HARTWOOD, Andrew & Grace
purchase from Harvey — 05604/1329

HAWICK HOLDINGS LTD.
re Rennick — 08412/3882

HOWARD, Ernest & Jane
sale to Singh — 05602/1149

HUMBER CASUALTY
re Etobicoke Automotive — 04569/0297

MATTER / CLIENT NUMBERS

H

HUMPHRIES, Carew P.
and Humphries   05708/1182

HUMREX HOLDINGS LIMITED
re incorporation   05125/0091

J

JAMAL, Nadir
re Estate of   04829/9072

JOHANNSEN, Peter
re Will   05504/3802

JONES, Henry
re Expropriation   04756/1262

JULIETTE'S BOUTIQUES LIMITED
re White   05002/0482

K

KNIGHT, Victoria
re Brownlee Mortgage   04682/0982

KHAN, Ali
purchase from Smythe   03801/0321

L

LEWIS, Walter
re Lewis   04919/1308
re Humber Management   04957/1308

LITTLE and CLELLAND
re Agreement   04697/1212

M

MAHARWOOD et al.
v. Pendergast et. al.   04965/1356

MARRIOTT, Victoria
re Lillian Vlaznezski   04835/0504

MARTIN, Mara & HANSON
re Marriage Contract   05003/1386

MARTINEZ, Tony & Mary
re discharge of mortgage   05221/1461

MATTHEWS, John R.
and Matthews

MAYHUE, Gordon
re Wills   09130/9012

McCLELLAND, William
and Holman

METHA, Julie
re Levin   09140/9016

N

NORDSTROM, Gordon
Estate of   08410/1780

O

1975311 ONTARIO LIMITED
et al. ats Porter Building Supplies   05005/1387

MATTER / CLIENT NUMBERS

P

PALMER, Marylynn
v. Rose — 05096/1461

PETERSON, Ryan & Kelly
re sale to Anderson — 05022/0598

PINDAR, Richard
ats Hadji — 09105/9003

POTTIN, Joyce
re Pottin — 04929/8925

PRENNAN-VANCE
re Corporate Affairs — 04905/1299

PRESTON, John
Re Centre Lease Agreement — 04683/1201

Q

QUADRINI, Robert J.
re Separation Agreement

R

RICHARDSON, Jason
re Estate of — 04657/0892

RIVEIRO, D
re Riveiro — 05061/1437

RODRIGUES, Elian J.
and Rodrigues — 09241/6804

ROUSSEAU, Jason & Dorothy
purchase from Shafer — 05605/1330

S

SMILEY, Roger
re Estate of Ronald Smiley — 02604/7132

SMITH BORDER COMPANY
re Corporate Affairs — 04941/1282

STEEB et al.
re 1723680 Ontario Limited — 04966/1357

T

TREMBLAY, Albert
re Estate of — 06604/9801

TRIMBLE, Donna
v. Scott — 05902/3285

U, V

VLASNEZSKI, Lillian
re Will — 04981/1372

W - Z

WEBSTER et al.
re Holland and others — 04930/1330

WHITE and others
ats Cochrane — 05046/1287

ZEKAS, Marguerite
re Will — 06641/1390

ADDRESS LIST

NAME, ADDRESS and Contact Name(s), if applicable	TELEPHONE (as applicable)		
	BUSINESS	FACSIMILE	RESIDENCE

A

ABC MORTGAGE LENDERS INC.
974 Raspwood Drive, Toronto ON M4V 8W5   416.225.9450   416.225.9451

ALGONQUIN PERMANENT TRUST COMPANY
500 Tower Road, Newmarket ON L6K 9V2   905.422.3300   905.422.3380

ANDERSON, Kevin J.
400 Duncan Dr, Unit 200, Mississauga ON L6X 4V9   905.338.2809

ANDERSON, Ronald & Kelly   (Ronald)
174 Prince William Avenue, Toronto ON M4Y 8C3   416.291.6609   416.444.0001

APPLEGATE HOLDINGS LIMITED
79 Legge Road, Suite 460, Newmarket ON L4V 9S3 905.789.4000   905.789.4100

ARMSTRONG, WARD & SIEGEL
Barristers & Solicitors
16 Montreal Street West, Whitby ON L4R 8C2   905.687.4682   905.687.4690
    Colin W. King
    Katherine R. Siegel
    Burt M. Ward

B

BROWN GELON-COMPANY LIMITED
26 Glenaden Avenue East, Toronto ON M8Y 2L7   416.965.4340   416.965.4341
    John Brown, President, Jennifer Gelon, CFO

BROWNLEE, Martin J., Barrister & Solicitor
30 Lake Crescent, Pickering ON L7Y 4J9   905.645.5350   905.645.5351

C

CAMPBELL, Judith
42 Gleneden Drive, Brampton ON L6R 3S9   905.578.8320

CENTENNIAL CONSULTING LTD.
4000 Birchmount Ave., Suite 500
Toronto ON M3D 4K9   416.439.5500   416.439.5505
    Michelle Wang, President

NAME, ADDRESS and Contact Name(s), if applicable	TELEPHONE (as applicable)		
	BUSINESS	FACSIMILE	RESIDENCE
CHAN, Mary S. 46 Stony Way, Unit 40, Scarborough ON M5J 7K2	416.891.3380		416.289.9214
COLLINS & YOUNG, Barristers & Solicitors 55 Main Street, Havelock ON K0L 9Z8	705.345.7898	705.345.7899	
COOKSON, OAKVILLE, MATTHEWS & PALMER Barristers & Solicitors Suite 73, Calgary-Dominion Centre P.O. Box 940, Calgary AB T2R 0B4	403.445.8200	403.445.8201	

D

DELOS-RAYES, Henry Armand R.R. #1, Honey Harbour, ON L9K 4S7			705.654.3289
DRYDALE, Howard E. 9 Bay Street, Calgary AB T2V 2C3	403.781.5777	403.781.5277	
DROHAN (MARTIN) LIMITED Suite 121, 44 Prince Street, Toronto ON M8R 5J9	416.324.9681.	416.324.9682	
DURHAM TECHNOLOGY INC. 300 Parkside Drive, Oshawa ON L2G 4G3	905.721.3300	905.721.3301	

E

EAST HARDWARE LIMITED Suite 400, 17 Princess Street South Toronto ON M8Y 3N5 Hoaln W. East, President	416.435.9800	416.435.9801	416.429.3850
EAST, Hoaln 76 Prince Albert Road, Toronto ON M4R 6N2			416.429.3850
ELVIDGE, Susan 1096 Kelly Court, Apt. 506, Mississauga ON L6K 4R2	416.424.6511		905.233.4561

F

590 STEPHEN DRIVE LIMITED 6397 Dufferin Street, Toronto ON M2K 6Z1	416.787.3244	416.787.3245	
FOX, WOLFE & LYONS, Barristers & Solicitors 976 City Centre Crescent, Mississauga ON L4V 8B2 Brianna T. Wolfe	905.552.0034	905.552.0035	

NAME, ADDRESS and Contact Name(s), if applicable	TELEPHONE (as applicable)		
	BUSINESS	FACSIMILE	RESIDENCE

G

GELON, Helena
295 Papineau Avenue, Saint-Thomas QC J4K 8D2   418.980.4485

GENERAL FOOD EQUIPMENT LIMITED
Suite 305, 1684 Cranston Rd., Mississauga ON L8V 4S2   905.323.7878   905.323.7879

GENERAL MOTORS LEASING
4200 Wyandotte Road, Windsor ON N8P 3J9   519.468.3820   519.468.3821

GEORGIAN TECHNOLOGY INC.
400 West Simcoe Street, Barrie ON L4M 2J9T   705.728.8200   705.728.8201
    Maria Griffiths, President

GORDON'S ART GALLERY INC.
430 Queen Street West, Toronto ON M3K 2L3   416.528.6988   416.528.6989
    Marc Tremblay, President

GRAHAM, HARVEY & RICHARDS
Barristers & Solicitors
85 Nelson Road, Brantford ON N2B 3J9   519.772.5667   519.772.5668

GREEN, John S.
487 Queen Anne Drive, Orillia ON L3V 4R1   705-551.6754   705.551.6755

GREEN, POMEROY & SHAPERO
Barristers & Solicitors
25 Mohawk Blvd., Hamilton ON L5C 9M8   905.686.3443   905.686.3444
    Janet Green

GRAHAM & PARKER, Barristers & Solicitors
2416 Pickering Place, Suite 660, Hamilton ON L3N 4G3   905.415.9000   905.415.9001
    Michael Cochrane

H

HARE, ROSS & WILKINSON, Barristers & Solicitors
94 Wimbleton Crescent, Suite 405, Barrie ON L4V 8X2   705.554.4891   705.554.4892
    David S. Ross

HENDERSON, MAXWELL & ARMSTONG
Barristers & Solicitors
8175 Ellesmere Avenue West, Toronto ON M9V 3K9   416.429.3234   416.429.3235

HOUGHTON, CHEUNG, Barristers & Solicitors
121 Richmond Street West, Suite 200
Suite 200, Toronto ON M8G 7M3   416.366.5444   416.366.5445
    Sarah G. Cheung

NAME, ADDRESS and Contact Name(s), if applicable	TELEPHONE (as applicable)		
	BUSINESS	FACSIMILE	RESIDENCE
HUMBER MANUFACTURING LTD. 480 Kipling Avenue, Toronto ON M8Z 5E1	416.790.6776	416.790.6777	
HUMPHRIES, Carew Philip 40 Oaklea Avenue, Oakville ON L2R 3V9	416.789.2381		905.431.2604
HUNEWOOD, Douglas 340 Dominion Avenue, Midland ON L4R 1N4			705.778.5442

I

INGLE, HENCHMAN & BRODER Barristers & Solicitors 857 Lombard Place, Winnipeg MB R3C 2J9	204.987.6777	204.987.6778	

J

JOHANNSEN, Peter 40 Bacchus Avenue, Ajax ON L2R 2V3			905.229.3451
JONES, Henry P. 68 Main Street North, Hamilton ON L8F 5H9			905.881.0034
JULIETTE'S BOUTIQUES LIMITED 946 Queen Street North, Toronto ON M4R 2B6 John P. Jason, President	416.323.1449	416.323.1440	

K

KINGSMAN, LESTER & MARTINEAU Barristers & Solicitors 90 Wentlock Gate, Halifax NS B4R 2S7 Gordon R. Martineau	902.665.8000	902.664.8001	

L

LEWIS, Walter 185 Timothy Drive, Toronto ON M4R 6T4			416.449.6539
LITTLE, BELL, SHAW & ROBINSON Barristers & Solicitors 410 Willow Avenue, Bracebridge ON P1L 2V6 Paul G. Shaw	705.654.9889	613.654.9881	

NAME, ADDRESS and Contact Name(s), if applicable	TELEPHONE (as applicable)		
	BUSINESS	FACSIMILE	RESIDENCE

M

MARRIOTT, Victoria
59 Hillcrest Avenue, Indianapolis IN 10340 — — 317.442.8775

MASON & WALKER, Barristers & Solicitors
200 Main Street, Suite 200, Orillia ON L3V 2R9 — 705-331.4550 — 705-331-4551

MAYHUE, Gordon
36 Ridley Avenue, Toronto ON M5M 4A9 — — 416.483.3748

McCLELLAND, WYERS & CHAE
Barristers & Solicitors
759 Main Street, Owen Sound ON N4K 5Z7 — 519.376.0075 — 519.376.0076
    Timothy J. Wyers

N

NORRIS, PALMER & HANSON
Barristers & Solicitors
4685 Georgia Street, Vancouver BC V7J 3K3 — 604.551.8444 — 604.551.8445
    Richard P. Norris

O

OSMOND, HESPLER & BRUNDI
Barristers & Solicitors
975 Albert Street, Regina SK S6V 4L9 — 306.940.2333 — 306.940.2334
    Marian Brundi

P

PINDAR, Richard
94 Royal Orchard Blvd., Thornhill ON L3K 4P9 — 647.380.9665 — 905.438.8891

PICOV, BLAIR & SCHMIDT
Barristers & Solicitors
480 Water Street, Peterborough ON K9H 8G7 — 705.877.4545 — 705.877.4546
    Cheryl S. Blair

POTTIN, Joyce
95 Peterborough Crescent, Hamilton ON L6B 5S8 — — 905.442.2100

PRESTON, John
890 Ballacaine Drive, Toronto ON M3H 6X3 — 416.990.4435 — 416.781.8921

NAME, ADDRESS and Contact Name(s), if applicable	TELEPHONE (as applicable) BUSINESS	FACSIMILE	RESIDENCE

R

RIVEIRO, Deborah
484 Morningside Drive, Acton ON L8K 7B6 — — 519.332.8975

RODRIGUES, Elian
7500 Yonge Street, Suite 305, Aurora ON L2K 7W3 — — 905.325.7865

ROSARIO, Enrico
105 Springdale Crescent, Oshawa, ON L2H 8D4 — — 905.325.7865

S

SIMPSON, STAINTON & CRAWFORD
Barristers & Solicitors
53 Suffolk Street, Guelph ON N1H 7B4 — 519.424.6744 — 519.424.6745
    Drew C. Crawford

SMILEY, Roger
135 Bond Street, Brockville ON K6V 5K9 — — 613.833.4521

SMITH, BROWN & BLACKWOOD
Barristers & Solicitors
25 Belfast Road, Toronto ON M8X 6G2 — 416.936.8870 — 416.936.8871

SMITH, FRASER, HAMID & LEE LLP
Barristers & Solicitors
75 Victoria Street, Suite 503, Toronto ON M5C 2B1 — 416.233.9985 — 416.233.9980
    John A. Hamid
    Leonard A. Blackwell
    Shelly A. Colangelo

SPEERS, Roger
560 Hillcrest Blvd., Toronto ON M4F 6P7 — — 416.483.3778

STEEB & KUBLICK, Barristers & Solicitors
480 Douglas Street, Suite 204, Cobourg ON K9A 9Y2 — 613.824.9872 — 613.824.9873

T

TASKER, MATTEA, AULD & GUESS
Barristers & Solicitors
185 Ladybrook Crescent, London ON N6H 3D2 — 519.543.3440 — 519.543.3441
    Donald L. Guess

TORONTO COURT REPORTERS
Suite 200, 60 Queen Street West — 416.430.2260 — 416-430.2261

NAME, ADDRESS and Contact Name(s), if applicable	TELEPHONE (as applicable) BUSINESS	FACSIMILE	RESIDENCE

U

UNDERHILL, PALLAZI, DeMARA & TOLFO
Barristers & Solicitors
4695 Peel Avenue Montreal QC H3S 8M4   514.334.7780   514.334.7781

V

VLASNEZSKI, Lillian
794 Pemberton Crescent, Toronto ON M4R 2C6   416.226.9830

W

WALKER SHERIDAN, Professional Corporation
300 Main Street, Brampton ON L1M 3C7   905.328.8000   905.328.8010

XYZ

YOUNG, McCANSE, PAINTER & TECKERT
Barristers & Solicitors
P.O. Box 4765, One Main Street
Fredericton NB E3J 7H4   506.665.0042   506.665.0043

PROOFREADER'S MARKS

Mark		Example
//	Align (line up)	// Barrister / // Solicitor
≡	Capitalize	judge McCartney
/	Do not capitalize (lowercase)	The following Acts will be
ℐ	Delete a word	As you requested, we enclose
ℐ	Delete a letter and close space	judgement
⌶	Move to the left	⌶ GST is charged
⌷	Indent (or move) to the right	IN WITNESS WHEREOF
⌷⌶	Centre	⌷ JUDGMENT ⌶
∧	Insert a letter	acknowledgment (insert e)
∨	Insert punctuation (from above)	Herein the "vendor"
∧	Insert punctuation (from below)	liens encumbrances, or debts

Symbol	Meaning	Example
#	Insert a space	Instrument No.#47501
__	Insert underscore or italics	the <u>Courts of Justice Act</u>
∧	Insert a word	The cost will ∧be calculated
—	Change a word	Sworn before me at the ~~Town~~ city of
↻	Move as shown	(City of London) in the
○	Spell out	①Park Ⓐve.
¶	Start a new paragraph	¶The following parties
...	Stet (leave as it was)	Lease, contracts, or agreements
∽	Transpose	It is their opinion that the
DS [	Double space	DS [Any requests for further information should be made to
SS [	Single space	SS [The exclusions listed in this contract are binding upon